Business Skills Exercises 5e

Loretta Barker

Retired Teacher
Fontana High School
Fontana, California

SOUTH-WESTERN
CENGAGE Learning

Australia • Brazil • Japan • Korea • Mexico • Singapore • Spain • United Kingdom • United States

Business Skills Exercises, Fifth Edition
Loretta Barker

Vice President of Editorial, Business:
Jack W. Calhoun

Vice President/Editor-in-Chief: Karen Schmohe

Senior Developmental Editor: Karen Caldwell

Consulting Editor: Kathy Schaefer

Editorial Assistant: Anne Merrill

Interim Marketing Manager: Kara Bombelli

Senior Media Editor: Sally Nieman

Manufacturing Planner: Charlene Taylor

Senior Marketing Communications Manager:
Sarah Greber

Art and Cover Direction, Production
Management, and Composition:
PreMediaGlobal

Cover Image(s): ©Frannyanne/shutterstock,
©South12th Photography/shutterstock,
©Sadovnikova Olga/shutterstock, ©firedark/
shutterstock, ©Ty Smith/istockphoto

Rights Acquisition Specialist, Text and Image:
Amber Hosea

For product information and technology assistance, contact us at
Cengage Learning Customer & Sales Support, 1-800-354-9706

For permission to use material from this text or product,
submit all requests online at **www.cengage.com/permissions**
Further permissions questions can be emailed to
permissionrequest@cengage.com

Library of Congress Control Number: 2011944637

ISBN-13: 978-1-111-57219-8

ISBN-10: 1-111-57219-4

South-Western
5191 Natorp Boulevard
Mason, OH 45040
USA

Cengage Learning products are represented in Canada by
Nelson Education, Ltd.

For your course and learning solutions, visit **www.cengage.com/school**

Visit our company website at **www.cengage.com**

Printed in the United States of America
1 2 3 4 5 6 7 16 15 14 13 12

CONTENTS

UNIT 3   GENERAL BUSINESS SKILLS

UNIT 4   RECORDS MANAGEMENT SKILLS

UNIT 5   REFERENCING SKILLS

UNIT 6   21st Century Skills

INTRODUCTION

You may fill this empty chair when you finish your studies.

No one is sitting at the workstation in the photograph above. The work done in an office will slow down until a qualified person fills this empty chair. In today's market, jobs are scarce with many people competing for the same position. Those candidates with the best skills will earn the jobs. You can become a qualified job candidate by studying hard and learning what is presented in this text-workbook. Persons like you who are well prepared for a job in business will fill many empty chairs such as this.

In job interviews, you likely will be asked, "What skills do you have?" To have good skills, you must spend time in class and at home doing drills and practice exercises. As a result of your efforts, your skills will improve each day! So that you will be prepared for your future, you should begin now to practice business skills that will help you get a job and succeed in that job.

OVERVIEW

Business Skills Exercises is divided into six units: Communication, Math, General Business, Records Management, Referencing, and 21st Century Skills. Each unit contains activities that will help improve your basic job skills. The units are described briefly in the following paragraphs. Read each description carefully. As you read, consider how improving these basic skills will help you when you apply for a job in business.

COMMUNICATION SKILLS

Good communication skills are vital in every job. Knowledge of proper grammar is essential for all office workers. Some basic rules of grammar are presented in this unit. Learning these grammar rules will help you communicate more effectively. It is important that you continue to study proper grammar throughout your education and strive to improve your business communication skills.

When preparing written documents, **proofreading** is an important step. The proofreading exercises in this unit will help you become a better proofreader. You will learn common proofreaders' marks and their meanings. As you follow the tips for proofreading and use proofreaders' marks to correct documents, your proofreading skills will improve. Proofreading is an essential part of communicating effectively in writing.

You will add many new words to your **vocabulary** as you complete the exercises in this unit. You will also encounter new words in other areas of learning. For example, many text-workbooks have word lists, glossaries, or vocabulary-building exercises. You should practice new words by using them in sentences, either orally or in writing. Using new words in sentences will help you remember their meanings.

Neat and legible **handwriting** is emphasized in this unit. As you practice proper handwriting techniques, you will also be improving your spelling skills. Good **spelling** is a necessity. Incorrectly spelled words within a document cause the reader to focus on the misspelled words rather than on the writer's message. When you add a word to your vocabulary, you should also learn to spell and pronounce that word correctly. One way to improve your spelling is to spell a word slowly over and over in your mind. Writing the word several times is also helpful. To repeat new words or to drill upon them helps you learn the sounds and the letters of the new words.

MATH SKILLS

Most jobs require basic math skills. The math activities in this unit will help prepare you for the types of calculations you may be expected to complete on a job. You will gain experience **improving number writing, proofreading amounts of money and other numbers, making change, calculating sale totals, preparing an invoice, writing receipts, maintaining a personal checking account, maintaining petty cash, and preparing cash drawer count reports.**

Comparing, matching, and **proofreading** are useful skills for an office worker. Exercises in this unit will give you practice determining whether certain numbers are exactly the same or slightly different from other numbers. When proofreading numbers, look for *transposed* numbers, which are two switched numbers. For example, if the number 3498 is written as 4398, the 3 and 4 are switched or transposed.

Throughout the unit, an emphasis is placed on **writing numbers legibly.** You will practice improving your number writing so that on the job you and others are able to easily read what you have written.

GENERAL BUSINESS SKILLS

You will continue to improve your **comparing, matching,** and **proofreading** skills in this unit. When proofreading names and addresses, be sure to read slowly and compare each letter in each word.

You will complete a variety of business forms such as **shipping labels, change of address forms, time records, insurance forms, telephone messages, property records, order forms, work orders,** and **more.** The importance of using proper hand **printing** is stressed in this unit. When hand printing, some forms require all capital letters only, and others require both capital and lowercase letters. Always keep in mind the person who will read what you have written. Print the letters and numbers in the boxes or spaces on the forms neatly and clearly. In an office environment, you may be required to write while you are feeling rushed. For example, a telephone call may require you to listen while you write information on a form or note pad. Take your time and write all names and numbers clearly so others will not have difficulty reading your message. Repeating the information back to the caller to confirm that you have written it correctly and legibly is also helpful.

RECORDS MANAGEMENT SKILLS

Three methods of filing information are presented: alphabetic, numeric, and chronological. With alphabetic (or name) filing, you will determine filing order following the indexing rules of filing. With numeric (or number) filing, you will file by numbers arranged in a certain way. Some offices have filing systems that use both letters of the alphabet and numbers, such as IBC496. With chronological (or time) filing, you will file according to dates. Different businesses use different filing methods, but most follow the standard filing rules that you will learn as you progress through this unit.

REFERENCING SKILLS

You may have used reference sources in a school, public library, home library, or on a computer. Your duties on the job will also require you to use reference books, charts, directories, and other sources of information. Some common reference materials are:

- telephone directory
- dictionary
- maps
- CD-ROM sources
- tax charts
- shipping charts

- ZIP Code directory
- price lists
- airline guides
- databases
- online sources
- newspapers

The exercises in this unit will help you build on your referencing skills. You will find answers to questions by referring to pages from common reference sources provided at the back of the text-workbook. Be sure to use your best handwriting or printing as you complete these referencing exercises.

21ST CENTURY SKILLS

Prioritizing tasks is an ongoing activity in an office setting. In this unit you will determine the order in which certain tasks should be completed. You will gain experience setting priorities in a business environment as well as setting personal priorities. Being able to prioritize tasks is a valuable skill that will make you an asset to your employer.

Having good time management skills is essential in today's office. If you manage your time efficiently, you are a more productive worker. The time and task management exercises in this unit will help you analyze and improve your time management skills.

The topic of ethics is presented in this unit. Individuals and companies make decisions based on a code of ethics. Ethical behavior is required of us daily in both personal and professional settings. Employers require their employees to be loyal and to follow the company's established ethics policy or business code of behavior. You will also learn about the ethical issues surrounding the use of e-mail at work.

Writing effective e-mail and using cell phones responsibly is also covered in this unit. E-mail is quick and easy to send but can be easily misinterpreted. You will learn the importance of writing professional and effective e-mail. You will also gain an understanding of the appropriate use of cell phones.

The Internet activities in this unit will help prepare you for the types of Internet searches you might encounter at work and at home. You will gain experience using the Internet for workplace tasks, homework assignments, and online shopping. The Internet makes it possible for you to get more information faster and easier than ever before. Understanding how to search efficiently on the Internet to complete common workplace tasks will make you a valued employee.

LEARNING GOALS

The activities in *Business Skills Exercises* are divided into six units. Each exercise has a learning goal. Read the goal before you begin the exercise, and work hard to meet the goal. Be sure to read and follow all instructions carefully. With practice, you will see how easy it is to reach the goals!

LEARNING OUTCOMES

After completing the exercises in this text-workbook, you should be able to:

- apply basic rules of grammar
- use proofreaders' marks when proofreading documents
- spell and define new words
- improve your hand printing and handwriting
- solve basic math problems
- proofread names and numbers
- complete a wide variety of business forms
- maintain a personal checking account
- put names, numbers, and dates in order for filing
- use reference sources to find information
- prioritize personal and workplace tasks
- improve your time management skills
- apply rules of ethical behavior
- write effective e-mail
- use cell phones responsibly
- search efficiently on the Internet

GOAL: Identify the main idea of a paragraph

_____ NAME

_____ CLASS

It is important to be able to identify the main ideas when writing or reading a paragraph, a letter, an article, or any body of text. The **main idea** is the single most important idea in a group of words. It is also referred to as the topic sentence. Identifying the main idea as you read will make your understanding of what you are reading much easier.

Read the paragraphs shown below. As you read, pay particular attention to the underlined sentences. The underlined sentence is the main idea, or topic sentence, of each paragraph.

> <u>Facebook is a social networking website that was established in 2004 and currently has over 600 million users.</u> It is currently the largest and most popular social networking service. Mark Zuckerberg and fellow Harvard computer science students Eduardo Saverin, Dustin Moskovitz, and Chris Hughes founded Facebook. Over the years, Facebook has grown from a Harvard-only website to an international phenomenon.*
>
> <u>A thesaurus is a collection of words and phrases listed with their synonyms and arranged alphabetically or by concepts.</u> This book serves a different purpose than a dictionary. A dictionary provides the spelling, definition, and pronunciation of a word you have in mind. A thesaurus gives you access to a broader vocabulary and helps you choose exactly the right word with which to express an idea.
>
> <u>Horticulture is the science of plant cultivation and soil preparation.</u> Horticultural scientists study both edible plants (fruits, vegetables, berries) and ornamental plants (trees, shrubs, flowers). The term horticulture means to cultivate gardens. Horticulturists conduct research on crop production, plant breeding, genetic engineering, insect and disease resistance, and more.
>
> *Source: http://www.facebook.com/press/info.php?founderbios (accessed April 13, 2011).

After you have read the above paragraphs, read them once again. The topic sentence is most often found at the beginning of a paragraph; however, occasionally it will be within the paragraph. Opening with a topic sentence will get your point across to the reader immediately. Notice that the sentences that are NOT underlined give additional information about the sentence that is underlined. Notice also that all sentences in a paragraph relate to the same subject.

Read the paragraphs below and underline the main idea of each paragraph.

1. Pyramids were built as burial tombs for Egyptian kings. Because Egyptians believed in life after death, they built burial tombs for their kings and filled them with treasures for their next life. The most famous pyramid was built for King Tutankhamen—King Tut.

2. The Kentucky Derby takes place every year at Churchill Downs in Kentucky. Three-year-old colts from around the country attempt to add this "Run for the Roses" crown to their list of races won. This exciting horse race is run the first Saturday of May.

3. Motorcycle racing is a dangerous sport. It is important that riders wear appropriate protective gear. They should also understand the risks involved.

4. The Home Decorating Showcase is in progress at the convention center. If you are planning remodeling projects for your home, be sure to attend. Experts will be available to answer any questions you may have.

5. Preparing a family tree is a fun way to learn about your ancestors and preserve your family's heritage. My grandmother is researching and preparing a family tree. It is interesting to see history come alive as she discovers our past family members.

6. On the night of the recital, the violinist played beautifully without making a single mistake. She had practiced her solo for weeks before the recital, and her preparation paid off.

7. Bill finally learned to key on a computer keyboard. He began his computer class in September and has been working hard all semester to master this skill. Now he will be able to complete tasks more efficiently.

8. Dr. Charles Mannes has announced the addition of Dr. Marcia Brunner to his staff. Dr. Brunner completed her residency at Mt. Pinion General Hospital. She is trained in reconstructive surgery and general surgery. Dr. Brunner will replace Dr. John Westin, who recently retired from practice.

9. Jordan is an accomplished horsewoman. She has won four championship titles since she began showing her horse, O'Break Danser. Next year she hopes to compete in the Olympics.

10. The ability to operate a computer is a necessity in today's workplace. In order to be better prepared for a job in business, you should learn to use the software programs that are commonly used in today's offices.

11. The annual Fourth of July picnic and parade will begin at 10:00 A.M. Be sure to bring your blankets and picnic baskets for this exciting event. The day will climax with a fireworks display over the lake.

12. In 1877 Thomas Edison invented the phonograph, a device for recording and replaying sound. It used a cylinder as a recording medium. Also invented in the 19th century was the gramophone, which used a disc rather than a cylinder.

13. Competing in off-road racing competitions is an expensive hobby. Drivers and owners of off-road vehicles spend thousands of dollars preparing their vehicles for races. Sometimes the vehicles are destroyed or damaged during a race.

14. When working in an office, it is important to have good reference sources close at hand. Reference sources can include a dictionary, thesaurus, and online websites.

15. Synthesis is the combination of separate parts, or elements, to create a new whole. The word synthesis comes from Greek words that mean "to place together." Types of synthesis include chemical synthesis, sound synthesis, and photosynthesis.

GOAL: Identify the subject of a sentence

_____ NAME

_____ CLASS

A **sentence** is a group of words that expresses a complete thought; in other words, it makes sense. All sentences are composed of subjects and predicates. The **complete subject** of a sentence tells who is speaking, who is spoken to, or who or what is spoken about. The **simple subject** is the main word within the complete subject. All other words in the sentence are called the **predicate**. The predicate, which includes the verb, tells you something about the subject. You will learn more about verbs in Exercise 5.

Complete Subject   The complete subject of a sentence may be one word or a group of words and may appear at any point in the sentence. To identify the complete subject, ask yourself these questions:

1. Who is speaking? The person speaking usually appears as *I* or *we*.

2. Who is spoken to? The person spoken to is usually addressed as *you*.

3. Who or what is spoken about? The person or thing spoken about will vary.

Read the sentences below. In these examples the complete subject of each sentence is underlined.

1. Person speaking
    a. I would like to vacation in Hawaii.
    b. We decided to have a family reunion in October.

2. Person spoken to
    a. Will you please close the window?
    b. You will receive an award at the meeting next month.

3. Person or thing spoken about
    a. He is thinking about purchasing a new ski boat.
    b. A single red rose is often given as a symbol of love.

Note: Look again at sentence 2a above. When a sentence is a question, the subject will not come first in the sentence.

EXERCISE 2a   Underline the complete subject in each of the following sentences. Remember to ask yourself the three questions above to help determine the complete subject.

1. I am anxious to attend the baseball game.

2. The climate in our region is usually mild.

3. The instruction book was difficult to understand.

4. You will enjoy a peaceful life in the country.

5. All branches of the company are linked by the internet.

6. She wanted investors to back a dot.com company.

7. We look forward to "casual Fridays" in our office.

8. Drive-through restaurants are not allowed in our city.

9. My best friend moved to New York.

10. Have you ever wished to live in a beachside community?

Simple Subject   The simple subject is the heart of the complete subject. It is the single most important word within the complete subject. Read the sentences below. In these examples the complete subject is underlined once and the simple subject is underlined twice.

1. A restaurant near the hotel has been selected as the meeting place.

2. The pilot program is sponsored by the Undersea Life Laboratory.

3. We ran in the citywide marathon on Saturday.

4. You should proofread your work carefully to avoid costly mistakes.

Note: In the last two sentences above, *We* and *You* are both the complete and simple subjects.

EXERCISE 2b   In each of the following sentences, underline the complete subject once and the simple subject twice. First ask yourself the three questions on the previous page to help determine the complete subject. Then identify the single most important word within the complete subject to determine the simple subject.

1. The birthday party was a wonderful success.

2. We must use teamwork to complete this project by Wednesday.

3. Ms. Viterna is organizing the benefit for the flood victims.

4. You should arrive at the meeting early to set up the podium for the speaker.

5. A new home improvement store is being built at the south end of town.

6. Our travel group is looking forward to the trip to Italy.

7. Will you take the dog to the veterinarian tomorrow afternoon?

8. The firefighters in our town organize a Community Muster each spring.

9. The majority of the voters were in favor of funding the grant.

10. I am glad the neighbors are excited about the block party.

GOAL: Identify nouns and pronouns

_____ NAME

_____ CLASS

Nouns   The word used to name a person, place, or thing is referred to as a **noun**. Nouns name something; for example, your house, a tree, a building, an animal, or your own name. There are two types of nouns: common and proper. **Common nouns** name *general* people, places, and things and are not capitalized unless they start a sentence or are part of a title. **Proper nouns** name a *specific* person, place, or thing and are capitalized no matter where they appear in a sentence. Some examples of common and proper nouns are shown in Figure 1-1.

Figure 1-1   Common and Proper Nouns

	Common Nouns	**Proper Nouns**
Person:	boy, teacher, dentist	John, Ms. Thomas, Dr. Rubin
Place:	city, beach, museum	St. Louis, Newport Beach, Museum of Fine Arts
Thing:	cat, cookie, book	Cheshire, Oreo, Charlotte's Web

Read the sentences below. In these examples the common nouns are underlined once and the proper nouns are underlined twice.

1. Both <u>Marsha</u> and <u>Bob</u> enjoy <u>spaghetti</u> at their favorite <u>Italian</u> <u>restaurant</u>.

2. Was your <u>teacher</u> able to attend the <u>concert</u> at <u>Red Rocks Amphitheater</u>?

3. <u>Alex</u> bought <u>hot dogs</u> during the <u>game</u> at <u>Dodger Stadium</u>.

EXERCISE 3a   In each of the following sentences, underline the common nouns once and the proper nouns twice. There may be more than one type of noun in a sentence and more than one common or proper noun in a sentence. If you are not certain whether or not a word is a noun, you may use a dictionary to help you identify the nouns.

1. Mary was excited to see the stars in the Andromeda Galaxy when she visited the planetarium.

2. Madison High School's senior class took a trip to San Francisco.

3. Lucy's parents told her of their plan to move to southern Arizona.

4. How many times has Dr. Portillo traveled to Asia?

5. The train slowed as it approached the city.

6. Why did Lakeisha transfer to the other class?

7. Tennis is Allison's favorite form of recreation.

8. How often does your family play board games?

9. Arthur is carefully planning his trip to Australia.

10. In Washington the monuments are popular with visitors.

Pronouns   A **pronoun** is a word used to replace a noun, a group of nouns, or another pronoun. You might think of pronouns as noun substitutes. Using a pronoun in place of a noun will make the sentence less awkward and repetitive. Unless it appears at the start of a sentence, a pronoun is generally not capitalized. An exception is the pronoun *I* which is always capitalized no matter where it appears in a sentence.

A list of pronouns is shown in Figure 1-2 below. There are more categories of pronouns than those shown here. The pronouns listed below are the most common. A **nominative pronoun** (also called a subjective pronoun) is the subject of the verb and carries out the action. An **objective pronoun** is the object of the verb and receives the action. A **possessive pronoun** shows possession or ownership.

Figure 1-2   Common Pronouns

Nominative Case		Objective Case		Possessive Case	
Singular	Plural	Singular	Plural	Singular	Plural
I	we	me	us	my	our
you	you	you	you	your	your
he/she/it	they	him/her/it	them	his/her/its	their

Study each pair of sentences below. Note how the nouns have been replaced with pronouns.

1. a. Andrea asked the teacher for an eraser.
   b. She asked her for an eraser.

2. a. Did Darren know that Don and Hiro also were going to the game?
   b. Did he know that they also were going to the game?

3. a. Mom and Dad were proud of Alberto's and my grades.
   b. They were proud of our grades.

EXERCISE 3b   For each underlined noun or group of nouns in the following sentences, write the correct pronoun substitute in the space to the right of the sentence. An example is provided.

Ex.   <u>Jacob and Jennifer</u> registered for classes today.   Ex. _____They_____

1.   <u>Mateo</u> did all of his homework before dinner.   1. _____

2.   After <u>James and Elizabeth</u> were married, they went on a   2. _____
     honeymoon to Europe.

3.   The soccer game was very exciting according to <u>Mary</u>.   3. _____

4.   <u>Rita</u> was thrilled to be hired by the advertising firm.   4. _____

5.   The freelance work was awarded to <u>Joshua</u>.   5. _____

6.   After the river receded, <u>Michael</u> was able to return home.   6. _____

7.   How many people do you need to play <u>Monopoly</u>?   7. _____

8.   <u>Phyllis and I</u> took our driver's tests on Monday.   8. _____

9.   <u>Ron's</u> dog, Benji, is going to compete in the World Trials.   9. _____

10. By the time Glen arrived, <u>Martin's Groceries</u> was closed.   10. _____

EXERCISE 3c   In each of the following sentences, identify the words in parenthesis by writing CN (common noun), PN (proper noun), or P (pronoun) in the space to the right of the sentence. There may be multiple nouns and/or pronouns in each sentence. An example sentence is given.

Ex.   (My) (brother) bought a (car) at (Norm's Used Autos).   Ex. __P, CN, CN, PN__

1.   Each (spring) our (trees) provide (us) with delicious   1. _____
     fresh (fruit).

2.   During (our) winter (break) from (school),   2. _____
     we traveled to (Mexico).

3.   In (New York City), (we) visited the (Empire State Building).   3. _____

4.   (Audrey) was excited that (she) had been accepted to (college). 4. _____

5.   Next (Monday) (she) will practice (her) speech for the (class).   5. _____

6.   The (committee) approved (their) request for a booth at the   6. _____
     (Montgomery County Fair).

7.   How many (times) did (Harry) try to ring the (bell) at the fair?   7. _____

8.   (Our) chickens laid an extraordinary number of (eggs)   8. _____
     this week.

9.   Is (Hank's Girl) still the favorite to win best of show   9. _____
     (Saturday)?

10. (My) (friends) watch the (Scripps National Spelling Bee),   10. _____
     which is broadcast each year from (Washington, D.C.).

Exercise 3   7

GOAL: Identify prepositions

NAME _____

CLASS _____

Prepositions are connecting words. They show relationships between nouns or pronouns and other words in a sentence. Prepositions are always followed by a noun or pronoun. Look closely at the word preposition. It is made of two parts: *pre*, which means before, and *position*. Therefore, a preposition comes *before* a noun or pronoun. Of course, not every word that is positioned before a noun or a pronoun is a preposition.

A list of prepositions is shown in Figure 1-3 below. There are more prepositions than those shown here. The prepositions listed below are the most common. Notice that a preposition may be one or more words.

A simple way to identify most prepositions is to imagine a dog and its doghouse. A dog can do many things described by prepositions, such as jump *over* its doghouse, hide *behind* it, sleep *against* it, or sit *in* front of it. Some prepositions cannot be identified using the dog/doghouse illustration, such as *among, during,* and *instead of.* These prepositions you should memorize.

Figure 1-3   Common Prepositions

about	behind	from	out
above	below	in	over
according to	beside	in addition to	through
after	between	instead of	to
against	beyond	into	toward
along	by	like	under
among	down	near	until
around	during	of	up
at	except	off	upon
before	for	on	with

Note: You can look in a dictionary to learn a word's *part of speech*—the role that a word or phrase plays in a sentence. Be aware that words defined as prepositions may also function as other parts of speech, depending on their use in a sentence.

Prepositional Phrase Prepositions are combined with other words into prepositional phrases. A **prepositional phrase** is a group of words beginning with a preposition and ending with a noun or pronoun. A prepositional phrase gives additional information about the subject of the sentence. A prepositional phrase can indicate location (in time or place), modify other parts of the sentence, or explain under what circumstances something happened. Read the sentences below. In these examples the prepositional phrase is underlined.

1. They were standing near the door.

2. The woman with the helmet is a motorcyclist.

3. The cashier gave the change to me.

The prepositions that introduce the prepositional phrases in the examples above are *near*, *with*, and *to*.

> Note: When *to* is used with a noun or pronoun, it is a preposition (for example, *to school*). When *to* is used with a verb, it is an **infinitive**—a verb form following the word *to* (for example, *to sleep*).

EXERCISE 4a Underline the prepositional phrase in each of the following sentences.

1. The dishes in the dishwasher are clean.

2. The boy with the ball ran fast.

3. Please pass the lemonade to them.

4. We spent the day at the beach.

5. The wind blew through the trees.

6. The deer disappeared into the forest.

7. Sally threw the ball over the fence.

8. The buildings in the city are very tall.

9. How many bubbles did she blow into the sky?

10. During dinner the conversation was animated.

Prepositional Object The noun or pronoun that ends the prepositional phrase is the **object** of the preposition that begins the phrase. Read the sentences below. In these examples the phrase is underlined once and the object is underlined twice. Notice how each preposition relates its object to the other words in the sentence.

1. During the long winter, we read books and played board games.

2. He scored the winning home run in the last inning.

3. The volunteers picked litter along the highway.

EXERCISE 4b   In each of the following sentences, underline the prepositional phrase once and the prepositional object twice.

1. All agreed she danced with style.

2. Place the planter beside the tall bookcase.

3. Please bring the bandages from the supply cabinet.

4. After the class, we ate lunch.

5. I read the journals written by my grandmother.

6. Among the guests was a noted author.

7. We waltzed under the stars.

8. I found my pencil between the books.

9. Our dog, Max, jumped over his doghouse.

10. Behind our home is a beautiful park.

Multiple Prepositional Phrases   A sentence may contain more than one prepositional phrase. Read the sentences below. In these examples the prepositional phrases are underlined. The remaining words in the sentence, the words not underlined, still make a complete sentence. However, note the contribution the prepositional phrases make to the sentences. They add greatly to your understanding of the subject.

1. Over the holidays, we decorated our neighbor's cabin near the lake.

2. I waved at him in addition to the crowd.

3. She sat beside the gazebo among the rosebushes waiting for the wedding photographer.

EXERCISE 4c   Underline the prepositional phrases in each of the following sentences.

1. She returned to the office before noon.

2. Our cats prefer to sleep in the sun instead of the shade.

3. The apartment on the hill by the river has a great view.

4. Our supervisor sits in the black chair during staff meetings.

5. Down the valley and over the plain the river wanders.

6. The tourist strolled around the museum beyond the main exhibit.

7. Until yesterday, all supplies had arrived except the tablecloths.

8. From the south, the train rolls along the track toward the next station.

9. I looked at my reflection in the mirror.

10. The boy with the green hair is standing near the third row of the auditorium and is causing a disturbance.

Prepositional Phrases and Subjects of Sentences   The subject of a sentence will *never* be found within a prepositional phrase. Being able to identify prepositions and prepositional phrases will allow you to more quickly and correctly identify the subject of a sentence.

Read the sentences below. In these examples, the prepositional phrases are crossed out and the subject of the sentence is underlined.

> **Note:** If necessary, turn to Exercise 2, page 3, to review the subject of a sentence.

1. <u>Dexter</u> carefully carved the turkey ~~with a sharp knife~~.

2. ~~Beyond the wall, around the church yard~~, <u>Mary</u> waited ~~for Roger~~.

3. ~~In the evening~~, <u>we</u> sometimes go ~~for a walk in the park~~.

EXERCISE 4d   For each of the following sentences, draw a line through the prepositional phrase or phrases, then underline the subject of the sentence.

1. At the street festival, we danced the tango.

2. Formal wear is required in the dining room.

3. Willa Cather was born in Back Creek Valley near Winchester, Virginia.

4. A gaggle of geese waddled past.

5. The student at the back of the room asked several pertinent questions.

6. Marco was pleased that he swam 100 laps instead of taking a nap.

7. Sylvia and Karen baked a cake from scratch over the weekend.

8. According to robotics experts, Dr. Krieger is a scientist of great renown.

9. The woman with the helmet is a motorcyclist.

10. I saw a spider spinning a web among the flowers behind the house.

GOAL: Identify verbs

_____ NAME

_____ CLASS

In Exercise 2 you learned about subjects and predicates. The predicate is the part of the sentence that tells you something about the subject. The core of the predicate is the **verb**. Verbs describe a subject's action, condition, or state of being. Think of the verb as the "engine" of the sentence. Without an engine, an automobile would go nowhere. You might say verbs bring sentences to life, as engines do for automobiles.

Action and Linking Verbs   Two types of verbs are action verbs and linking verbs. These verbs function as their names imply. An **action verb** is a verb that describes an action. Examples of action verbs are _run, jump, sing, fly, lift,_ and _drive._ Read the following sentence.

1. Adam <u>drove</u> the car. _Drove_ is the verb. It is an action verb; it describes Adam's action.

A **linking verb** is a verb that links, or connects, the subject of a sentence to information about that subject. Linking verbs describe a condition or state of being for the subject; they do not show action. Examples of linking verbs are _am, is, are, was, were, be, being, been, become, seem, look, taste,_ and _sound._ Read the following sentences.

2. Adam <u>looks</u> tired. _Looks_ is the verb. It is a linking verb; it tells Adam's condition.

3. Adam <u>is</u> in the office. _Is_ is the verb. It is a linking verb; it tells Adam's state of being.

There are verbs that can be action verbs in some sentences and linking verbs in other sentences, depending on their role in each individual sentence. These include verbs that express the senses. Examples are _taste, look, feel, smell, appear, sound, prove, remain, grow,_ and _turn._ Follow this rule of thumb: If you can substitute _is, am,_ or _are_ for the verb in question, and the sentence is still logical, it is probably a linking verb. If, after the verb substitution, the sentence does not make sense, it is probably an action verb. Read the following sentences. _Smells_ is the verb in both sentences.

4a. Adam <u>smells</u> the popcorn.   5a. The popcorn <u>smells</u> good!

Determine whether _smells_ is functioning as an action or linking verb using the verb substitution rule of thumb.

4b. Adam _is_ the popcorn.

Does this make sense? No! In this sentence _is_ cannot be substituted for _smells._ That means _smells_ is an action verb in sentence 4a. Adam performed the action of smelling the popcorn.

5b. The popcorn _is_ good!

Does this sound logical? Yes, _is_ can be substituted for _smells._ This lets you know that _smells_ is a linking verb in sentence 5a. It connects the subject _popcorn_ with information about that subject, that it smells good.

EXERCISE 5a For each of the following sentences, complete two steps. First, underline the verb in the sentence. Then indicate whether the verb is an action verb or a linking verb by writing the capital letter *A* (for action) or *L* (for linking) on the blank line next to the sentence. An example is provided. For verbs that can be either an action or linking verb, remember to follow the verb substitution rule of thumb to help determine their function in the sentence.

Ex. I <u>tasted</u> the pie.

Ex. _____A_____

1. Audrey feels better today.

1. _____

2. The manager addressed the staff.

2. _____

3. Robert Walsh is the manager.

3. _____

4. Traffic moves slowly at rush hour.

4. _____

5. The economy appears bright.

5. _____

6. He was a pilot and adventurer.

6. _____

7. Manny sent an e-mail to members.

7. _____

8. Please raise the window blinds.

8. _____

9. The jacket seems comfortable.

9. _____

10. She grew into a tall woman.

10. _____

Verb Phrase When the subject of a sentence has two or more verbs working together as one verb, it is said to have a **verb phrase**. A verb phrase is formed by the combination of one or more **helping verbs** followed by the main verb. The helping verbs (also known as *auxiliary verbs*) are *am, is, are, was, were, be, being, been, have, has, had, do, did, does, will, would, shall, should, ought, can, could, may, might,* and *must.* Study and learn this list of helping verbs so that you are able to recognize them in a sentence.

A few things to keep in mind about helping verbs: some are helpers only; for example, *might, would,* and *will.* Others can be helping verbs or can stand alone as the main verb of a sentence; for example, *was, do,* and *have.* Sometimes there is another word separating the helping verb from the main verb. When you see an *-ing* verb such as *jumping,* look for one or more helping verbs nearby.

Read the sentences below. In these examples the verb phrase is underlined.

1. She <u>will</u> not <u>approve</u> the new budget.
    Will is the helping verb; *approve* is the main verb. This verb phrase is separated by *not,* which is an adverb and not part of the verb phrase.

2. The cat <u>must have been chasing</u> the mouse.
    Must, have, and *been* are helping verbs; *chasing* is the main verb.

3. You <u>can learn</u> about verb phrases.
    Can is the helping verb; *learn* is the main verb.

EXERCISE 5b   Underline the verb phrase in each of the following sentences.

1. Her family <u>has been traveling</u> to the mountains on vacation for years.
2. Anyone <u>can appreciate</u> the new ice cream flavors.
3. You <u>should have asked</u> for help with the report.
4. Anthony <u>is working</u> on the presentation.
5. We <u>are waiting</u> for the revised insurance information.
6. Marta Johansen <u>will be making</u> the arrangements for the trip to Europe.
7. She <u>might not have listened</u> to the entire speech.
8. The money <u>may have been invested</u> in mutual funds.
9. <u>Would</u> you <u>deliver</u> the files to Mr. Kinney's office?
10. Juan <u>did explain</u> the procedure for counting inventory.

GOAL: Improve proofreading skills and use proofreaders' marks

_____ NAME

_____ CLASS

Proofreading is the skill of detecting errors in written documents. These errors may be in keying, spelling, grammar, punctuation, format, or content. Proofreading is the last step—and a very important step—in preparing any document.

Turn to the proofreaders' marks in the _Reference Sources_ on page 266 of this text. Look carefully at each mark and study its meaning. Always use these common proofreaders' marks to correct a document. Doing so will ensure that the proper corrections are made to the document regardless of who revises it.

Read the tips for proofreading given in Figure 1-4. These guidelines explain how to proofread. Follow these tips when checking any type of document, and you will become a better proofreader.

Figure 1-4   Tips for Proofreading

- Try to allow some time between writing a document and proofreading it. This prepares you to read what is actually keyed rather than what you expect to be keyed.

- Use a guide—an envelope, an index card, or a folded piece of paper. Move the guide down line by line as you read so that you focus on one line at a time.

- If you are reading a document that has been keyed from a written draft, place the two documents next to each other and use guides to proofread the keyed document line by line against the original.

- Double-check all figures by proofreading numbers aloud or with another person.

- Check for only one type of error at a time. Read the document several times, each time focusing on a different aspect, such as spelling, punctuation, grammar, word choice, or missing words.

- Read the document backwards. This is especially helpful when checking for spelling errors.

- Print the document and proofread the printed copy. You may notice errors that you previously overlooked.

- Ask another person to proofread the document. Fresh eyes will likely spot any errors you may have missed.

Practice your proofreading skills by proofreading the document on the next page.

Proofread the following letter. Use proofreaders' marks to make corrections. The letter contains ten errors: two in capitalization, two in number use, and six in spelling or keying.

May 12, 20—

Mr. Tran Nguyen
Two Gilbert Ave.
Baltimore, MD 21218-4515

Dear Mr. Nguyen:

Thank you for asking about the tech training program at Bell college. Whether your are seeking your first job, refreshing your skills, or hoping to move to an administrative position, our program will give you the technological skills you need for success.

5 occupations that generate the most intrest in our program relate to computers. They are computer engineers, computer support specialists, computer systems analysts, database administrators, and desktop publishing specialists. Our tech training program will prepare y ou for these high-growth positions.

Many jobs, including non-technical jobs, also require technological skills. for example, almost every worker must know how to use cellular phones and telephone systems with multiple lines, call forwarding, and voice mail. Also beneficial is experience with word processing software, e-mail software, fax machines, company intranets, an the Internet.

If you are seeking an adminastrative position in almost any field, you will need additional technological skills in using accounting, billing, and human resources software. Our experienced instructors can help you gain these skills.

The enclosed brochure describes the tech training program in full. If I canbe of further help, please write to me again.

Sincerely,

Janie Lopez
Program Coordinator

cf

Enclosure

GOAL: Improve proofreading skills and use
proofreaders' marks

_____ NAME

_____ CLASS

EXERCISE 7a   Review the proofreaders' marks in the *Reference Sources* on page 266 and review the tips for proofreading in Exercise 6. Next, proofread the following letter. Use proofreaders' marks to make corrections. The letter contains eight errors.

November 6, 20—

Mr. Jeremy Ward
361 Labelle Street
Wheeling, WV 26003-1418

Dear Jeremy:

Congradulations on your appointment to teach employment skills at the Wheeling Job Bank! I would be glad to provide some specific suggestions for your students on what employers mean when they say that they expect you tobe responsible at work.

- You're supposed to show up on time.

- You're not supposed to call in sick unless you really are are sick.

- You're supposed to do you work wihtout being told repeatedly to do it.

- If you're going to be late getting to work or finishing a task, you're supposed to let your supervisor know.

- Your not supposed to make personal calls on company time.

I hope this advise will be helpfull to you and your students. If I can be of any further assistance, please let me know.

Sincerely,

Robert Edison

mf

EXERCISE 7b Proofread the report below using proofreaders' marks to make all necessary corrections.

During the Great Depression, the American writer Eudora Welty got a job asa publicity agent with the Works Progres Administration. She traveled through her State of Mississippi writing about how people were managing during those difficult times—and taking photgraphs. Begininng with a small Eastman Kodak camera with a bellows, she made what she later called a a record of "life in those times" and "of a time and place."

The pictures, taken in Mississippi in the nineteen thirties, show the rural poor and convey the want and worry of the Great depression But more than that they show the photo-grapher's wide-ranging curiosaty and unstinting empathy—which would mark her work as a writer, too.

Welty has remarked, "I was taking photographs of human human beings be cause they were real life and they were there in front of me and that the reality. I was the recorder of it. . . . These people . . . kept alive on the determination to get back to work and to make a living again. . . . The photographs speak for themselves."*

---

*Sources: *Eudora Welty: Photographs,* Jackson, MS: University Press of Mississippi, 1989, p. xiv and pp. xvi-xvii.
Eudora Welty as Photographer, T.A. Frail, April 2009, www.smithsonianmag.com/arts-culture/The-Writers-Eye.html

GOAL: Improve spelling and handwriting of proper names

_____ NAME

_____ CLASS

Look at the sample letters of the alphabet in Figure 1-5. Look at the size and shape of each capital letter and each lowercase letter. Note how the letter fits on the line. Follow your instructor's directions for using script or block letters to complete Exercises 8-12. As you complete the handwriting exercises in this unit, refer to the sample in Figure 1-5 to improve the size and shape of your letters.

Figure 1-5   Sample of Script Letters   Sample of Block Letters

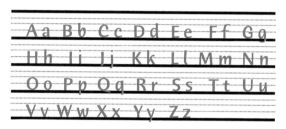

The capital cities and states or territories shown below are divided into pronunciation syllables. Do not confuse these syllabic word divisions with the end-of-line word divisions shown in the dictionary. Pronounce the city and state or territory in syllables. Spell and write the city and state or territory one time in syllables and twice as a complete word. _Do not write too fast_. Lincoln, Nebraska, is shown as an example of the correct way to complete this exercise.

These proper names may appear on the unit test. Spend time in study and in drill at home learning which city is the capital of which state or territory.

Lin coln, Ne bras ka   _Phoe nix, Ar i zo na_

Lin coln, Ne bras ka   _____

Lincoln, Nebraska   _____

Lincoln, Nebraska   _____

Al ba ny, New York

_____

_____

_____

Rich mond, Vir gi nia

_____

_____

_____

Ta lla ha ssee, Flor i da

_____

_____

_____

Des Moines, I o wa

_____

_____

_____

Pierre, South Da ko ta

_____

_____

_____

San Juan, Puer to, Ri co

_____

_____

_____

Den ver, Co lo ra do

_____

_____

_____

Co lum bus, O hi o

_____

_____

_____

GOAL: Improve spelling and handwriting of proper names

_____ NAME

_____ CLASS

As you write and spell the proper names in this exercise, follow the same procedure that you used in Exercise 8. Pronounce the city and state or territory in syllables. Spell and write the city and state or territory one time in syllables and twice as complete words. _Do not write too fast._ Refer to the sample writing in Figure 1-5, page 21, to improve the size and shape of your letters.

These proper names may appear on the unit test. Spend time in study and in drill at home learning which city is the capital of which state or territory.

Con cord, New Hamp shire

Mont go me ry, A la ba ma

Chey enne, Wy o ming

Salt Lake Ci ty, U tah

Harr is burg, Penn syl va nia

Sa lem, Or e gon

Bis marck, North Da ko ta

Sa cra men to, Ca li for nia

Ba ton Rouge, Lou i si a na

Je ffer son Ci ty, Mi ssour i

Pa go Pa go, A mer i can Sa mo a

GOAL: Improve spelling and handwriting of proper names

———————————————— NAME

———————————————— CLASS

As you write and spell the proper names in this exercise, follow the same procedure that you used to complete previous handwriting and spelling exercises. Pronounce the city and state or territory in syllables. Spell and write the city and state or territory one time in syllables and twice as complete words. *Do not write too fast.* Refer to the sample writing in Figure 1-5, page 21, to improve the size and shape of your letters.

These proper names may appear on the unit test. Spend time in study and in drill at home learning which city is the capital of which state or territory.

Ra leigh, North Car o li na ————————

In di a na po lis, In di a na ————————

————————

————————

————————

————————

————————

————————

Do ver, De la ware ————————

Bos ton, Ma ssa chu setts ————————

————————

————————

————————

————————

————————

————————

Charle ston, West Vir gi nia ————————

Hart ford, Co nnec ti cut ————————

————————

————————

————————

————————

————————

————————

He le na, Mon ta na

_____

_____

_____

Au gus ta, Maine

_____

_____

_____

St. Paul, Mi nne so ta

_____

_____

_____

Tren ton, New Jer sey

_____

_____

_____

Char lotte A mal ie, Vir gin I slands

_____

_____

_____

GOAL: Improve spelling and handwriting of proper names

_____ NAME

_____ CLASS

As you write and spell the proper names in this exercise, follow the same procedure that you used to complete previous handwriting and spelling exercises. Pronounce the city and state or territory in syllables. Spell and write the city and state or territory one time in syllables and twice as complete words. _Do not write too fast_. Refer to the sample writing in Figure 1-5, page 21, to improve the size and shape of your letters.

These proper names may appear on the unit test. Spend time in study and in drill at home learning which city is the capital of which state or territory.

O lym pi a, Wa shing ton _____

Aus tin, Tex as _____

_____

_____

_____

_____

_____

_____

Ju neau, A las ka _____

O kla ho ma Ci ty, O kla ho ma _____

_____

_____

_____

_____

_____

_____

Ha gat na, Guam _____

Frank fort, Ken tu cky _____

_____

_____

_____

_____

_____

_____

Car son Ci ty, Ne va da

_____

_____

_____

Spring field, I lli nois

_____

_____

_____

Pro vi dence, Rhode I sland

_____

_____

_____

Jack son, Mi ssi ssi ppi

_____

_____

_____

At lan ta, Geor gia

_____

_____

_____

To pe ka, Kan sas

_____

_____

_____

GOAL: Improve spelling and handwriting of
proper names

_____ NAME

_____ CLASS

As you write and spell the proper names in this exercise, follow the same procedure that you used to complete previous handwriting and spelling exercises. Pronounce the city and state or territory in syllables. Spell and write the city and state or territory one time in syllables and twice as complete words. *Do not write too fast.* Refer to the sample writing in Figure 1-5, page 21, to improve the size and shape of your letters.

These proper names may appear on the unit test. Spend time in study and in drill at home learning which city is the capital of which state or territory.

Lan sing, Mi chi gan

Li ttle Rock, Ar kan sas

Co lum bi a, South Car o li na

Mont pel ier, Ver mont

Boi se, I da ho

Ma di son, Wi scon sin

Ho no lu lu, Ha wa ii

San ta Fe, New Mex i co

Nash ville, Te nne ssee

A nna po lis, Mar y land

Sai pan, Nor thern Ma ri a na I slands

GOAL: Improve vocabulary and spelling

_____ NAME

_____ CLASS

The words in Column 1 are among those most frequently misspelled. The words are divided into pronunciation syllables in Column 2. Do not confuse these syllabic word divisions with end-of-line word divisions. The definitions in Column 3 will help you add the words to your vocabulary. These definitions are also called _synonyms_.

Study the terms and their definitions before completing the exercise on the next page. Pronounce the words as they are divided in Column 2. Learn the correct spellings and definitions. These terms may appear on the unit test.

COLUMN 1	COLUMN 2	COLUMN 3
1. absence	ab sence	nonattendance, nonappearance, want, lack
2. apology	a po lo gy	confession, excuse, regret, amends, plea
3. breathe	breathe	respire, inhale, exhale, draw in, sniff, smell
4. competition	com pe ti tion	contest, event, match, race, game, meet
5. describe	de scribe	explain, recount, illustrate, narrate, express
6. especially	es pe cia lly	particularly, notably, primarily, above all
7. financier	fi nan cier	banker, investor, backer, speculator, broker
8. guidance	gui dance	leadership, direction, supervision, management
9. immediate	i mme di ate	instant, now, current, urgent, pressing
10. jewelry	jewel ry	jewels, gems, trinkets, baubles, adornments
11. literature	li te ra ture	writing, prose, classics, novel, poetry, story
12. minuscule	mi nu scule	tiny, very small, minute, microscopic, little
13. noticeable	no ti cea ble	obvious, clear, conspicuous, apparent, evident
14. peculiar	pe cul iar	distinctive, strange, bizarre, odd, unusual
15. principle	prin ci ple	standard, belief, rule, fundamental law, doctrine
16. receive	re ceive	get, obtain, accept, acquire, take in, inherit
17. sacrifice	sa cri fice	give up, surrender, let go, forfeit, part with
18. stationary	sta tio nar y	motionless, immobile, fixed, stable, permanent
19. together	to ge ther	jointly, mutually, collectively, concurrently, simultaneously
20. utilize	u til ize	use, apply, employ, exercise, implement, operate

The definitions of the vocabulary words that you studied on the previous page appear in Column 1 below. In the space provided in Column 2, write the term that correctly matches the definitions in Column 1.

COLUMN 1	COLUMN 2
1. writing, prose, classics, novel, poetry, story	1. _____
2. motionless, immobile, fixed, stable, permanent	2. _____
3. respire, inhale, exhale, draw in, sniff, smell	3. _____
4. banker, investor, backer, speculator, broker	4. _____
5. use, apply, employ, exercise, implement, operate	5. _____
6. nonattendance, nonappearance, want, lack	6. _____
7. standard, belief, rule, fundamental law, doctrine	7. _____
8. particularly, notably, primarily, above all	8. _____
9. instant, now, current, urgent, pressing	9. _____
10. give up, surrender, let go forfeit, part with	10. _____
11. confession, excuse, regret, amends, plea	11. _____
12. jointly, mutually, collectively, concurrently	12. _____
13. obvious, clear, conspicuous, apparent, evident	13. _____
14. explain, recount, illustrate, narrate, express	14. _____
15. leadership, direction, supervision, management	15. _____
16. get, obtain, accept, acquire, take in, inherit	16. _____
17. contest, event, match, race, game, meet	17. _____
18. jewels, gems, trinkets, baubles, adornments	18. _____
19. distinctive, strange, bizarre, odd, unusual	19. _____
20. tiny, very small, minute, microscopic, little	20. _____

GOAL: Improve vocabulary and spelling

_____ NAME

_____ CLASS

The words in Column 1 are among the most frequently misspelled. The words are divided into pronunciation syllables in Column 2. The definitions in Column 3 will help you add the words to your vocabulary. Study the terms and their definitions before completing the exercise on the next page. Pronounce the words as they are divided in Column 2. Learn the correct spellings and definitions. These terms may appear on the unit test.

	COLUMN 1	COLUMN 2	COLUMN 3
1.	acceptable	ac cept a ble	satisfactory, suitable, adequate, sufficient
2.	apparent	a ppar ent	obvious, clear, evident, noticeable, conspicuous
3.	budget	bu dget	financial plan, statement, estimate, allowance
4.	completely	com plete ly	wholly, thoroughly, entirely, totally, fully
5.	difference	di fference	dissimilarity, distinction, contrast, variety, diversity
6.	exaggerate	ex a gge rate	overstate, embellish, boast, amplify, inflate
7.	foreign	for eign	unknown, unfamiliar, strange, alien, exotic
8.	harass	ha rass	annoy, pester, bother, hassle, tease, irritate
9.	immense	i mmense	huge, gigantic, vast, enormous, tremendous
10.	judgment	judg ment	decision, ruling, finding, verdict, conclusion
11.	livelihood	live li hood	living, income, means, resources, salary, earnings
12.	miscellaneous	mi sce lla ne ous	various, assorted, mixed, diverse, eclectic
13.	numerous	nu me rous	many, plentiful, abundant, countless, several
14.	penniless	pe nni less	impoverished, destitute, bankrupt, insolvent, broke
15.	privilege	priv ilege	freedom, prerogative, opportunity, advantage
16.	recognize	re cog nize	distinguish, identify, remember, know, recall
17.	salutation	sal u ta tion	greeting, address, salute, welcome, regards
18.	statistics	sta tis tics	figures, data, information, facts, stats
19.	tragedy	tra ge dy	misfortune, adversity, disaster, catastrophe
20.	vacuum	va cuum	void, space, gap, emptiness, nothingness

The definitions of the vocabulary words that you studied on the previous page appear in Column 1 below. In the space provided in Column 2, write the term that correctly matches the definitions in Column 1.

COLUMN 1	COLUMN 2
1. unknown, unfamiliar, strange, alien, exotic	1. _____
2. figures, data, information, facts, stats	2. _____
3. financial plan, statement, estimate, allowance	3. _____
4. many, plentiful, abundant, countless, several	4. _____
5. void, space, gap, emptiness, nothingness	5. _____
6. satisfactory, suitable, adequate, sufficient	6. _____
7. freedom, prerogative, opportunity, advantage	7. _____
8. misfortune, adversity, disaster, catastrophe	8. _____
9. decision, ruling, finding, verdict, conclusion	9. _____
10. dissimilarity, distinction, contrast, variety	10. _____
11. distinguish, identify, remember, know, recall	11. _____
12. obvious, clear, evident, noticeable, conspicuous	12. _____
13. living, income, means, resources, salary	13. _____
14. annoy, pester, bother, hassle, tease, irritate	14. _____
15. impoverished, destitute, bankrupt, insolvent	15. _____
16. overstate, embellish, boast, amplify, inflate	16. _____
17. greeting, address, salute, welcome, regards	17. _____
18. various, assorted, mixed, diverse, eclectic	18. _____
19. wholly, thoroughly, entirely, totally, fully	19. _____
20. huge, gigantic, vast, enormous, tremendous	20. _____

GOAL: Improve vocabulary and spelling

_____ NAME

_____ CLASS

Study the frequently misspelled words in Column 1 and their definitions in Column 3 before completing this exercise. Pronounce the words as they are divided in Column 2. Learn the correct spellings and definitions. These terms may appear on the unit test.

COLUMN 1	COLUMN 2	COLUMN 3
1. accidentally	ac ci dent ally	by chance, by mistake, unwittingly, unintentionally
2. argument	ar gu ment	case, reasoning, evidence, proof, debate
3. bulletin	bu lle tin	statement, communiqué, announcement, notice
4. conference	con ference	meeting, discussion, convention, talk, gathering
5. disappoint	di sa ppoint	dissatisfy, fail, let down, mislead, frustrate
6. exceed	ex ceed	surpass, go beyond, outdo, beat, top
7. formerly	for mer ly	previously, before, earlier, prior, in the past
8. healthy	heal thy	fit, well, strong, in good physical condition
9. immigrant	i mmi grant	settler, refugee, migrant, foreigner, newcomer
10. kernel	ker nel	core, center, root, heart, essence, gist
11. loyalty	loy al ty	faithfulness, devotion, allegiance, reliability
12. mischief	mis chief	misbehavior, naughtiness, trouble, disobedience
13. obstacle	ob sta cle	hindrance, obstruction, barrier, impediment
14. perceive	per ceive	observe, notice, discern, see, look, regard
15. probably	pro ba bly	most likely, possibly, presumably, conceivably
16. recommend	re co mmend	approve, endorse, support, suggest, urge
17. satisfactory	sa tis fac tory	acceptable, suitable, pleasing, adequate, enough
18. subsidize	sub si dize	finance, support, fund, sponsor, back, underwrite
19. transparent	trans par ent	see-through, clear, translucent, lucid, sheer
20. valuable	val ua ble	expensive, high-priced, precious, costly, worthwhile

Read the definitions in Column 1. Circle the *correctly spelled* word in Column 2 that matches the definitions in Column 1.

COLUMN 1	COLUMN 2
1. fit, well, in good physical condition	1. helthy, heallthy, haelthy, healthy
2. finance, support, fund, sponsor	2. subsedize, subsadize, subsidize, subsidise
3. case, reasoning, evidence, proof	3. argument, arrgument, argumant, arghument
4. misbehavior, naughtiness, trouble	4. mischeif, mischief, mischef, misschief
5. dissatisfy, fail, let down, mislead	5. dissappoint, disapoint, disappoint, disippoint
6. most likely, possibly, presumably	6. probably, probabely, probley, probibly
7. faithfulness, devotion, allegiance	7. loyalty, loyilty, loyallty, loyelty
8. by chance, by mistake, unwittingly	8. accidentilly, accidentally, axidentally, accidentaly
9. expensive, high-priced, precious	9. valuble, valuabl, valuable, valluable
10. settler, refugee, migrant, newcomer	10. imigrant, immigrent, immagrant, immigrant
11. observe, notice, discern, regard	11. perceive, perceve, percieve, perseive
12. hindrance, obstruction, impediment	12. obsticle, obbstacle, obstacle, obstacel
13. surpass, go beyond, outdo, top	13. excceed, excede, exseed, exceed
14. statement, announcement, notice	14. bulletin, buletin, bulleten, bullitin
15. approve, endorse, support, urge	15. recomend, reccommend, recommand, recommend
16. core, center, root, heart, essence	16. kernnel, karnel, kernel, kernell
17. meeting, discussion, gathering	17. conferance, conference, confrence, conferrence
18. acceptable, suitable, pleasing	18. satisfactory, satisfactry, sattisfactory, satisfactery
19. previously, before, earlier, prior	19. formally, formerly, formarly, formerlly
20. see-through, clear, translucent	20. transparant, transperant, transparent, transpurent

GOAL: Improve vocabulary and spelling

NAME _____

CLASS _____

Study the frequently misspelled words in Column 1 and their definitions in Column 3 before completing this exercise. Pronounce the words as they are divided in Column 2. Learn the correct spellings and definitions. These terms may appear on the unit test.

COLUMN 1	COLUMN 2	COLUMN 3
1. accommodate	a cco mmo date	make suitable, adapt, adjust, reconcile, comply
2. auditor	au di tor	assessor, examiner, inspector, accountant, actuary
3. bureau	bur eau	agency, office, department, branch, division
4. congratulate	con gra tu late	applaud, cheer, praise, salute, wish joy to
5. disastrous	di sas trous	catastrophic, devastating, destructive, ruinous
6. excellent	ex ce llent	brilliant, exceptional, outstanding, superb
7. fraternity	fra ter ni ty	brotherhood, association, alliance, club, society
8. heartily	hear til y	enthusiastically, vigorously, energetically, zealously
9. important	im por tant	significant, vital, crucial, central, chief, main
10. kindergarten	kin der gar ten	nursery school, play group, day nursery, play school
11. maintenance	main ten ance	preservation, provision, care, continuance, support
12. mischievous	mis chie vous	naughty, unruly, prankish, impish, ill-behaved
13. occasion	o cca sion	event, incident, affair, happening, occurrence
14. permanent	per ma nent	lasting, enduring, eternal, stable, unending
15. procedure	pro ce dure	process, method, system, protocol, policy
16. reference	re ference	source material, original text, book, article, writing
17. schedule	sche dule	agenda, timetable, calendar, program, plan
18. subtle	su btle	suggestive, indirect, implied, insinuated, inferred
19. trespass	tres pass	intrude, invade, infringe, encroach, violate
20. variety	va ri e ty	difference, diversity, variation, medley, assortment

Look at the definitions in Column 2. Find the word in Column 1 that correctly matches the definition. In Column 3 write the *letter* of the matching word from Column 1.

COLUMN 1		COLUMN 2	COLUMN 3
A. accommodate	1.	agenda, timetable, calendar, program, plan	1. _____
B. auditor	2.	brilliant, exceptional, outstanding, superb	2. _____
C. bureau	3.	suggestive, indirect, implied, insinuated	3. _____
D. congratulate	4.	intrude, invade, infringe, encroach, violate	4. _____
E. disastrous	5.	nursery school, play group, day nursery	5. _____
F. excellent	6.	make suitable, adapt, adjust, reconcile, comply	6. _____
G. fraternity	7.	significant, vital, crucial, central, chief, main	7. _____
H. heartily	8.	lasting, enduring, eternal, stable, unending	8. _____
I. important	9.	source material, original text, book, article	9. _____
J. kindergarten	10.	naughty, unruly, prankish, impish, ill-behaved	10. _____
K. maintenance	11.	agency, office, department, branch, division	11. _____
L. mischievous	12.	difference, diversity, variation, medley	12. _____
M. occasion	13.	brotherhood, association, alliance, club, society	13. _____
N. permanent	14.	process, method, system, protocol, policy	14. _____
O. procedure	15.	applaud, cheer, praise, salute, wish joy to	15. _____
P. reference	16.	event, incident, affair, happening, occurrence	16. _____
Q. schedule	17.	preservation, provision, care, continuance	17. _____
R. subtle	18.	enthusiastically, vigorously, energetically	18. _____
S. trespass	19.	catastrophic, devastating, destructive, ruinous	19. _____
T. variety	20.	assessor, examiner, inspector, accountant	20. _____

GOAL: Improve vocabulary and spelling

———————————————————— NAME

———————————————————— CLASS

Study the frequently misspelled words in Column 1 and their definitions in Column 3 before completing this exercise. Pronounce the words as they are divided in Column 2. Learn the correct spellings and definitions. These terms may appear on the unit test.

	COLUMN 1	COLUMN 2	COLUMN 3
1.	accuracy	a ccu ra cy	correctness, exactness, precision, reliability
2.	author	au thor	writer, novelist, essayist, founder, creator
3.	business	busi ness	job, work, occupation, venture, commerce
4.	conscience	con science	moral sense, scruples, principles, qualms
5.	disbursement	dis burse ment	payment, outlay, spending, expenditure, cost
6.	exhilarate	ex hi la rate	excite, elate, thrill, invigorate, uplift, cheer
7.	fundamental	fun da men tal	basic, primary, central, grassroots, elemental
8.	height	height	tallness, stature, elevation, altitude, loftiness
9.	inadequate	i na de quate	insufficient, lacking, scarce, meager, insubstantial
10.	knowledge	know ledge	learning, education, understanding, insight, wisdom
11.	management	ma nage ment	administration, supervision, authority, direction
12.	occur	o ccur	happen, take place, transpire, ensue, come about
13.	permissible	per mi ssi ble	allowable, permitted, lawful, sanctioned, admissible
14.	pronunciation	pro nun ci a tion	articulation, voicing, diction, elocution, intonation
15.	referred	re ferred	passed on, relegated, handed over, transferred
16.	security	se cur i ty	safety, refuge, sanctuary, protection, defense
17.	sufficient	su ffi cient	enough, adequate, ample, satisfactory, acceptable
18.	truly	tru ly	really, actually, indeed, honestly, in fact, sincerely
19.	verification	ver i fi ca tion	validation, confirmation, proof, corroboration, authentication
20.	wholly	who lly	completely, altogether, entirely, totally, fully

The definitions of the vocabulary words that you studied on the previous page appear in Column 1 below. In the space provided in Column 2, write the term that correctly matches the definitions in Column 1.

COLUMN 1	COLUMN 2
1. insufficient, lacking, scarce, meager	1. _____
2. really, actually, indeed, honestly, in fact	2. _____
3. articulation, voicing, diction, elocution	3. _____
4. correctness, exactness, precision, reliability	4. _____
5. passed on, relegated, handed over, transferred	5. _____
6. administration, supervision, authority, direction	6. _____
7. job, work, occupation, venture, commerce	7. _____
8. basic, primary, central, grassroots, elemental	8. _____
9. completely, altogether, entirely, totally, fully	9. _____
10. safety, refuge, sanctuary, protection, defense	10. _____
11. writer, novelist, essayist, founder, creator	11. _____
12. allowable, permitted, lawful, sanctioned	12. _____
13. payment, outlay, spending, expenditure	13. _____
14. validation, confirmation, proof, corroboration	14. _____
15. happen, take place, transpire, ensue	15. _____
16. enough, adequate, ample, satisfactory	16. _____
17. moral sense, scruples, principles, qualms	17. _____
18. learning, education, understanding, insight	18. _____
19. tallness, stature, elevation, altitude, loftiness	19. _____
20. excite, elate, thrill, invigorate, uplift, cheer	20. _____

GOAL: Improve vocabulary and spelling

_____ NAME

_____ CLASS

Study the frequently misspelled words in Column 1 and their definitions in Column 3 before completing this exercise. Pronounce the words as they are divided in Column 2. Do not confuse these syllabic word divisions with end-of-line word divisions. Learn the correct spellings and definitions. These terms may appear on the unit test.

	COLUMN 1	COLUMN 2	COLUMN 3
1.	acquire	a cquire	obtain, get, gain, attain, buy, procure
2.	awkward	aw kward	self-conscious, embarrassed, clumsy, inept
3.	calendar	ca len dar	agenda, schedule, date book, almanac, docket
4.	conscientious	con sci en tious	careful, thorough, reliable, hard-working
5.	discipline	di sci pline	correction, order, control, restraint, obedience
6.	existence	ex is tence	life, being, survival, essence, continuation
7.	gauge	gauge	measure, assess, weigh, determine, estimate
8.	heroes	he roes	champions, distinguished for action, brave, valiant
9.	independent	in de pen dent	separate, free, unattached, self-supporting
10.	label	la bel	tag, ticket, name, identification, description
11.	maneuver	ma neu ver	plan, trick, plot, scheme, tactic, manipulation
12.	modified	mo di fied	changed, adapted, varied, adjusted, altered
13.	omitted	o mi tted	left out, ignored, neglected, disregarded, excluded
14.	perseverance	per se ver ance	insistence, firmness, persistence, resolve, determination
15.	publicly	pub li cly	openly, plainly, overtly, candidly, aboveboard
16.	regardless	re gard less	despite, anyway, aside from, notwithstanding
17.	seize	seize	grab, take, snatch, grasp, clutch, appropriate
18.	turnover	tur no ver	yield, output, productivity, volume, aggregate
19.	vicinity	vi ci ni ty	proximity, nearness, neighborhood, environs, region
20.	withhold	with hold	hold back, deduct, reserve, keep, delay, deny

Read each sentence carefully. Look at the definitions in parentheses. In the *Answers* column, write the vocabulary word that matches the definition.

1. Everyone should have (champions) to look to for inspiration.

   1. _____

2. A paragraph has been (excluded) from the contract.

   2. _____

3. Long-range planning of product (output) is important to successful businesses.

   3. _____

4. We made a few wrong turns on our trip, but we had fun (anyway).

   4. _____

5. Isabelle was preparing to (procure) a new computer.

   5. _____

6. Our task was to (ticket) all new inventory for our department.

   6. _____

7. When will they (snatch) our telephones for texting in class?

   7. _____

8. The court clerk will update the judge's (docket).

   8. _____

9. The actress (candidly) announced her dislike of the movie's script.

   9. _____

10. Employers often reward (reliable) workers with salary increases.

    10. _____

11. We did not have an address for the restaurant, but we knew it was in the (neighborhood).

    11. _____

12. The young boy on the stage was (self-conscious).

    12. _____

13. It was only through (determination) that I was able to pass my driver's test.

    13. _____

14. Ben was surprised at the amount of taxes his employer was required to (deduct) from his paycheck.

    14. _____

15. His political opponent's shameless (plot) caused Elliott to lose the election.

    15. _____

16. The (survival) of the plane crash victims depended on their ability to keep calm.

    16. _____

17. Our (changed) homeowner's rules were presented to all homeowners on Friday.

    17. _____

18. Brisco was excited to become (self-supporting) when he reached his 18th birthday.

    18. _____

19. (Restraint) can be difficult if you don't exercise self-control.

    19. _____

20. Our instructor asked us to (estimate) the weight of an egg.

    20. _____

Unit 1

GOAL: Improve vocabulary and spelling

NAME _____

CLASS _____

Study the frequently misspelled words in Column 1 and their definitions in Column 3 before completing this exercise. Pronounce the words as they are divided in Column 2. Learn the correct spellings and definitions. These terms may appear on the unit test.

COLUMN 1	COLUMN 2	COLUMN 3
1. acquit	a cquit	let off, clear, absolve, free, exonerate, release
2. bankruptcy	ban krupt cy	insolvency, ruin, liquidation, economic failure
3. candidate	can di date	office seeker, nominee, applicant, contestant
4. conscious	con scious	aware, mindful, cognizant, awake, alert
5. dissatisfied	di ssa tis fied	unhappy, disgruntled, displeased, disappointed
6. experience	ex per i ence	knowledge, skill, understanding, know-how
7. genius	gen ius	prodigy, gifted, intellectual, master, sage, brain
8. hierarchy	hi er ar chy	ranking, pecking order, placing, chain of command
9. indispensable	in di spen sa ble	crucial, vital, essential, necessary, imperative
10. laboratory	la bora tor y	workroom, testing ground, experiment room, research facility
11. material	ma ter i al	matter, substance, element, component, fabric, cloth
12. monotonous	mo no ton ous	dull, wearying, repetitive, boring, tedious, tiresome
13. operation	o per a tion	process, action, maneuver, procedure, plan, method
14. personnel	per sonn el	employees, staff, workforce, human resources
15. pursue	pur sue	strive, try, aspire, attempt, undertake, seek
16. reimburse	re im burse	repay, pay back, compensate, return, recompense
17. separate	se pa rate	divide, part, split, sever, undo, disconnect
18. superfluous	su per flu ous	extra, redundant, unnecessary, excessive, extravagant
19. superintendent	su per in ten dent	manager, supervisor, administrator, overseer, director
20. visible	vi si ble	apparent, noticeable, obvious, clear, evident

Look at the definitions in Column 1. Circle the *correctly spelled* word in Column 2 that matches the definitions in Column 1.

COLUMN 1	COLUMN 2
1. matter, substance, element, fabric	1. materrial, meterial, material, materiel
2. divide, part, split, sever, undo	2. seperate, sepparate, seprate, separate
3. insolvency, ruin, economic failure	3. bankruptcy, bankrupcy, bankrutpcy, bankrupptcy
4. ranking, pecking order, placing	4. higharchy, higherarchy, hierarchy, heirarchy
5. aware, mindful, cognizant, awake	5. connscious, conscious, consciouss, connscience
6. strive, try, aspire, attempt, undertake	6. purrsue, persue, pursoo, pursue
7. extra, redundant, unnecessary, excessive	7. superflouous, superfluous, sooperfluous, superfluouss
8. let off, clear, absolve, free, release	8. acquitt, akquit, acqwit, acquit
9. process, action, maneuver, procedure	9. operation, opperation, operasion, oparation
10. knowledge, skill, understanding	10. expereince, expperience, experience, experiencce
11. apparent, noticeable, obvious, clear	11. vissible, visible, visable, vizible
12. employees, staff, workforce	12. perssonel, personal, personel, personnel
13. office seeker, nominee, applicant	13. canidate, candedate, canndidate, candidate
14. repay, pay back, compensate, return	14. reimburse, reimmburse, reimberse, reimburce
15. manager, supervisor, administrator	15. superintenndent, superentendent, superintendent, superintendant
16. workroom, testing ground, research facility	16. laboratary, laborratory, labratory, laboratory
17. dull, wearying, repetitive, boring	17. monotonous, monotinous, monotonus, monotenous
18. prodigy, gifted, intellectual, sage	18. genus, genious, genius, geinus
19. crucial, vital, essential, necessary	19. indispensible, indespensable, indispansible, indispensable
20. unhappy, disgruntled, displeased	20. dissatisfied, disatisfied, dissatissfied, dissattisfied

GOAL: Improve vocabulary and spelling

NAME _____

CLASS _____

Study the frequently misspelled words in Column 1 and their definitions in Column 3 before completing this exercise. Pronounce the words as they are divided in Column 2. Learn the correct spellings and definitions. These terms may appear on the unit test.

COLUMN 1	COLUMN 2	COLUMN 3
1. adequate	a de quate	enough, satisfactory, suitable, ample, sufficient
2. bargain	bar gain	good buy, discount, markdown, good deal, reduction
3. career	ca reer	work, job, vocation, occupation, profession
4. consensus	con sen sus	agreement, accord, harmony, consent, concurrence
5. economic	e co no mic	financial, business, budgetary, commercial, industrial
6. explanation	ex pla na tion	clarification, detail, enlightenment, elaboration
7. genuine	gen u ine	real, authentic, actual, sincere, honest, heartfelt
8. hindrance	hin drance	obstacle, barrier, impediment, interference
9. individual	in di vi dual	person, somebody, self, being, character
10. laboriously	la bor i ous ly	arduously, carefully, painstakingly, with difficulty
11. mathematics	mathe ma tics	arithmetic, reckoning, calculation, science of numbers
12. morale	mo rale	confidence, assurance, resolve, spirit, conviction
13. opinion	o pin ion	belief, view, idea, sentiment, notion, theory
14. physician	phy si cian	doctor, general practitioner, surgeon, M.D.
15. qualification	qua li fi ca tion	requirement, prerequisite, condition, criterion
16. relevant	re le vant	pertinent, applicable, germane, related, significant
17. supersede	su per sede	override, succeed, replace, supplant, displace
18. tyranny	tyr a nny	oppression, dictatorship, autocracy, domination, cruelty
19. volume	vol ume	quantity, amount, expanse, bulk, mass, size
20. witness	wit ness	observer, bystander, onlooker, attester, spectator

The definitions of the vocabulary words that you studied on the previous page appear in Column 1 below. In the space provided in Column 2, write the word that correctly matches the definitions in Column 1.

COLUMN 1	COLUMN 2
1. arithmetic, calculation, science of numbers	1. _____
2. good buy, discount, markdown, reduction	2. _____
3. oppression, dictatorship, autocracy, domination	3. _____
4. clarification, detail, enlightenment, elaboration	4. _____
5. doctor, general practitioner, surgeon, M.D.	5. _____
6. observer, bystander, onlooker, attester, spectator	6. _____
7. obstacle, barrier, impediment, interference	7. _____
8. enough, satisfactory, suitable, ample, sufficient	8. _____
9. pertinent, applicable, germane, related, significant	9. _____
10. belief, view, idea, sentiment, notion, theory	10. _____
11. agreement, accord, harmony, consent, concurrence	11. _____
12. requirement, prerequisite, condition, criterion	12. _____
13. quantity, amount, expanse, bulk, mass, size	13. _____
14. work, job, vocation, occupation, profession	14. _____
15. real, authentic, actual, sincere, honest, heartfelt	15. _____
16. override, succeed, replace, supplant, displace	16. _____
17. confidence, assurance, resolve, spirit, conviction	17. _____
18. person, somebody, self, being, character	18. _____
19. financial, business, budgetary, commercial	19. _____
20. arduously, carefully, painstakingly, with difficulty	20. _____

Unit 1

GOAL: Improve vocabulary and spelling

_____ NAME

_____ CLASS

Study the frequently misspelled words in Column 1 and their definitions in Column 3 before completing this exercise. Pronounce the words as they are divided in Column 2. Learn the correct spellings and definitions. These terms may appear on the unit test.

	COLUMN 1	COLUMN 2	COLUMN 3
1.	adjacent	ad ja cent	neighboring, near, close by, next to, adjoining
2.	beautiful	beau ti ful	gorgeous, good-looking, stunning, attractive, striking
3.	category	ca te gor y	group, class, sort, grade, type, kind, league
4.	courteous	cour te ous	polite, well-mannered, considerate, civil, gracious
5.	efficient	e ffi cient	competent, productive, proficient, effective, capable
6.	facilities	fa ci li ties	amenities, services, conveniences, restrooms
7.	government	go vern ment	administration, rule, authority, regulation, regime
8.	hospitality	hos pi tal i ty	welcome, kindness, generosity, graciousness, courtesy
9.	ingenious	in gen ious	clever, resourceful, inventive, original, imaginative
10.	language	lan guage	communication, speech, tongue, dialect, jargon
11.	mechanics	me cha nics	workings, logistics, procedures, technicalities
12.	mysterious	mys ter i ous	strange, unexplained, unsolved, puzzling, peculiar
13.	opponent	o ppo nent	foe, competitor, challenger, enemy, rival, adversary
14.	possession	po sse ssion	control, ownership, tenure, proprietary, custody
15.	quantity	quan ti ty	amount, number, size, volume, allotment, sum
16.	remittance	re mi ttance	payment, allowance, transmittal, money sent
17.	severely	se vere ly	harshly, sternly, strictly, cruelly, relentlessly
18.	tangible	tan gi ble	touchable, real, solid, concrete, physical, substantial
19.	unanimous	u na ni mous	agreed, undisputed, undivided, unified, harmonious
20.	voucher	vou cher	coupon, ticket, receipt, record, check, certificate

Look at the definitions in Column 2. Find the term in Column 1 that correctly matches the definitions. In Column 3 write the *letter* of the matching term from Column 1.

COLUMN 1	COLUMN 2	COLUMN 3
A. adjacent	1. workings, logistics, procedures, technicalities	1. _____
B. beautiful	2. touchable, real, solid, concrete, physical, substantial	2. _____
C. category	3. group, class, sort, grade, type, kind, league	3. _____
D. courteous	4. control, ownership, tenure, proprietary, custody	4. _____
E. efficient	5. payment, allowance, transmittal, money sent	5. _____
F. facilities	6. neighboring, near, close by, next to, adjoining	6. _____
G. government	7. amenities, services, conveniences, restrooms	7. _____
H. hospitality	8. coupon, ticket, receipt, record, check, certificate	8. _____
I. ingenious	9. polite, well-mannered, considerate, civil, gracious	9. _____
J. language	10. amount, number, size, volume, allotment, sum	10. _____
K. mechanics	11. agreed, undisputed, undivided, unified, harmonious	11. _____
L. mysterious	12. foe, competitor, challenger, enemy, rival, adversary	12. _____
M. opponent	13. competent, productive, proficient, effective, capable	13. _____
N. possession	14. harshly, sternly, strictly, cruelly, relentlessly	14. _____
O. quantity	15. gorgeous, good-looking, stunning, attractive, striking	15. _____
P. remittance	16. strange, unexplained, unsolved, puzzling, peculiar	16. _____
Q. severely	17. communication, speech, tongue, dialect, jargon	17. _____
R. tangible	18. welcome, kindness, generosity, graciousness	18. _____
S. unanimous	19. administration, rule, authority, regulation, regime	19. _____
T. voucher	20. clever, resourceful, inventive, original, imaginative	20. _____

GOAL: Improve vocabulary and spelling

NAME _____

CLASS _____

Study the frequently misspelled words in Column 1 and their definitions in Column 3 before completing this exercise. Pronounce the words as they are divided in Column 2. Learn the correct spellings and definitions. These terms may appear on the unit test.

COLUMN 1	COLUMN 2	COLUMN 3
1. advantageous	ad van ta geous	beneficial, profitable, favorable, worthwhile, helpful
2. beginning	be gi nning	origin, starting point, outset, commencement, birth
3. cemetery	ce me ter y	graveyard, burial ground, memorial park, resting place
4. dangerous	dan ge rous	unsafe, hazardous, risky, treacherous, perilous
5. elementary	e le men ta ry	basic, simple, uncomplicated, fundamental, primary
6. familiar	fa mil iar	well-known, common, frequent, recognizable
7. gorgeous	gor geous	beautiful, elegant, attractive, striking, good-looking
8. humiliate	hu mi li ate	disgrace, put down, demean, humble, debase
9. inoculate	i no cu late	immunize, vaccinate, inject, protect, prevent
10. leisurely	lei sure ly	unhurriedly, lazily, slowly, lingeringly, calmly
11. magnificent	mag ni fi cent	superb, wonderful, splendid, glorious, outstanding
12. narrative	narr a tive	story, tale, account, anecdote, yarn, description
13. opportunities	o ppor tu ni ties	chances, occasions, favorable circumstances, possibilities
14. poverty	po ver ty	scarcity, shortage, lack, need, deficiency, poor
15. questionnaire	ques tio nnaire	survey, poll, inquiry, canvass, sampling, census
16. requisition	re qui si tion	call for, request, order, require, buy, demand
17. similar	si mi lar	alike, same, comparable, parallel, related, akin
18. temperament	tem pera ment	nature, character, personality, disposition, attitude
19. university	u ni ver si ty	college, institution of higher learning, campus, school
20. waive	waive	forgo, abandon, surrender, give up, relinquish

Read each sentence carefully. Look at the definitions in parentheses. In the *Answers* column, write the vocabulary word that matches the definition.

ANSWERS

1. The couple strolled (lazily) along the lakeshore.

1. _____

2. Our (campus) is especially beautiful in the fall.

2. _____

3. Without proper gear, it would be (risky) to climb down the cliff.

3. _____

4. There are many (possibilities) for those who work hard.

4. _____

5. Our (order) for new computer monitors was misplaced.

5. _____

6. Marilee was often referred to as (striking).

6. _____

7. The conference location is (favorable) to all participants.

7. _____

8. Melvin was required to (surrender) his rights to the property.

8. _____

9. We must each do our part to help those in (need).

9. _____

10. The music teacher told us that learning scales is (basic) to becoming a good musician.

10. _____

11. Have you ever been asked to complete a (survey)?

11. _____

12. The (starting point) of the novel is set in London, England.

12. _____

13. Hawaiian sunsets are absolutely (splendid).

13. _____

14. A nurse should have a compassionate (personality).

14. _____

15. Our English assignment was to write a (description) of our summer vacation.

15. _____

16. The streets of the city were very (well-known) to our taxi driver.

16. _____

17. The farmer who lives down the road from us asked us to help him (vaccinate) his chickens!

17. _____

18. She purchased (comparable) souvenirs for each family member.

18. _____

19. It is wrong to (demean) another person.

19. _____

20. On Veterans Day, a ceremony was held at our local (memorial park).

20. _____

GOAL: Improve vocabulary and spelling

_____ NAME

_____ CLASS

Study the frequently misspelled words in Column 1 and their definitions in Column 3 before completing this exercise. Pronounce the words as they are divided in Column 2. Learn the correct spellings and definitions. These terms may appear on the unit test.

COLUMN 1	COLUMN 2	COLUMN 3
1. advisable	ad vi sa ble	wise, prudent, sensible, desirable, commendable
2. behavior	be ha vior	actions, deeds, demeanor, manner, conduct
3. changeable	change a ble	variable, unreliable, unpredictable, erratic
4. deficiency	de fi cien cy	lack, need, loss, scarcity, shortage, inadequacy
5. embarrass	em barr ass	shame, mortify, upset, humiliate, fluster
6. fascinate	fa scin ate	charm, attract, allure, enthrall, captivate
7. grammar	gra mmar	language rules, sentence structure, syntax
8. humorous	hu mor ous	funny, amusing, entertaining, witty, comical
9. intelligence	in te lli gence	aptitude, intellect, cleverness, brains, smarts
10. lengthen	leng then	extend, elongate, stretch, prolong, increase
11. memento	me men to	souvenir, reminder, keepsake, token, remembrance
12. naturally	na tur a lly	of course, as expected, instinctively, unsurprisingly
13. optimistic	op ti mis tic	hopeful, positive, confident, cheerful, buoyant
14. precede	pre cede	lead, come first, go before, pave the way, herald
15. quotation	quo ta tion	citation, passage, extract, reference, excerpt
16. resign	re sign	leave, quit, give notice, abdicate, retire, step down
17. simultaneous	si mul ta ne ous	concurrent, in unison, synchronous, instantaneous
18. tenant	te nant	occupant, renter, resident, lodger, boarder
19. unmistakable	un mi sta ka ble	evident, apparent, obvious, recognizable, distinct
20. warrant	warr ant	guarantee, attest, vouch, ensure, certify, secure

Look at the definitions in Column 2. Find the term in Column 1 that correctly matches the definitions. In Column 3 write the *letter* of the matching term from Column 1.

COLUMN 1	COLUMN 2	COLUMN 3
A. advisable	1. aptitude, intellect, cleverness, brains, smarts	1. _____
B. behavior	2. guarantee, attest, vouch, ensure, certify, secure	2. _____
C. changeable	3. lead, come first, go before, pave the way, herald	3. _____
D. deficiency	4. concurrent, in unison, synchronous, instantaneous	4. _____
E. embarrass	5. souvenir, reminder, keepsake, token, remembrance	5. _____
F. fascinate	6. actions, deeds, demeanor, manner, conduct	6. _____
G. grammar	7. evident, apparent, obvious, recognizable, distinct	7. _____
H. humorous	8. charm, attract, allure, enthrall, captivate	8. _____
I. intelligence	9. wise, prudent, sensible, desirable, commendable	9. _____
J. lengthen	10. citation, passage, extract, reference, excerpt	10. _____
K. memento	11. occupant, renter, resident, lodger, boarder	11. _____
L. naturally	12. hopeful, positive, confident, cheerful, buoyant	12. _____
M. optimistic	13. variable, unreliable, unpredictable, erratic	13. _____
N. precede	14. extend, elongate, stretch, prolong, increase	14. _____
O. quotation	15. lack, need, loss, scarcity, shortage, inadequacy	15. _____
P. resign	16. funny, amusing, entertaining, witty, comical	16. _____
Q. simultaneous	17. shame, mortify, upset, humiliate, fluster	17. _____
R. tenant	18. of course, as expected, instinctively, unsurprisingly	18. _____
S. unmistakable	19. leave, quit, give notice, abdicate, retire, step down	19. _____
T. warrant	20. language rules, sentence structure, syntax	20. _____

GOAL: Improve vocabulary and spelling

_____ NAME

_____ CLASS

Study the frequently misspelled words in Column 1 and their definitions in Column 3 before completing this exercise. Pronounce the words as they are divided in Column 2. Learn the correct spellings and definitions. These terms may appear on the unit test.

	COLUMN 1	COLUMN 2	COLUMN 3
1.	allotted	a llott ed	rationed, doled out, distributed, designated
2.	believe	be lieve	consider, think, suppose, deem, presume, hold
3.	committee	co mmi ttee	advisory group, board, council, commission
4.	definitely	de fi nite ly	exactly, precisely, certainly, surely, positively
5.	emergency	e mer gen cy	crisis, disaster, accident, urgency, tragedy
6.	favorite	fa vo rite	preferred, best-liked, favored, beloved, popular
7.	grandeur	gran deur	splendor, magnificence, majesty, dignity, greatness
8.	hungry	hun gry	ravenous, starving, empty, famished, craving
9.	interest	in terest	concern, attention, notice, curiosity, awareness
10.	liaison	li ai son	link, connection, contact, intermediary, go-between
11.	memorandum	me mo ran dum	memo, note, communication, message, letter
12.	necessary	ne ce ssar y	needed, essential, required, principal, unavoidable
13.	original	o rig i nal	earliest, first, introductory, initial, primary
14.	predominant	pre do mi nant	main, major, chief, principal, primary, prevailing
15.	readjustment	re a djust ment	rearrangement, change, modification, correction, alteration
16.	restaurant	res tau rant	eating place, dining room, eatery, bistro, café
17.	solemn	so lemn	somber, grave, serious, sad, grim, brooding
18.	territory	terr i tor y	area, land, region, province, terrain, boundary
19.	unnecessary	un ne ce ssar y	needless, dispensable, unessential, superfluous
20.	wealthiest	weal thi est	richest, most affluent, most prosperous, most well-off

Read each sentence carefully. Look at the definitions in parentheses. In the *Answers* column, write the vocabulary word that matches the definition.

1. We went to the store to purchase the (required) items for our vacation.

1. _____

2. The newly discovered (region) has not been explored.

2. _____

3. The (council) will meet on Thursday evening at 7:00 P.M.

3. _____

4. The trapeze artists were the (major) attraction at the circus.

4. _____

5. We plan to meet our friends at the (bistro) tomorrow evening.

5. _____

6. Our food for the weekend backcountry hike was (rationed).

6. _____

7. The attendees were (famished) by the time they were excused for lunch.

7. _____

8. In our city, the (most affluent) families live on Nobb Hill.

8. _____

9. The (contact) for the two companies was not able to join them due to a flight delay.

9. _____

10. I (certainly) plan to go to my school's end-of-year celebration.

10. _____

11. The scientist made a (modification) to her experiment parameters.

11. _____

12. Betsy had a (beloved) childhood pet.

12. _____

13. The (needless) destruction of the forest upset many people.

13. _____

14. The (initial) settlers to the area learned to live off the land.

14. _____

15. I (hold) that freedom is essential to our way of life.

15. _____

16. The (message) I wrote needs to be proofread and revised.

16. _____

17. Have you ever seen such (splendor) as the Canadian Rockies?

17. _____

18. The students remained (serious) during the assembly about texting and driving.

18. _____

19. The hospital attendants worked tirelessly during the (disaster).

19. _____

20. He reads library books about aviation to satisfy his (curiosity).

20. _____

Well done! You have completed the exercises for Unit 1. Before your instructor administers the Unit 1 Test, review the exercises in this unit. Do not begin the Unit 2 exercises until your instructor has approved Unit 1.

Go Digital!

For additional activities visit www.cengage.com/school/bse

GOAL: Improve number writing

_____ NAME

_____ CLASS

Have you ever looked at a handwritten message, either written by you or someone else, and been unable to read the numbers? It is important to take the time to write numbers properly and legibly, especially when working with others who need to be able to easily read what you have written. Refer to the sample numbers in Figure 2-1 to improve the size and shape of the numbers you write as you complete the exercises in this text-workbook.

Figure 2-1   Sample of Number Writing

0 1 2 3 4 5 6 7 8 9

On each of the seven lines below, write the number 0 once at the left of the line. Next, write the number 1 on each line next to the 0. Continue writing each number—2, 3, 4, 5, 6, 7, 8, and 9—across all lines. When you have finished, each of the seven lines should have the numbers 0 through 9, as shown in Figure 2-1. Keep the size and shape of the numbers the same as you write each number. _Do not write fast._

_____

_____

_____

_____

_____

_____

_____

Use the lines below to practice writing any numbers that need more improvement.

_____

_____

_____

_____

_____

Look at Column 1. Amounts of money ($23.00, $7.25, etc.) have been written in the column. Notice that the dollar sign ($) is not used. Instead of a decimal point, a line down the column divides the dollars and cents amounts. Look at the first three amounts in Column 1. Notice that the 7 in the second amount (7.25) is lined up beneath the 3 in the first amount (23.00). The third amount of money ($326.50) must be lined up beneath the figures above it, with the 3 in this amount farther to the left than the 2 in the first amount. Lining up your figures makes addition easier and more accurate.

Complete Columns 2 and 3 by writing the amounts shown on the lines in the columns (the first amount of $245.50 has been written for you). Write each number neatly and line up the figures properly. Not all lines in the columns will have amounts written on them; use only the number of lines needed. Add the amounts in each column and write the total dollars and cents on the bottom row for each column. Add the columns a second time to verify your answers.

COLUMN 1		COLUMN 2			COLUMN 3		
Total Expenses			**Total Expenses**			**Total Expenses**	
23	00	245.50	245	50	45.30		
7	25	7.00			185.00		
326	50	25.25			26.50		
12	05	106.00			329.45		
9	20	37.10			250.90		
		6.75			13.40		
		123.00			150.25		
		89.42					
		118.40					
378	00						

GOAL: Improve number writing

Write the Social Security numbers shown in Column 1 in the boxes provided in Column 2. An example is shown. Remember that numbers must be written clearly so that you and others are able to read them easily.

COLUMN 1	COLUMN 2
Ex. 288-40-9337	Ex. 2 8 8 – 4 0 – 9 3 3 7
1. 752-01-6652	1. ☐☐☐–☐☐–☐☐☐☐
2. 363-29-4417	2. ☐☐☐–☐☐–☐☐☐☐
3. 518-90-0674	3. ☐☐☐–☐☐–☐☐☐☐
4. 760-32-8843	4. ☐☐☐–☐☐–☐☐☐☐
5. 256-88-1953	5. ☐☐☐–☐☐–☐☐☐☐
6. 516-38-2086	6. ☐☐☐–☐☐–☐☐☐☐
7. 360-98-4441	7. ☐☐☐–☐☐–☐☐☐☐
8. 890-33-7674	8. ☐☐☐–☐☐–☐☐☐☐
9. 161-64-8065	9. ☐☐☐–☐☐–☐☐☐☐
10. 690-19-4247	10. ☐☐☐–☐☐–☐☐☐☐

GOAL: Improve number writing

_____ NAME

_____ CLASS

In Exercise 25 you learned to write numbers in a column. In the columns in that exercise, a vertical line divided the dollars and cents amounts. In the columns in this exercise, vertical lines divide individual figures in the amount. Look at the example in Column 1. You might use ledger forms such as these working in an accounting office, keeping books for businesses, or preparing a budget.

Complete Columns 2 and 3 by writing the amounts shown on the lines in the columns. Write each number neatly and line up the figures properly. Add the amounts in each column and write the total at the bottom of each column. Add the columns a second time to verify your answers.

COLUMN 1	COLUMN 2	COLUMN 3

COLUMN 1

AMOUNT	
12 9 7 4 80	1
1 8 29	2
5 40	3
4 2 9 7 12	4
10 4 8 2 00	5
4 2 7 92	6
	7
	8
	9
28 2 0 5 53	10

COLUMN 2

429.67
2,981.00
24.77
17,180.62
55.55

COLUMN 3

937.43
3,569.00
547.92
18.43
26,428.30
674.24
8.70

GOAL: Improve number writing

_____ NAME

_____ CLASS

Write the claim numbers shown in Column 1 in the spaces provided in Column 2. Write each number neatly. _Do not write fast._ Concentrate on improving the size and shape of each number as you write. An example is shown.

<u>COLUMN 1</u>   <u>COLUMN 2</u>

Ex. **627-82-0091-B**   Ex.

Claim Number From Health Insurance Card

| 6 | 2 | 7 | 8 | 2 | 0 | 0 | 9 | 1 | B |

1. **274-13-3579-T**   1.

Claim Number From Health Insurance Card

2. **496-18-3495-J**   2.

Claim Number From Health Insurance Card

3. **283-68-0947-Y**   3.

Claim Number From Health Insurance Card

4. **095-27-8841-R**   4.

Claim Number From Health Insurance Card

5. **703-89-5615-D**   5.

Claim Number From Health Insurance Card

GOAL: Proofread amounts of money

_____ NAME

_____ CLASS

When working with numbers, it is important to pay attention to details. Being able to identify slight, but potentially significant, differences in figures will help you become a more valuable employee. Proofread the figures below. Look closely at the amount of money in Column 1, then at the amount of money in Column 2. If the two amounts are exactly alike, circle the _Y_ for Yes in Column 3. If the two amounts are not exactly alike, circle the _N_ for No in Column 3. An example is shown.

COLUMN 1	COLUMN 2	COLUMN 3
Ex. $565.55	$575.55	Ex. Y Ⓝ
1. $385.58	$385.58	1. Y N
2. $821.70	$827.10	2. Y N
3. $339.85	$339.35	3. Y N
4. $289.54	$298.54	4. Y N
5. $650.61	$650.61	5. Y N
6. $928.90	$928.98	6. Y N
7. $545.25	$454.25	7. Y N
8. $6,539.00	$6,539.00	8. Y N
9. $2,280.82	$2,280.82	9. Y N
10. $1,777.75	$1,717.75	10. Y N
11. $3,234.73	$3,234.37	11. Y N
12. $7,471.51	$7,471.15	12. Y N
13. $5,545.55	$5,545.65	13. Y N
14. $18,239.27	$18,329.27	14. Y N
15. $23,850.90	$23,850.90	15. Y N
16. $78,859.80	$78,859.80	16. Y N
17. $41,758.90	$41,758.90	17. Y N
18. $84,587.00	$84,587.00	18. Y N
19. $16,863.55	$16,862.55	19. Y N
20. $77,943.18	$77,934.18	20. Y N

GOAL: Proofread account numbers

_____ NAME

_____ CLASS

Proofread the account numbers in Column 1 and Column 2. Concentrate on paying attention to details as you proofread. If the two numbers are exactly alike, circle the _Y_ for Yes in Column 3. If the two numbers are not exactly alike, circle the _N_ for No in Column 3.

COLUMN 1	COLUMN 2	COLUMN 3
1. WIY3306	WIY3036	1. Y N
2. PJW0817	PWJ0817	2. Y N
3. QEU6639	QEU6639	3. Y N
4. BWV1530	BWV1530	4. Y N
5. RSE3402	RSE3402	5. Y N
6. BDA9053	BDA9052	6. Y N
7. PZH0403	PZH0403	7. Y N
8. GRM5917	GRN5917	8. Y N
9. EMS2953	EMS2953	9. Y N
10. MVE7645	MYE7645	10. Y N
11. KLA6037	KLA6031	11. Y N
12. AHW3026	AHW3026	12. Y N
13. EBB4583	EPB4583	13. Y N
14. BCJ0934	BCJ0934	14. Y N
15. VQO6171	VQC6171	15. Y N
16. CRO9469	CRO9469	16. Y N
17. FDJ1242	FOJ1242	17. Y N
18. NRL3636	NRL3663	18. Y N
19. HOH9727	HOH9727	19. Y N
20. DOG4598	DGO4598	20. Y N

GOAL: Proofread credit card numbers

_____ NAME

_____ CLASS

Improve your skill at identifying differences in figures by comparing the credit card numbers on the computer display with the credit card numbers on the hard copies. If the two numbers are exactly alike, circle the _Y_ for Yes in the Answers column. If the two numbers are not exactly alike, circle the _N_ for No in the Answers column.

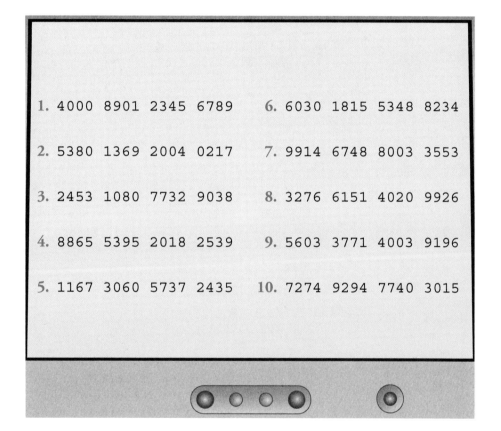

1. 4000 8901 2345 6789   6. 6030 1815 5348 8234

2. 5380 1369 2004 0217   7. 9914 6748 8003 3553

3. 2453 1080 7732 9038   8. 3276 6151 4020 9926

4. 8865 5395 2018 2539   9. 5603 3771 4003 9196

5. 1167 3060 5737 2435   10. 7274 9294 7740 3015

ANSWERS

1. Y   N

2. Y   N

3. Y   N

4. Y   N

5. Y   N

6. Y   N

7. Y   N

8. Y   N

9. Y   N

10. Y   N

1. 4000 8901 2345 6789   6. 6030 1815 5348 8239

2. 5380 1368 2004 0217   7. 9974 6748 8003 3553

3. 2453 1080 7723 9038   8. 3276 6151 4020 9926

4. 8865 5395 2018 2539   9. 5603 3771 4003 9196

5. 1167 3060 5737 2465   10. 7274 9249 7740 3015

GOAL: Make change using the count-back
method

_____ NAME

_____ CLASS

Employees of businesses such as stores and fast-food restaurants accept money from customers for items they purchase. Employees must return the proper amount of change to customers. Most businesses have computerized cash registers that indicate the amount of money to be returned. However, some businesses still use the simple "cash drawer," which is not computerized. Also, if a computerized cash register fails to work, employees must be able to "count" the proper change.

When returning change to customers, be sure to count the change rather than just handing it to them. The **count-back method** means counting the change to customers one coin or bill at a time. Using the count-back method to count change as you hand it to customers allows you to verify the amount due back and assures customers that they are receiving the proper amount of money. To count back change, begin with the smallest coins and work up to the larger bills as shown below.

Coins

$ .01	pennies
.05	nickels
.10	dimes
.25	quarters
.50	half-dollar coins
1.00	one-dollar coins

Bills

$ 1.00	dollar bills
5.00	five-dollar bills
10.00	ten-dollar bills
20.00	twenty-dollar bills
50.00	fifty-dollar bills
100.00	one-hundred-dollar bills

Example: You work at a fast-food restaurant. A customer orders a hamburger, side salad, and small soft drink, which totals $4.63. The customer hands you a $5 bill. To use the count-back method, begin with the amount of the purchase ($4.63), and starting with the smallest coin, "count" the change to add up to $5.00 as follows:

Counting money from the cash drawer:

- take from the drawer $.01 (1 penny)   and say to yourself $4.64
- take from the drawer $.01 (1 penny)   and say to yourself $4.65
- take from the drawer $.10 (1 dime)   and say to yourself $4.75
- take from the drawer $.25 (1 quarter)   and say to yourself $5.00

Counting money to the customer:

Count the change to the customer just as you counted it when you took it from the cash drawer. The change you should give the customer in the example is two pennies, one dime, and one quarter.

Write in the *Take From Cash Drawer* column each coin or bill you would remove from the cash drawer to make the proper change for the sale. In the *Say To Customer* column, write the amount you would say to the customer as you hand them their change. Use half-dollar coins ($.50 or 50 cents) where appropriate. An example is shown.

	TOTAL OF SALE	CUSTOMER GIVES YOU	TAKE FROM CASH DRAWER	SAY TO CUSTOMER
Ex.	$4.82	$10.00	$ .01	$ 4.83
			.01	4.84
			.01	4.85
			.05	4.90
			.10	5.00
			5.00	10.00
1.	$5.04	$ 6.00		
2.	$2.35	$ 5.00		
3.	$8.67	$10.00		
4.	$7.24	$10.00		
5.	$3.97	$20.00		

GOAL: Make change when given extra coins

In Exercise 32 you learned how to make change using the count-back method. You learned to begin with the amount of the purchase and, starting with the smallest coin in your cash drawer, "count" the change to add up to the bill(s) the customer gave you.

Sometimes a sale will add up to an amount that would result in the customer receiving pennies or almost a dollar's worth of change. Some customers may not want to receive pennies or numerous coins. The customer may give you a coin or coins in addition to the bill(s) to reduce the amount of change he or she will receive.

Study the example below to learn how to "count" back change when you are given extra coins.

Example: You work at the checkout counter of a drugstore. A customer's purchases total $15.02. The customer gives you a $20 bill and a nickel ($.05 or 5 cents). The change for the $15 will be counted from the $20 bill given to you. The change for the 2 cents will be counted from the nickel.

Counting money from the cash drawer:

- take from the drawer $.01 (1 penny)   and say to yourself $15.03
- take from the drawer $.01 (1 penny)   and say to yourself $15.04
- take from the drawer $.01 (1 penny)   and say to yourself $15.05
- take from the drawer $5.00 (a $5 bill)   and say to yourself $20.05

Counting money to the customer:

Count the change to the customer just as you counted it when taking it from the cash drawer. The change you should give the customer in this example is three pennies and one five-dollar bill.

Write in the *Take From Cash Drawer* column each coin or bill you would remove from the cash drawer to make the proper change for the sale. In the *Say To Customer* column, write the amount you would say to the customer as you hand them their change. An example is shown.

	TOTAL OF SALE	CUSTOMER GIVES YOU	TAKE FROM CASH DRAWER	SAY TO CUSTOMER
Ex.	$ 5.03	$10.05	$ .01	$ 5.04
			.01	5.05
			5.00	10.05
1.	$ 8.23	$10.25		
2.	$12.74	$15.75		
3.	$17.19	$20.20		
4.	$24.16	$30.20		
5.	$43.68	$50.75		

GOAL: Calculate sale totals and make change

_____ NAME

_____ CLASS

In Exercise 32 you learned to make change using the count-back method, and in Exercise 33 you learned to make change when a customer gives you extra coins. In this exercise you will determine the total of each sale. Then, using the knowledge you have gained in previous exercises, you will make the proper change for each sale.

You have been hired as a cashier at a local discount store. As part of your training, your supervisor assigns you to different departments so that you will become familiar with the store and the variety of products it sells.

When a customer makes a purchase, you will need to calculate the total cost. When making change, remember to begin with the smallest coins and work up to the larger bills. Give the customer the fewest coins and bills possible.

1. a. In the electronics department, a customer purchases a network-ready printer/scanner/copier/fax machine for $399.99, plus tax of $30.99. Add these two amounts and write the total in the _Total Of Sale_ column below.
    b. The customer gives you $450.00. Determine the change and count it back to the customer, completing the _Take From Cash Drawer_ and _Say To Customer_ columns as you have done in previous exercises.

TOTAL OF SALE	CUSTOMER GIVES YOU	TAKE FROM CASH DRAWER	SAY TO CUSTOMER
$_____	$450.00	$_____	$_____
		_____	_____
		_____	_____
		_____	_____
		_____	_____
		_____	_____
		_____	_____
		_____	_____

2. a. Another customer in the electronics department purchases a computer hard drive. The cost of the hard drive is $99.99, plus tax of $7.76. Calculate the sale total.
    b. The customer gives you $120.00. Determine the change and count it back to the customer.

TOTAL OF SALE	CUSTOMER GIVES YOU	TAKE FROM CASH DRAWER	SAY TO CUSTOMER
$_____	$120.00	$_____	$_____
		_____	_____
		_____	_____
		_____	_____

3. You are now working in the housewares department. A customer purchases an upright vacuum for $57.80, plus tax of $4.61. The customer gives you $70.50. Fill in the columns below following the procedure used for problems 1 and 2.

TOTAL OF SALE	CUSTOMER GIVES YOU	TAKE FROM CASH DRAWER	SAY TO CUSTOMER
$ _____	$70.50	$ _____	$ _____
		_____	_____
		_____	_____
		_____	_____
		_____	_____
		_____	_____
		_____	_____
		_____	_____
		_____	_____

4. Another customer in the housewares department purchases a coffee maker for $26.50, plus tax of $2.58. The customer gives you $40.10. Fill in the columns below.

TOTAL OF SALE	CUSTOMER GIVES YOU	TAKE FROM CASH DRAWER	SAY TO CUSTOMER
$ _____	$40.10	$ _____	$ _____
		_____	_____
		_____	_____
		_____	_____

5. In the jewelry department, a customer purchases a necklace for $75.99, plus tax of $5.89. The customer gives you $100.00. Fill in the columns below.

TOTAL OF SALE	CUSTOMER GIVES YOU	TAKE FROM CASH DRAWER	SAY TO CUSTOMER
$ _____	$100.00	$ _____	$ _____
		_____	_____
		_____	_____
		_____	_____
		_____	_____
		_____	_____
		_____	_____
		_____	_____

GOAL: Prepare a sales receipt and make change

_____ NAME

_____ CLASS

A **sales receipt** is a document issued by a business showing the details of a customer's purchase. The sales receipt shows the location and date of the purchase, the items purchased, the amount of the sale, and the method of payment. Most businesses provide written receipts to customers as proof of their purchase.

You have been hired as a part-time sales clerk at McCroary Stationers. Your job is to assist the customer with his/her purchase, prepare a sales receipt, accept money, and return the appropriate amount of change to the customer.

A customer wants to purchase:

- two black ink cartridges at $17.49 each
- one color cartridge pack at $46.69 each
- one #2 yellow pencils, 48-pack, at $4.50 each
- two reams of multipurpose copy paper at $9.48 each

Complete the sales receipt on the next page as follows:

1. Use the current date.

2. The sales receipt number is 271.

3. Use your initials for the sales clerk.

4. For each item purchased, list the quantity, description, and price.

5. Calculate the amount for each item by multiplying the quantity by the price.

6. Calculate the subtotal of the sales receipt.

7. Using the 8.25% sales tax chart found in the _Reference Sources_ section of this text-workbook, determine the tax on the subtotal.

8. Calculate the total amount the customer owes.

9. The customer is paying with cash. Check the box to indicate the method of payment.

10. The customer gives you $150.00. Determine the change and count it back to the customer, completing the _Total Of Sale, Take From Cash Drawer,_ and _Say To Customer_ columns on the next page.

McCroary Stationers
1442 Main Street
Spencer, IA 51301

Date: _____

Receipt # _____   Sales Clerk _____

Qty.	Description	Price	Amount
		Subtotal	
		Tax	
		Total	

Payment Method:

☐ Cash

☐ Credit Card No. _____

☐ Check No. _____

☐ Other _____

TOTAL OF SALE	CUSTOMER GIVES YOU	TAKE FROM CASH DRAWER	SAY TO CUSTOMER
$ _____	$150.00	$ _____	$ _____
		_____	_____
		_____	_____
		_____	_____
		_____	_____

GOAL: Prepare an invoice

NAME _____

CLASS _____

An **invoice** is a document issued by a seller that lists the details of a transaction between a seller and a buyer. An invoice shows the products or services delivered, quantities, date, parties involved, prices, shipping charges, and the total amount due. An invoice is also called a bill or statement, and it indicates that the buyer must pay the seller according to the payment terms. The buyer has a maximum number of days to pay for the goods or services. Buyers are sometimes offered discounts if the total due is paid within a specified time.

You have been hired as an order clerk at Brandell Lumber & Hardware. When contractors place an order for supplies, it is your job to prepare the invoice.

Mr. Bob Jones placed the following order of building materials:

Quantity	Item No.	Description	Unit Price
2 lbs.	65-08	2 ½" galvanized screws	$6.58 per pound
3 lbs.	65-02	2 ½" galvanized nails	$4.24 per pound
16 ea.	29-03	2×8×10 boards	$6.48 each
5 ea.	27-01	2×6×10 boards	$4.82 each
8 ea.	50-45	4×4×12 posts	$10.87 each

Complete the invoice on the next page as follows:

1. The invoice number is 20-942.

2. Use the current date.

3. Mr. Jones' mailing address is 8632 Skyhawk Drive, Monroe, WA 98272. His telephone number is 360-555-1236.

4. The order will be shipped to 4976 West Creek Road, Monroe, WA 98272.

5. Mr. Jones is paying with his Brandell credit card, #BJ572-4397.

6. Delivery will be made by Brandell truck.

7. For each item purchased, list the quantity, item no., description, and unit price.

8. Calculate the amount for each item by multiplying the quantity by the unit price.

9. Calculate the subtotal of the invoice.

10. Calculate the tax by multiplying the subtotal by 7.50%. Be sure to round up to the nearest cent.

11. The shipping charge for delivery by Brandell truck is $79.

12. Calculate the invoice total.

INVOICE

BRANDELL LUMBER & HARDWARE
239 Center Street
Monroe, WA 98272

Invoice No.: _____

Invoice Date: _____

Name: _____

Mailing Address: _____

_____

Telephone: (_____) _____

Shipping Address: _____

_____

Payment Method: ☐ Check

☐ Brandell credit card # _____

☐ Other _____

Delivery Method: ☐ Customer pick-up

☐ Brandell truck

Quantity	Item No.	Description	Unit Price	Amount
			Subtotal	
			Tax	
			Shipping	
			Total Due	

Payment is due within 30 days of the invoice date.

GOAL: Write amounts of money on receipts

NAME _____

CLASS _____

There are a variety of ways to write amounts of money on business forms such as receipts or checks. In a law office, amounts of money may be written in a special way on legal forms and records. Your relatives and friends may write amounts of money in slightly different ways. Other textbooks may show even more variations. For the exercises in this text-workbook, write amounts of money as shown in the examples in Figure 2-2.

Figure 2-2 Examples of Writing Amounts of Money on Business Forms

Amount of Money		
$54.00	*Fifty-four and no/100* ~~~~~~~~~~	DOLLARS
$35.85	*Thirty-five and 85/100* ~~~~~~~~~~	DOLLARS
$192.66	*One hundred ninety-two and 66/100* ~~~~~	DOLLARS
$3,207.50	*Three thousand two hundred seven and 50/100* ~~	DOLLARS
75¢	*Only seventy-five cents* ~~~~~~~~~~	~~DOLLARS~~

Use the receipt shown in Figure 2-3 as a guide as you complete the receipt forms in this exercise. As you read the instructions below the form, note that the numbered steps correspond with the circled numbers and letters shown on the form.

Figure 2-3 Stub and Receipt Form

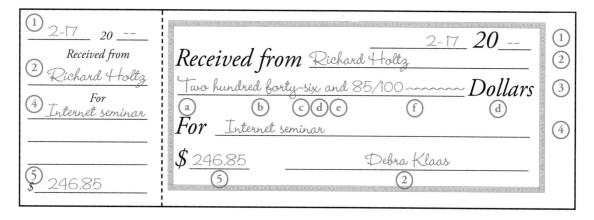

1. Write the date in figures: 2-17. After the *20*, write the current year.

2. The name after *Received from*, Richard Holtz, is the person who paid the money. The name at the bottom of the receipt, Debra Klaas, is the person who received the money.

3. Write the amount of money in both words and figures following these guidelines:

   a. Begin the first word of the amount as close to the left edge of the form as you can. Use a capital letter for the first word only. The words *hundred, forty,* and *six* do not have capital letters.

   b. Do not use a comma or the word *and* after the word *hundred* for an amount of money more than $100.

   c. Use a hyphen to divide numbers greater than twenty.

   d. Since the word *Dollars* appears at the end of the line, do not write the word *Dollars* anywhere else on the line.

   e. Write the word *and* between the dollars and cents amounts. An ampersand (&) may be used instead.

   f. Write the cents amount as a figure and as a part of 100 (or $1). Use a diagonal (/) to divide the cents amount and the 100. After the cents amount, use a wavy line to fill in the space before the word Dollars at the end of the line. Do not leave any blank space on the line.

4. After *For,* write the reason the money was paid.

5. After the *$,* write in figures the amount you wrote in words in Step 3.

EXERCISE 37a Write each amount of money as you would on a receipt. Write neatly and small. Space is limited on a receipt, and the entire written amount must fit on the line.

1. $48.95 _____ DOLLARS

2. $114.02 _____ DOLLARS

3. $219.00 _____ DOLLARS

4. $94.50 _____ DOLLARS

5. 19¢ _____ DOLLARS

6. $2,413.90 _____ DOLLARS

EXERCISE 37b   Complete the following receipt forms using the information provided for each form.

Form 1:   Use the current date. Write a receipt to Abe Rosewald for a contribution in the amount of $500.00. Sign the receipt with your own name.

_____ 20 _____
Received from
_____
For
_____
_____
_____
$ _____

_____ 20 _____
Received from _____
_____ Dollars
For _____
$ _____   _____

Form 2:   Use the current date. Write a receipt to Debra Martinez for a monthly payment in the amount of $198.75. Sign the receipt with your own name.

_____ 20 _____
Received from
_____
For
_____
_____
_____
$ _____

_____ 20 _____
Received from _____
_____ Dollars
For _____
$ _____   _____

Form 3:   Use the current date. Write a receipt to Matthew Wayne for tennis lessons in the amount of $50.00. Sign the receipt with your own name.

_____ 20 _____
Received from
_____
For
_____
_____
_____
$ _____

_____ 20 _____
Received from _____
_____ Dollars
For _____
$ _____   _____

Exercise 37

Form 4: Use the current date. Write a receipt to Sally Strommer for cookware in the amount of $85.79. Sign the receipt with your own name.

_____ 20 _____	_____ 20 _____
Received from	*Received from* _____
_____	_____ *Dollars*
For	*For* _____
_____	*$* _____ _____
_____	
$ _____	

Many businesses use receipts that have duplicate copies instead of stubs. Often there are multiple receipts on a page. The receipts are perforated so the customer's copy can be easily torn out and given to them. Writing receipts in duplicate allows the business to retain copies of fully completed receipts instead of only receipt stubs.

Some businesses allow customers to make payments on their accounts. In that case, the receipts may have spaces for recording the customer's previous balance and balance due. The payment is subtracted from any previous balance to determine the balance due. If there is no previous balance or balance due, a zero (-0-) is written on those lines.

EXERCISE 37c Complete the receipts on the next page using the information provided below for each receipt. Use the current date, determine any balance due, and sign your name next to *By*.

Receipt #287: $150.27 in cash is received from Ellison Brooks for service of a refrigerator. Mr. Brooks is paying the service charge in full. He has no previous balance.

Receipt #288: Check #2381 for $100.00 is received from Sally Scott for payment on her account. Ms. Scott's previous balance is $349.00.

Receipt #289: $985.60 is received from Alejandro Medina for the purchase of a dishwasher. Mr. Medina is paying the full amount with credit card #462-736-7002. He has no previous balance.

BENITO'S APPLIANCES
9802 Bell Avenue
Surprise, AZ 85374

287

Date _____

Received From _____ $ _____

Amount _____ DOLLARS

For _____

Previous Balance _____

This Payment _____

Balance Due _____

☐ Cash
☐ Check # _____
☐ Card # _____

YOUR RECEIPT - THANK YOU

By _____

BENITO'S APPLIANCES
9802 Bell Avenue
Surprise, AZ 85374

288

Date _____

Received From _____ $ _____

Amount _____ DOLLARS

For _____

Previous Balance _____

This Payment _____

Balance Due _____

☐ Cash
☐ Check # _____
☐ Card # _____

YOUR RECEIPT - THANK YOU

By _____

BENITO'S APPLIANCES
9802 Bell Avenue
Surprise, AZ 85374

289

Date _____

Received From _____ $ _____

Amount _____ DOLLARS

For _____

Previous Balance _____

This Payment _____

Balance Due _____

☐ Cash
☐ Check # _____
☐ Card # _____

YOUR RECEIPT - THANK YOU

By _____

To open a checking account, you must complete a signature card. A **signature card** is a document a customer signs when opening an account at a financial institution, such as a bank or credit union. On this card you sign your name the way you plan to sign it on the front of your checks. The way you sign your name on the front of your checks is also the way you sign your name on the back of checks to be deposited in your checking account.

You must put money in the account to open a checking account. This is known as making a **deposit**. Before making a deposit, you must **endorse** (sign) all the checks you will deposit into your account. In Figure 2-4 Jacob endorsed the back of the one check he deposited.

Figure 2-4   Endorsement

A **deposit ticket** (or deposit slip) is a form that must be completed each time a deposit is made in an account. To make a deposit in your account, you may take the deposit to your financial institution, mail the deposit (in a standard envelope or in one provided for that purpose), or make the deposit at an **ATM** (Automated Teller Machine). Policies vary as to whether a deposit ticket is required when depositing money through an ATM. Be sure to understand and follow the procedures required by your financial institution. Look at Figure 2-5 on the next page to see how Jacob completed his deposit ticket. As you read the instructions that follow the figure, note that the numbered steps correspond with the circled numbers shown on the deposit ticket.

Figure 2-5 Deposit Ticket Showing a $500 Deposit

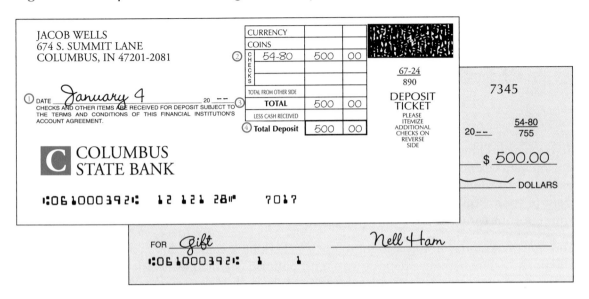

1. The *Date* with the month spelled out is written: January 4. You may also use abbreviations such as Jan. 4 or 1–4. After the *20*, the current year is written.

2. Three types of money to be deposited are: *Currency* (one-dollar bill, five-dollar bill, ten-dollar bill, etc.), *Coins* (pennies, nickels, dimes, etc.), and *Checks*. In Figure 2-5 the lines for currency (bills) and coins have no amounts written on them because only a check is being deposited. On the first line for *Checks*, the **ABA** (American Bankers Association) number is written: 54-80. This number is found on the check to be deposited. Look at Figure 2-5 under the check number 7345 and you will see the fraction format 54-80 over 755. Some banks do not require that this number be written on the deposit ticket. Some banks prefer that the check number (7345) or the check writer's name (Nell Ham) be written on the deposit ticket. If you do write the number in the fraction format, always use the *top* number given to that bank by the American Bankers Association. Do not use the bottom number from the Federal Reserve System. The format for the ABA number may vary, but it typically appears in small print near the top of the check. On the deposit ticket on the same *Checks* line, to the right of the ABA number that was written, the deposit amount of 500.00 is written. A line down the column divides the dollars and cents.

3. On the *Total* line the deposit amount of 500.00 is written.

4. Since Jacob is depositing the entire amount of the check and is receiving no cash, the *Less Cash Received* line is left blank and the *Total Deposit* of 500.00 is written again. You will learn more about the parts of a deposit ticket in a later exercise in this unit.

You should keep a current record of your account balance in a check register. A **check register** is a log of all transactions in a checking account. You must record each transaction in the register every time you make a deposit, write a check, make an ATM withdrawal, or make a **POS** (point of sale) purchase with a debit card.

Look at Figure 2-6 to see how Jacob's $500 deposit is recorded in his check register. As you read the instructions below the check register, note that the numbered steps correspond with the circled numbers above the check register.

Figure 2-6 Check Register

① CHECK NO.	② DATE	③ TRANSACTION DESCRIPTION	AMOUNT OF PAYMENT OR WITHDRAWAL	④ AMOUNT OF DEPOSIT		⑤ BALANCE	
	1-4	Deposit		500	00	500	00
		gift from Aunt Nell					

1. The *Check No.* column is left blank because a check was not written.

2. The *Date* of the deposit is written: 1-4.

3. The *Transaction Description* is written: Deposit. On the second line for this transaction, the description is written: gift from Aunt Nell.

4. The *Amount of Deposit* is written: 500.00. A line down the column divides the dollars and cents.

5. The *Balance* is the same as the amount of the deposit because Jacob is opening an account. You will learn more about maintaining a balance in later exercises in this unit.

Use the forms shown on page 90 to open a checking account in YOUR NAME.

1. Use your name to endorse the back of the check you are depositing. Refer to Figure 2-4 on page 87 as you sign the endorsement.

2. Complete the deposit ticket. Use the current date. Refer to Figure 2-5 on page 88 and the instructions below the figure as you complete the deposit ticket.

3. Record the deposit in the check register. Use the current date. Refer to Figure 2-6 above and the instructions below the figure as you complete the check register.

Exercise 38

Back of Check

Deposit Ticket

CURRENCY		
COINS		
C H E C K S		
TOTAL FROM OTHER SIDE		
TOTAL		
LESS CASH RECEIVED		
Total Deposit		

YOUR NAME
4289 CENTER AVENUE APT. G-9
GARWOOD, NJ 07027-1389

DATE _____ 20 ____
CHECKS AND OTHER ITEMS ARE RECEIVED FOR DEPOSIT SUBJECT TO
THE TERMS AND CONDITIONS OF THIS FINANCIAL INSTITUTION'S
ACCOUNT AGREEMENT.

25-43
1709

**DEPOSIT
TICKET**
PLEASE
ITEMIZE
ADDITIONAL
CHECKS ON
REVERSE
SIDE

G GARWOOD
CITY BANK

⑆06⑈0003792⑇ ⑈2 ⑈2⑈ 28⑈ 7017

3772

20 --   23-62
              1246

$ 900.00

_____ DOLLARS

FOR _college tuition_____   _Catherine Jackson_

⑆06⑈0003792⑇ ⑈   ⑈

Check Register

CHECK NO.	DATE	TRANSACTION DESCRIPTION	AMOUNT OF PAYMENT OR WITHDRAWAL		AMOUNT OF DEPOSIT	BALANCE

GOAL: Write checks and fill out check stubs

NAME

CLASS

In Exercise 38 you learned how to open a checking account. You endorsed a check, completed a deposit ticket, and made the first entry in the check register.

In this exercise you will learn how to write checks and fill out check stubs. Use the completed check stub and check shown in Figure 2-7 as guides as you complete this exercise.

Figure 2-7   Check Stub and Check

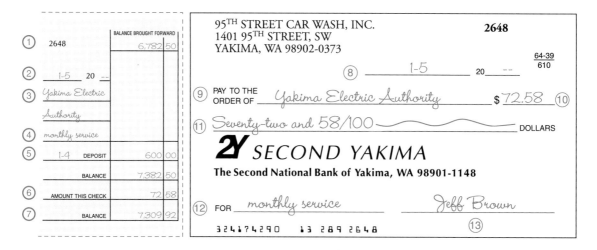

Completing the Check Stub   Always fill out the check stub before writing a check. Making a habit of completing the check stub first will ensure that you do not forget to complete the stub or have to try to recall later to whom and for what a check was written. If a stub is not filled out before a check is written, the account balance reflected on the stub will be incorrect.

1. The check stub number (2648) corresponds with the check number. You do not need to record check numbers on stubs as you do in a check register. Check stubs are usually pre-printed with the check numbers. Check numbers are printed in consecutive order; for example, 2648, 2649, 2650, etc.

2. The date is written either in figures (1-5) or spelled out (January 5). The current year is written after the *20*.

3. On the line(s) below the date, to whom the check will be written is recorded: Yakima Electric Authority.

4. On the next available line, the reason the check will be written is recorded: monthly service.

5. A deposit of $600.00 was made on 1-4. Deposits are recorded on the next available check stub. That same check stub is used the next time a check is written, whether a check is written on the same day the deposit was made or on a later day. When a deposit is recorded on a check stub, the deposit amount ($600.00) is added to the Balance Brought Forward amount ($6,782.50) to calculate a new Balance ($7,382.50).

6. The amount of the check is written in the *Amount This Check* space: 72.58. Note that dollar signs and decimal points are not written on a check stub. A vertical line divides the dollars and cents.

7. The amount of the check ($72.58) is subtracted from the Balance Brought Forward amount, or from the Balance amount if a deposit has been made ($7,382.50), to calculate the current Balance ($7,309.92).

Completing the Check   After all the information is recorded on the check stub, the check can be written.

8. The date is written either in figures or spelled out. The current year is written after the *20*.

9. After *Pay To The Order Of*, the name of the person or company to whom the check is being written is filled out. You may abbreviate a word in a long business name such as Company (Co.), Incorporated (Inc.), Limited (Ltd.), International (Intl.), or Association (Assn.).

10. The amount of the check is written in figures close to the dollar sign to prevent any possible tampering with the check amount.

11. Follow the same procedure for writing amounts on checks as you used for writing amounts on receipts in Exercise 37.

12. After *For*, the reason the check is being written is recorded.

13. The signature on a check must match the signature written on the signature card when the account was opened.

You work in the offices of 95th Street Car Wash, Inc. Your responsibilities include writing checks and making deposits. Using the transaction information provided below and on the next two pages, complete the check stubs and checks on the following pages. Be sure to complete each transaction in the order given. Sign your name on the signature line of each check. Remember to fill out the check stub *before* writing a check.

Check 2649:   Write a check for $85.23 to Madison Gas Works for the heating bill. Use January 7 of the current year as the date. Calculate the new Balance. Record it at the bottom of check stub 2649 and as the Balance Brought Forward at the top of check stub 2650.

Check 2650:   Write a check for $53.29 to Yakima Telephone Co. for the telephone bill. Use January 8 of the current year as the date. Calculate the new Balance. Record it on check stub 2650 and as the Balance Brought Forward on check stub 2651.

Deposit: You made a deposit of $650.00 for your employer on January 9. Record the deposit on check stub 2651. Calculate the new Balance and record it just below the Deposit amount.

Check 2651:   Write a check for $350.00 to Metropolitan Water Services for water usage. Use January 11 of the current year as the date. Calculate and record the new Balance and the Balance Brought Forward.

2649	BALANCE BROUGHT FORWARD	7,309	92
_____ 20___			
DEPOSIT			
BALANCE			
AMOUNT THIS CHECK			
BALANCE			

95TH STREET CAR WASH, INC.   **2649**
1401 95TH STREET, SW
YAKIMA, WA 98902-0373

$\frac{64\text{-}39}{610}$

_____ 20_____

PAY TO THE
ORDER OF _____ $ _____

_____ DOLLARS

2Y *SECOND YAKIMA*
The Second National Bank of Yakima, WA 98901-1148

FOR _____ _____

⑃24⑃74290   ⑃3 289 2649

2650	BALANCE BROUGHT FORWARD		
_____ 20___			
DEPOSIT			
BALANCE			
AMOUNT THIS CHECK			
BALANCE			

95TH STREET CAR WASH, INC.   **2650**
1401 95TH STREET, SW
YAKIMA, WA 98902-0373

$\frac{64\text{-}39}{610}$

_____ 20_____

PAY TO THE
ORDER OF _____ $ _____

_____ DOLLARS

2Y *SECOND YAKIMA*
The Second National Bank of Yakima, WA 98901-1148

FOR _____ _____

⑃24⑃74290   ⑃3 289 2650

2651	BALANCE BROUGHT FORWARD		
_____ 20___			
DEPOSIT			
BALANCE			
AMOUNT THIS CHECK			
BALANCE			

95TH STREET CAR WASH, INC.   **2651**
1401 95TH STREET, SW
YAKIMA, WA 98902-0373

$\frac{64\text{-}39}{610}$

_____ 20_____

PAY TO THE
ORDER OF _____ $ _____

_____ DOLLARS

2Y *SECOND YAKIMA*
The Second National Bank of Yakima, WA 98901-1148

FOR _____ _____

⑃24⑃74290   ⑃3 289 2651

Check 2652: Write a check for $73.86 to Industrial Services for cleaning supplies. Use January 12 of the current year as the date. Calculate and record the new Balance and the Balance Brought Forward.

Check 2653: Write a check for $761.52 to Washington Electrical Authority for the electric bill. Use January 15 of the current year as the date. Calculate and record the new Balance and the Balance Brought Forward.

Exercise 39

Deposit: You made a deposit of $823.67 for your employer on January 16. Record the deposit on check stub 2654. Calculate the new Balance and record it just below the Deposit amount.

Check 2654: Write a check for $359.20 to Allbright Laundry Service for towel laundering. Use January 18 of the current year as the date. Calculate the new Balance. This amount would also be carried forward to check stub 2655 on the next page of stubs and checks.

	BALANCE BROUGHT FORWARD	
2652		
_____ 20 ___		
DEPOSIT		
BALANCE		
AMOUNT THIS CHECK		
BALANCE		

95TH STREET CAR WASH, INC.   **2652**
1401 95TH STREET, SW
YAKIMA, WA 98902-0373
                                                          64-39
                                                          610
_____ 20_____

PAY TO THE
ORDER OF _____ $ _____

_____ DOLLARS

2Y *SECOND YAKIMA*
The Second National Bank of Yakima, WA 98901-1148

FOR _____   _____

⑊324⑊74290   ⑊3 289 2652

	BALANCE BROUGHT FORWARD	
2653		
_____ 20 ___		
DEPOSIT		
BALANCE		
AMOUNT THIS CHECK		
BALANCE		

95TH STREET CAR WASH, INC.   **2653**
1401 95TH STREET, SW
YAKIMA, WA 98902-0373
                                                          64-39
                                                          610
_____ 20_____

PAY TO THE
ORDER OF _____ $ _____

_____ DOLLARS

2Y *SECOND YAKIMA*
The Second National Bank of Yakima, WA 98901-1148

FOR _____   _____

⑊324⑊74290   ⑊3 289 2653

	BALANCE BROUGHT FORWARD	
2654		
_____ 20 ___		
DEPOSIT		
BALANCE		
AMOUNT THIS CHECK		
BALANCE		

95TH STREET CAR WASH, INC.   **2654**
1401 95TH STREET, SW
YAKIMA, WA 98902-0373
                                                          64-39
                                                          610
_____ 20_____

PAY TO THE
ORDER OF _____ $ _____

_____ DOLLARS

2Y *SECOND YAKIMA*
The Second National Bank of Yakima, WA 98901-1148

FOR _____   _____

⑊324⑊74290   ⑊3 289 2654

GOAL: Maintain a personal checking account

NAME

CLASS

In Exercise 38 you opened a checking account in your name by depositing a check into the account and recording the deposit in your check register. In this exercise you will manage your checking account by making deposits, withdrawing cash from an ATM, using your debit card for purchases, and writing checks.

All transactions you make are listed below. As you read each transaction, complete the necessary forms on the following three pages. Remember to write each transaction in your check register to maintain a current record of your account balance.

1. **August 1:** You receive your semi-monthly paycheck of $382.22. Endorse the back of the check and deposit it in your checking account. The ABA number of the check is 25-72.

2. **August 4:** You withdraw $100 cash from the ATM.

3. **August 5:** Your college tuition is due. Write a check to Wellington College for $900.

4. **August 6:** You sell a dresser online and receive a check from the buyer for $35. Endorse the back of the check and deposit it in your checking account. The ABA number is 23-41.

5. **August 10:** Your portion of the rent is due. Write a check for $170 to Thompson Property Management.

6. **August 13:** At Market City you pay $32.40 for groceries with your debit card.

7. **August 15:** You receive your semi-monthly paycheck of $450.85. Endorse the back of the check and deposit it in your checking account. The ABA number is 25-72.

8. **August 18:** You withdraw $100 cash from the ATM.

9. **August 20:** Your car payment of $150 is due. Write a check to Gibson Motors.

10. **August 20:** It is your turn to pay for cable service. Write a check to Altman's Cable Co. for $65.

11. **August 22:** You pay $29.27 for household supplies at Towne Mart with your debit card.

12. **August 27:** You purchase college textbooks with your debit card at Book Nook for $50.83.

Check Register

CHECK NO.	DATE	TRANSACTION DESCRIPTION	AMOUNT OF PAYMENT OR WITHDRAWAL		AMOUNT OF DEPOSIT		BALANCE	
		Deposit			900	00	900	00
		college tuition						

Deposit Ticket 1

ENDORSE HERE

_____

_____

_____

DO NOT WRITE, STAM~~P~~
RESERVED FOR FI~~N~~

YOUR NAME
4289 CENTER AVENUE APT. G-9
GARWOOD, NJ 07027-1389

DATE _____ 20 _____
CHECKS AND OTHER ITEMS ARE RECEIVED FOR DEPOSIT SUBJECT TO
THE TERMS AND CONDITIONS OF THIS FINANCIAL INSTITUTION'S
ACCOUNT AGREEMENT.

G GARWOOD
CITY BANK

⑈061000392⑈ 12 121 28⑈ 7017

CURRENCY		
COINS		
CHECKS		
TOTAL FROM OTHER SIDE		
TOTAL		
LESS CASH RECEIVED		
Total Deposit		

25-43
1709

**DEPOSIT
TICKET**
PLEASE
ITEMIZE
ADDITIONAL
CHECKS ON
REVERSE
SIDE

Deposit Ticket 2

ENDORSE HERE

_____

_____

_____

DO NOT WRITE, STAM~~P~~
RESERVED FOR FI~~N~~

YOUR NAME
4289 CENTER AVENUE APT. G-9
GARWOOD, NJ 07027-1389

DATE _____ 20 _____
CHECKS AND OTHER ITEMS ARE RECEIVED FOR DEPOSIT SUBJECT TO
THE TERMS AND CONDITIONS OF THIS FINANCIAL INSTITUTION'S
ACCOUNT AGREEMENT.

G GARWOOD
CITY BANK

⑈061000392⑈ 12 121 28⑈ 7018

CURRENCY		
COINS		
CHECKS		
TOTAL FROM OTHER SIDE		
TOTAL		
LESS CASH RECEIVED		
Total Deposit		

25-43
1709

**DEPOSIT
TICKET**
PLEASE
ITEMIZE
ADDITIONAL
CHECKS ON
REVERSE
SIDE

Deposit Ticket 3

ENDORSE HERE

_____

_____

_____

DO NOT WRITE, STAM~~P~~
RESERVED FOR FI~~N~~

YOUR NAME
4289 CENTER AVENUE APT. G-9
GARWOOD, NJ 07027-1389

DATE _____ 20 _____
CHECKS AND OTHER ITEMS ARE RECEIVED FOR DEPOSIT SUBJECT TO
THE TERMS AND CONDITIONS OF THIS FINANCIAL INSTITUTION'S
ACCOUNT AGREEMENT.

G GARWOOD
CITY BANK

⑈061000392⑈ 12 121 28⑈ 7019

CURRENCY		
COINS		
CHECKS		
TOTAL FROM OTHER SIDE		
TOTAL		
LESS CASH RECEIVED		
Total Deposit		

25-43
1709

**DEPOSIT
TICKET**
PLEASE
ITEMIZE
ADDITIONAL
CHECKS ON
REVERSE
SIDE

Exercise 40

YOUR NAME
4289 CENTER AVENUE APT. G-9
GARWOOD, NJ 07027-1389

1642

$\dfrac{25\text{-}43}{1709}$

_____ 20_____

PAY TO THE
ORDER OF _____ $ _____

_____ DOLLARS

Ⓖ _GARWOOD CITY BANK_
4th STREET PLAZA, GARWOOD, NJ 07027

FOR _____   _____

⑆0⑆10003924   ⑆2 ⑆2⑆ ⑆642⑆

YOUR NAME
4289 CENTER AVENUE APT. G-9
GARWOOD, NJ 07027-1389

1643

$\dfrac{25\text{-}43}{1709}$

_____ 20_____

PAY TO THE
ORDER OF _____ $ _____

_____ DOLLARS

Ⓖ _GARWOOD CITY BANK_
4th STREET PLAZA, GARWOOD, NJ 07027

FOR _____   _____

⑆0⑆10003924   ⑆2 ⑆2⑆ ⑆643⑆

YOUR NAME
4289 CENTER AVENUE APT. G-9
GARWOOD, NJ 07027-1389

1644

$\dfrac{25\text{-}43}{1709}$

_____ 20_____

PAY TO THE
ORDER OF _____ $ _____

_____ DOLLARS

Ⓖ _GARWOOD CITY BANK_
4th STREET PLAZA, GARWOOD, NJ 07027

FOR _____   _____

⑆0⑆10003924   ⑆2 ⑆2⑆ ⑆644⑆

YOUR NAME
4289 CENTER AVENUE APT. G-9
GARWOOD, NJ 07027-1389

1645

$\dfrac{25\text{-}43}{1709}$

_____ 20_____

PAY TO THE
ORDER OF _____ $ _____

_____ DOLLARS

Ⓖ _GARWOOD CITY BANK_
4th STREET PLAZA, GARWOOD, NJ 07027

FOR _____   _____

⑆0⑆10003924   ⑆2 ⑆2⑆ ⑆645⑆

GOAL: Learn to deposit currency and coins into a checking account

NAME _____

CLASS _____

Some businesses, such as fast-food restaurants or convenience stores, receive many bills (currency) and coins. A deposit of only currency and coins usually is made each day. Bills and coins are counted and placed in special wrappers obtained from the financial institution. The wrappers have monetary values printed on them.

Look at the currency and coins below. The wrappers around the bills have values of $1,000 (twenty-dollar bills), $500 (tens), $250 (fives), and $50 (ones). The coins are in wrappers with values of $25 (one-dollar coins), $10 (quarters and half-dollars), $5 (dimes), $2 (nickels), and 50¢ (pennies).

Complete the deposit ticket on the next page as follows:

1. Write the *Date* of March 14. After the *20*, write the current year.

2. Add the amounts (in dollars) shown on the bundles of bills to calculate the total value of all the bills. Write this amount on the deposit ticket on the line beside *Currency*. A vertical line divides the dollars and cents amounts.

3. Add the amounts (in dollars and cents) shown on the rolls of coins to calculate the total value of all the coins. Write this amount on the deposit ticket on the line beside *Coins*.

4. Add the *Currency* and *Coins* amounts to calculate the total value of all the bills and coins. Write this amount on the last line of the deposit ticket beside *Total*.

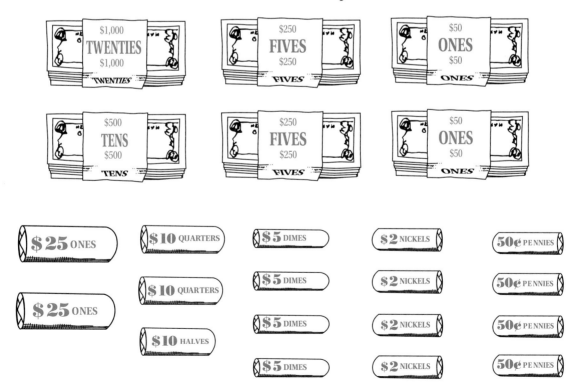

DEPOSIT TICKET

The Corner Store
805 Eisenhower Avenue
McKinney, TX 75071-8050

$\dfrac{91\text{-}7429}{3241}$

DATE _____, 20 _____

CHECKS AND OTHER ITEMS ARE RECEIVED FOR DEPOSIT SUBJECT
TO THE RULES AND REGULATIONS OF THIS FINANCIAL INSTITUTION

CB COMMERCE BANK

The Commerce Bank of McKinney, TX 75071-4969

⑂⑧⑊⑊⑤⑦⑆⑊⑊ ⑆⑆ ⑊⑊⑦ ⑥⑊⑊

		DOLLARS	CENTS
CURRENCY			
COINS			
CHECKS	1.		
List Singly ● Be sure each item is endorsed	2.		
	3.		
	4.		
Total From Other side			
Total Items	TOTAL		

Use reverse side for additional listing or attach tape

After the deposit has been made, it must be written in the company's check register. Update the check register below by recording the deposit just made. Be sure to calculate the new balance.

CHECK NO.	DATE	TRANSACTION DESCRIPTION	AMOUNT OF PAYMENT OR WITHDRAWAL	AMOUNT OF DEPOSIT	BALANCE
					4 2 8 5 39
438	3-6	Cola Distributors beverages	3 6 0 00		3 9 2 5 39
439	3-10	Delicious Bread Co. bakery products	1 5 0 00		3 7 7 5 39

GOAL: Write petty cash receipts and update a
petty cash book

_____ NAME

_____ CLASS

Many companies pay large expenses such as bills with checks and pay small expenses with cash. **Petty cash** is cash kept on hand for payment of minor items. The word "petty" means _small_ or _minor_. Examples of small expenses are a roll of tape, one postage stamp, or the fee to have a small package delivered.

One person, acting as a petty cash administrator, usually maintains the **petty cash fund**. The fund is typically kept in one place, such as a metal box, and has a specified amount of bills and coins for ready use when a petty cash payment is needed. Often the person who receives money from the petty cash fund has spent his or her own money for a small item. The company owes that person and **reimburses,** or pays back, the person from the petty cash fund. The person being reimbursed gives the petty cash administrator a cash register receipt for the money that was spent.

A **petty cash book** is kept as a record of all petty cash paid. Every time money is spent from the petty cash fund, the details of the transaction are written into the petty cash book. A **petty cash receipt** is a form showing the details of a petty cash payment. A petty cash receipt, as shown in Figure 2-8, or another type of form such as a voucher, is written and placed with the petty cash fund. In some offices, both the cash register receipt for a petty cash item and a voucher or petty cash receipt are used with the petty cash fund.

Figure 2-8   Petty Cash Receipt

Industrial Supplies Co.
PETTY CASH RECEIPT

① No. _____202_____   Date _____11-7_____ 20 __   ②

Received of Industrial Supplies Co. $_____5.68_____   ③

③ _Five and 68/100_ ~~~~~~~~~~~~~~~~~~ Dollars

④ For _paper clips and index cards_

Account Charged: _Office Supplies_   Signed _Peter Bachman_

⑤   ⑥

1. The receipt _No._ is written: 202. Each receipt has a different number. Receipt numbers are written in consecutive order, such as 1, 2, 3, 4, etc. The next receipt number will be 203.

2. The *Date* is written: 11-7. The date to be written on the receipt is always the date on which you are writing the receipt.

3. Follow the procedure for writing amounts of money as you learned in Exercise 37.

4. After *For*, the item(s) bought or the reason the money was spent is recorded.

5. After *Account Charged*, the account to be charged for the expense is recorded.

6. The person receiving money for petty cash items signs the receipt to show that he or she was given the money.

Complete the four petty cash receipt forms using the information provided for each form. The receipts then would be placed in the petty cash box.

Form 1: Write receipt number 203 for $25.96 for file folders. Use 11-8 of the current year as the date. The account charged is Office Supplies. Sign the name of Thelma Green, the person receiving the money.

```
┌─────────────────────────────────────────────────────────────────┐
│ Industrial Supplies Co.                                           │
│ PETTY CASH RECEIPT                                                │
├───────────────────────────────────────────────────────────────────┤
│ No. _____            Date _____ 20 ____           │
│                                                                   │
│ Received of Industrial Supplies Co.            $_____       │
│                                                                   │
│ _____ Dollars    │
│                                                                   │
│ For _____           │
│                                                                   │
│ _____            │
│                                                                   │
│ Account Charged: _____  Signed _____          │
└───────────────────────────────────────────────────────────────────┘
```

Form 2: Write receipt number 204 for 65 cents for postage due on a package. Use 11-10 of the current year as the date. The account charged is Postage. Sign the name of Sally Logan. Refer to Figure 2-2 on page 81 to review how amounts of less than one dollar are written.

```
┌─────────────────────────────────────────────────────────────────┐
│ Industrial Supplies Co.                                           │
│ PETTY CASH RECEIPT                                                │
├───────────────────────────────────────────────────────────────────┤
│ No. _____            Date _____ 20 ____           │
│                                                                   │
│ Received of Industrial Supplies Co.            $_____       │
│                                                                   │
│ _____ Dollars    │
│                                                                   │
│ For _____           │
│                                                                   │
│ _____            │
│                                                                   │
│ Account Charged: _____  Signed _____          │
└───────────────────────────────────────────────────────────────────┘
```

Form 3:   Write receipt number 205 for $23.14 for repairs to the photocopier. Use 11-20 of the current year as the date. The account charged is Repairs. Sign the name of Ellie Watkins.

Industrial Supplies Co.
PETTY CASH RECEIPT

No. _____   Date _____ 20 ____

Received of Industrial Supplies Co. $_____

_____Dollars

For _____

_____

Account Charged: _____   Signed _____

Form 4:   Write receipt number 206 for $16.62 for printer paper. Use 11-29 of the current year as the date. The account charged is Office Supplies. Sign the name of Ricardo Mejia.

Industrial Supplies Co.
PETTY CASH RECEIPT

No. _____   Date _____ 20 ____

Received of Industrial Supplies Co. $_____

_____Dollars

For _____

_____

Account Charged: _____   Signed _____

Figure 2-9 on the next page shows the petty cash book for Industrial Supplies Co. Study the entries that have been made in the book. Some companies start each month with a specific amount of money in the petty cash fund; some companies add money to the petty cash fund as it is needed. Industrial Supplies Co. replenishes its fund to a balance of $100 at the beginning of each month.

Figure 2-9 Petty Cash Book

Date	Receipt No.	Paid To	Account Charged	For	Amount	Deposit	Balance
		Industrial Supplies Co. **PETTY CASH BOOK**					
11-1		Balance Forward					22.72
11-1		Deposit				77.28	100.00
11-3	200	B. Daly	Office Sup.	tele. msg. book	6.87		93.13
11-6	201	S. Selters	Office Sup.	legal pads	14.93		78.20
11-7	202	P. Bachman	Office Sup.	clips, cards	5.68		72.52

Update the petty cash book above by entering the information from the four petty cash receipts you completed. Fill in each appropriate column and subtract each receipt amount from the previous balance to obtain a current balance of the petty cash fund.

It is now the beginning of the month, December 1. The petty cash fund at Industrial Supplies Co. needs to be replenished. Calculate the amount of money that must be added to the petty cash fund to replenish the balance to $100. Fill in each appropriate column in the petty cash book above to show the deposit and the new balance.

GOAL: Prepare cash drawer count reports

_____ NAME

_____ CLASS

At the end of each workday or shift, a cashier must count the money in the cash drawer. Each bill and coin value (denomination) is shown on a separate line of a *Cash Drawer Count Report*.

Bills, or currency, are $20, $10, $5, and $1. Coins are one-dollars ($1), half-dollars ($.50), quarters ($.25), dimes ($.10), nickels ($.05), and pennies ($.01).

Use Figure 2-10 as a guide as you complete the reports in this exercise.

Figure 2-10 Cash Drawer Count Report

Column 1	Column 2	Column 3			
Quantity	**× Value (Denomination)**	**= Amount**			
30	$20.00 Bills	6	0	0	00
50	10.00 Bills	5	0	0	00
75	5.00 Bills	3	7	5	00
180	1.00 Bills	1	8	0	00
25	1.00 Coins		2	5	00
13	.50 Coins			6	50
67	.25 Coins		1	6	75
46	.10 Coins			4	60
85	.05 Coins			4	25
170	.01 Coins			1	70
	Total in Cash Drawer	1	7	1	3	80

Complete Reports 1 and 2 on the next page as follows:

1. Complete Report 1 line by line. Multiply the number in Column 1 (Quantity) by the denomination in Column 2 (Value). Write the total value in Column 3 (Amount).
2. Calculate the total of Column 3. Write the total at the bottom of Column 3 (Total in Cash Drawer).
3. Follow the same procedure to complete Report 2.

Report 1

Column 1	Column 2	Column 3				
Quantity	**× Value (Denomination)**	**= Amount**				
45	$20.00 Bills					
37	10.00 Bills					
48	5.00 Bills					
94	1.00 Bills					
5	1.00 Coins					
3	.50 Coins					
82	.25 Coins					
76	.10 Coins					
48	.05 Coins					
325	.01 Coins					
	Total in Cash Drawer					

Report 2

Column 1	Column 2	Column 3				
Quantity	**× Value (Denomination)**	**= Amount**				
37	$20.00 Bills					
50	10.00 Bills					
26	5.00 Bills					
85	1.00 Bills					
7	1.00 Coins					
10	.50 Coins					
48	.25 Coins					
69	.10 Coins					
57	.05 Coins					
229	.01 Coins					
	Total in Cash Drawer					

Well done! You have completed the exercises for Unit 2. Before your instructor administers the Unit 2 Test, review the exercises in this unit. Do not begin the Unit 3 exercises until your instructor has approved Unit 2.

Go Digital!

For additional activities visit www.cengage.com/school/bse

GOAL: Proofread names of persons

_____ NAME

_____ CLASS

Misspelling a client's name can reflect poorly on both you and your employer. This proofreading exercise will help refine your skill at paying attention to detail. Look closely at the name in Column 1, then at the name in Column 2. If the two names are exactly alike, circle the *Y* for Yes in Column 3. If the two names are not exactly alike, circle the *N* for No in Column 3. An example is shown.

COLUMN 1	COLUMN 2	COLUMN 3		
Ex. Robert Sumner	Robert Summer	Ex.	Y	**N**
1. Stanislaus Macumber	Stanislaus Macumber	1.	Y	N
2. Carmen Rezotto	Carman Rezotto	2.	Y	N
3. John Marquette	John Marquete	3.	Y	N
4. Franklin Carrerro	Franklin Carrerro	4.	Y	N
5. Lawrence C. Holtzclaw	Lawrence G. Holtzclaw	5.	Y	N
6. Clyde Breseno	Clyde Breseno	6.	Y	N
7. Constansa Ruiz	Constansa Ruiz	7.	Y	N
8. Louisa Manson	Louise Manson	8.	Y	N
9. Lori C. Conneaughey	Lori C. Conneaghey	9.	Y	N
10. Michelle Petersen	Michelle Peterson	10.	Y	N
11. Daniel Roubian	Daniel Roubian	11.	Y	N
12. Malcolm P. Howard	Malcolm P. Howard	12.	Y	N
13. Gregg Mitchell	Greg Mitchell	13.	Y	N
14. Linsay Thomas	Linsay Thomes	14.	Y	N
15. Vincent Fuschettio	Vincent Fuschettio	15.	Y	N
16. Kenneth L. Goings	Kenneth I. Goings	16.	Y	N
17. Eugene Kebede	Eugene Kebede	17.	Y	N
18. Yolanda Gilbert	Yolanda Gilbert	18.	Y	N
19. Franco Perelli	Franco Peretti	19.	Y	N
20. Linda Garrison	Lynda Garrison	20.	Y	N

GOAL: Proofread names of persons

NAME _____

CLASS _____

Look closely at the handwritten name in Column 1, then at the keyed name in Column 2. If the two names are exactly alike, circle the *Y* for Yes in Column 3. If the two names are not exactly alike, circle the *N* for No in Column 3. An example is shown.

COLUMN 1	COLUMN 2	COLUMN 3
Ex. Arvin Webster	Arvin Webster	Ex. ⓎN
1. Davison Tuggle	Davison Tuggle	1. Y N
2. Steven Parke	Steven Park	2. Y N
3. Luyan Chiang	Luyan Chaing	3. Y N
4. Earlene Champagn	Earlene Champaign	4. Y N
5. Rex L. Deardoff	Rex L. Deardoff	5. Y N
6. Nestor Garcia	Nester Garcia	6. Y N
7. Daniela Camden	Daniela Camden	7. Y N
8. Wilfred Abbott	Wilfred Abott	8. Y N
9. Ming-Chia Chung	Ming-Chiia Chung	9. Y N
10. Forsythia G. Batcha	Forsythia C. Batcha	10. Y N
11. Simon R. Spreyberry	Simon R. Spreyberry	11. Y N
12. Cynthia Hodgerson	Cynthia Hogderson	12. Y N
13. Marcha L. Ortkiese	Marcha L. Ortkiese	13. Y N
14. Madilyn Brooks	Madelyn Brooks	14. Y N
15. Levi G. Shepard	Levi G. Shepard	15. Y N
16. Miceela D. Salas	Miceela D. Salas	16. Y N
17. Maxmilian Dean	Maximilian Dean	17. Y N
18. Luann Van Noorden	Luann Van Noorden	18. Y N
19. Emanuel Earaerts	Emanuel Eeraerts	19. Y N
20. Esther Quiroga	Esther Qiroga	20. Y N

GOAL: Proofread dates

_____ NAME

_____ CLASS

Being able to verify dates is a useful skill for an entry-level office worker. Writing or reading a date incorrectly could lead to disorder in the office schedule. Months and days having only a single digit may be preceded by a zero (0). For example, March 2 may be written as 3-2 or 03-02. Years may be written in full or using only the last two digits; for example, 2012 or 12. Look at the date in Column 1, then at the date in Column 2. If the two dates are the same, circle the *Y* for Yes in Column 3. If the two dates are not the same, circle the *N* for No in Column 3. An example is shown.

	COLUMN 1	COLUMN 2		COLUMN 3	
Ex.	February 5, 1999	02-05-99	Ex.	(Y)	N
1.	07-04-95	July 4, 1995	1.	Y	N
2.	December 1, 2006	12-10-06	2.	Y	N
3.	08-23-97	August 23, 1997	3.	Y	N
4.	September 15, 1992	09-15-92	4.	Y	N
5.	11-17-07	November 11, 2007	5.	Y	N
6.	January 22, 1993	01-22-98	6.	Y	N
7.	05-20-01	May 26, 2001	7.	Y	N
8.	October 15, 2006	10-15-06	8.	Y	N
9.	10-02-04	October 20, 2004	9.	Y	N
10.	March 8, 2008	08-03-08	10.	Y	N
11.	04-01-91	April 7, 1991	11.	Y	N
12.	December 10, 2002	10-10-02	12.	Y	N
13.	08-31-05	August 31, 2005	13.	Y	N
14.	November 12, 2009	11-12-08	14.	Y	N
15.	09-07-90	September 7, 1990	15.	Y	N
16.	October 30, 2001	10-03-01	16.	Y	N
17.	03-18-92	March 18, 1992	17.	Y	N
18.	January 13, 1994	01-31-94	18.	Y	N
19.	01-15-06	April 15, 2006	19.	Y	N
20.	June 26, 1996	06-26-96	20.	Y	N

GOAL: Proofread names of businesses

NAME _____

CLASS _____

Look closely at the business name in Column 1, then at the business name in Column 2. If the two names are exactly alike, circle the *Y* for Yes in Column 3. If the two names are not exactly alike, circle the *N* for No in Column 3. An example is shown.

	COLUMN 1	COLUMN 2		COLUMN 3
Ex.	Hampton Motorworks	Hamton Motorworks	Ex.	Y (N)
1.	Francis Chiropractic	Frances Chiropractic	1.	Y N
2.	Auto Electric Specialists	Auto Electric Specialists	2.	Y N
3.	Maywood Shops, Inc.	Maywood Shops, Inc.	3.	Y N
4.	Bellwood Consortium	Bellewood Consortium	4.	Y N
5.	Dayne Mold Supplies	Dayne Mold Suppliers	5.	Y N
6.	Checks For Cash	Checks for Cash	6.	Y N
7.	Pacific Finance	Pacific Financial	7.	Y N
8.	Veterans Memorial Hospital	Veterans' Memorial Hospital	8.	Y N
9.	Janson's Portfolio Service	Janson's Portfolio Service	9.	Y N
10.	Food For Thought Institute	Food-For-Thought Institute	10.	Y N
11.	Peach Tree Apartments	Peach Tree Apartments	11.	Y N
12.	First National Bank of Tray	First National Bank of Troy	12.	Y N
13.	Above Board Catering	Above Board Catering	13.	Y N
14.	A-American Self-Storage	American Self-Storage	14.	Y N
15.	Ferro Electronics Group	Ferro Electronic Group	15.	Y N
16.	Merlin Drive Upholstery	Merlin Drive Upholstery	16.	Y N
17.	Golden Eagle Travel, Inc.	Golden Eagle Travel, Inc.	17.	Y N
18.	Archer's Haven	Archer's Haven	18.	Y N
19.	China Motels	Chino Motels	19.	Y N
20.	Sam's Army Navy Store	Sam's Army Navy Store	20.	Y N

GOAL: Proofread names of businesses

_____ NAME

_____ CLASS

Work to improve your proofreading skills as you look closely at the handwritten business name in Column 1 and the keyed business name in Column 2. If the two names are exactly alike, circle the *Y* for Yes in Column 3. If the two names are not exactly alike, circle the *N* for No in Column 3.

COLUMN 1	COLUMN 2	COLUMN 3
1. A-1 Radiator Works	A-1 Radiator Works	1. Y N
2. Creative Images	Creative Image	2. Y N
3. Robert Lee Tours	Roberta Lee Tours	3. Y N
4. Leonard's Auditing Firm	Leonard's Auditing Firm	4. Y N
5. Stardust Motel	Stardust Motel	5. Y N
6. Dance Expressions, Ltd.	Dance Expressions, Ltd.	6. Y N
7. Jay Medical-Dental Labs	Jay Medical-Dental Lab	7. Y N
8. Romine Tractor Co.	Romine Tractor Co.	8. Y N
9. Ron's Auto Parts	Rons Auto Parts	9. Y N
10. Chilton Waterbeds	Chiltan Waterbeds	10. Y N
11. J and W Development Co.	J & W Development Co.	11. Y N
12. Daffodil Tours, Inc.	Daffodil Tours, Inc.	12. Y N
13. Copernicus Tree Surgeons	Capernicus Tree Surgeons	13. Y N
14. Rosenwald Reality Group	Rosenwald Realty Group	14. Y N
15. Loran Floral Products	Loran Floral Products, Inc.	15. Y N
16. Gretna Electric Authority	Gretna Electric Authority	16. Y N
17. Tocca Research Institute	Tocca Research Institute	17. Y N
18. Fremont Data Services	Freemont Data Services	18. Y N
19. Viceroy Square Apts.	Viceroy Square Apts.	19. Y N
20. Earlna Bakery, Inc.	Earlna Bakeries, Inc.	20. Y N

GOAL: Proofread ZIP Codes

NAME _____

CLASS _____

Incorrectly written ZIP Codes can cause delayed or undelivered mail. Improve your eye for detail by comparing the handwritten ZIP Code in Column 1 and the keyed ZIP Code in Column 2. If the two codes are exactly alike, circle the *Y* for Yes in Column 3. If the two codes are not exactly alike, circle the *N* for No in Column 3.

COLUMN 1	COLUMN 2	COLUMN 3
1. 30354-1120	30354-1120	1. Y N
2. 65442-0485	65442-0435	2. Y N
3. 17709-0385	17109-0385	3. Y N
4. 80229-3170	80229-3170	4. Y N
5. 02173-6034	02173-6034	5. Y N
6. 70129-0823	70129-0823	6. Y N
7. 20028-3412	20028-3472	7. Y N
8. 52720-0176	52720-0176	8. Y N
9. 79420-2245	79490-2245	9. Y N
10. 00918-0406	00918-0406	10. Y N
11. 44142-2258	44142-2258	11. Y N
12. 60646-1275	60646-1275	12. Y N
13. 96820-3089	96820-0389	13. Y N
14. 27108-0276	27108-0276	14. Y N
15. 33040-7795	33040-7759	15. Y N
16. 91710-2138	91701-2138	16. Y N
17. 64520-0142	64520-0142	17. Y N
18. 03687-2237	03678-2237	18. Y N
19. 93748-1345	93748-1345	19. Y N
20. 88632-6490	86832-6490	20. Y N

GOAL: Proofread street addresses

_____ NAME

_____ CLASS

Street addresses are comprised of both numbers and letters, so you must pay particular attention to their accuracy. Compare the street addresses in Column 1 and Column 2. If the two addresses are exactly alike, circle the _Y_ for Yes in Column 3. If the two addresses are not exactly alike, circle the _N_ for No in Column 3.

COLUMN 1	COLUMN 2	COLUMN 3
1. 4177 Sierra Vista Dr.	4777 Sierra Vista Dr.	1. Y N
2. 782 Bower Rd.	782 Bower Rd.	2. Y N
3. 838 Karo Blvd., Apt. C-4	838 Karo Blvd., Apt. G-4	3. Y N
4. 1400 Barton Rd., #2311	1400 Barton Rd., #3211	4. Y N
5. 2155 Francisco Ave., S.	2155 Francisco Ave., S.	5. Y N
6. 3629 Longmeadow St., N	3629 Longmeadow St., N	6. Y N
7. 19878 Seven Mile Rd., W	19878 Seven Mile Dr., W	7. Y N
8. 2849 Will Rogers Lane	2849 Will Rogers Lane	8. Y N
9. 2872 Payne Way	2372 Payne Way	9. Y N
10. 9433 Hearthside Dr.	9344 Hearthside Dr.	10. Y N
11. 871 Drabbington Way	871 Drabbington Way	11. Y N
12. 14287 2nd Ave., NW	14287 2nd Ave., NE	12. Y N
13. 958 Lusk Center Dr.	958 Lusk Center Dr.	13. Y N
14. 2339 Massasoit Ct.	2339 Massasoit Ct.	14. Y N
15. 7488 Tucson Rd.	7488 Tucson Rd.	15. Y N
16. 27 Newport Circle	27 Newport Circle	16. Y N
17. 113885 Ponderosa Dr.	13885 Ponderosa Dr.	17. Y N
18. 831 N.E. 115th St., Apt. 4C	831 N.E. 115th St., Apt. 4C	18. Y N
19. 728 St. Ignatius Place	728 St. Ignacius Place	19. Y N
20. 928 Missola Drive	938 Missola Drive	20. Y N

GOAL: Proofread cities, states, and ZIP Codes

_____ NAME

_____ CLASS

Compare the cities, states, and ZIP Codes in Column 1 and Column 2. If the two cities, states, and codes are exactly alike, circle the _Y_ for Yes in Column 3. If the two cities, states, and codes are not exactly alike, circle the _N_ for No in Column 3.

COLUMN 1	COLUMN 2	COLUMN 3
1. Orem, UT 84097-3304	Orem, UT 84097-3304	1. Y N
2. Fort Devens, MA 01433-2874	Fort Devens, MA 01433-2874	2. Y N
3. Fontana, WI 53125-9327	Fontana, WA 53125-9327	3. Y N
4. Myakka City, FL 33551-8347	Myakka City, FL 33551-8447	4. Y N
5. Carolina, PR 00979-1827	Carolena, PR 00979-1827	5. Y N
6. Hueytown, AL 35020-6693	Hueytown, AL 35020-6693	6. Y N
7. Pittsburg, CA 94565-2828	Pittsburgh, CA 94565-2828	7. Y N
8. New Salem, IL 62357-4593	New Salem, IL 62375-4593	8. Y N
9. Fairbanks, AK 99701-3487	Fairbanks, AR 99701-3487	9. Y N
10. Clitherall, MN 56524-8349	Clitherall, MN 56524-8349	10. Y N
11. Medford, OK 73759-2913	Medford, OH 73759-2913	11. Y N
12. Henrieville, UT 84736-1634	Henrieville, UT 84736-1684	12. Y N
13. Daly City, GA 94015-1652	Daly City, CA 94015-1652	13. Y N
14. Grand Glaise, AR 72056-6217	Grand Glaise, AR 72056-6217	14. Y N
15. Maurepas, LA 70449-3182	Maurapas, LA 70449-3182	15. Y N
16. Palm Bay, FL 32905-2306	Palm Bay, FL 33905-2306	16. Y N
17. Woonsocket, RI 02895-1437	Woonsocket, RI 02895-1437	17. Y N
18. Quilcene, WA 98376-4731	Quilcene, WA 98367-4731	18. Y N
19. Scottsdale, AZ 85253-4177	Scottdale, AZ 85253-4177	19. Y N
20. Elmendorf, TX 78112-3976	Elmendorf, TX 78112-3976	20. Y N

GOAL: Print information on business forms

———————————————— NAME

———————————————— CLASS

Information must be printed in special boxes or spaces on some business forms. Refer to the sample letters in Figure 3-1 to improve your printing as you complete forms in this unit requiring all capital letters.

Figure 3-1 Sample of All Capital Letters

A B C D E F G H I J K L M N O P Q R S T U V W X Y Z

EXERCISE 52a Print the information in Column 1 on the shipping labels in Column 2 using all capital letters. Leave a blank box between words to indicate a space. Abbreviate the addresses where appropriate. If necessary, refer to the USPS Abbreviations pages in the *Reference Sources* section. A completed form is shown as an example.

<u>COLUMN 1</u>   <u>COLUMN 2</u>

Ex.

Sutter Business Supplies
Lisa Ling
268 Palmetto Highway
   Suite 200
Idaho Falls, Idaho
   83401-2191

SHIP TO: (Fill in only if different from billing address)

| S | U | T | T | E | R | | B | U | S | I | N | E | S | S | | S | U | P | P | L | I | E | S | | |
Firm Name

| L | I | S | A | | L | I | N | G | |
ATTENTION

| 2 | 6 | 8 | | P | A | L | M | E | T | T | O | | H | W | Y | | S | T | E | | 2 | 0 | 0 | |
Street Address   Floor, Room or Suite No.

| I | D | A | H | O | | F | A | L | L | S | | | I | D | 8 | 3 | 4 | 0 | 1 | — | 2 | 1 | 9 | 1 |
City   State   ZIP

1.

Commercial Door Experts
Jeff Milne
486 Telephone Road
New Haven, Connecticut
   06511-2847

SHIP TO: (Fill in only if different from billing address)

Firm Name

ATTENTION

Street Address   Floor, Room or Suite No.

City   State   ZIP

COLUMN 1	COLUMN 2

COLUMN 1   **COLUMN 2**

2.

Abacus Interiors
Wilfredo Henriquez
492 Front Street
    Suite 750
Albuquerque, New Mexico
    87101-6029

SHIP TO: (Fill in only if different from billing address)

Firm Name

ATTENTION

Street Address   Floor, Room
                                                        or Suite No.

City   State   ZIP

Some business forms must have information printed with proper names and addresses beginning with a capital letter followed by lowercase letters. Refer to the sample letters in Figure 3-2 to improve your printing as you complete forms in this unit.

Figure 3-2   Sample of Capital and Lowercase Letters

Aa Bb Cc Dd Ee Ff Gg Hh Ii
Jj Kk Ll Mm Nn Oo Pp Qq
Rr Ss Tt Uu Vv Ww Xx Yy Zz

EXERCISE 52b   *Print* the information in Column 1 on the airline baggage forms in Column 2. Use a capital letter followed by lowercase letters. Abbreviate the addresses where appropriate. If necessary, refer to the USPS Abbreviations pages in the *Reference Sources* section. A completed form is shown as an example.

COLUMN 1   **COLUMN 2**

Ex.

Annie Van Olden
762 Cathedral Street
Livonia, Michigan
    48150-4197

AIR TRANSPORT ASSOCIATION
BAGGAGE IDENTIFICATION LABEL

Bend Tab To Release

Annie Van Olden
NAME
762 Cathedral St.
ADDRESS
Livonia   MI   48150-4197
CITY   STATE   ZIP

1.

Gerri Smith
726 Marigold Court
Myrtle Beach,
    South Carolina
    29577-2263

AIR TRANSPORT ASSOCIATION
BAGGAGE IDENTIFICATION LABEL

Bend Tab To Release

NAME

ADDRESS

CITY   STATE   ZIP

COLUMN 1	COLUMN 2

2.

Enrique Gomez
942 Cheyenne Lane
Lakeland, Florida
33810-4897

AIR TRANSPORT ASSOCIATION
BAGGAGE IDENTIFICATION LABEL

Bend Tab To Release

NAME

ADDRESS

CITY   STATE   ZIP

3.

Barry Martin
207 Hipawai Place
Honolulu, Hawaii
96822-1825

AIR TRANSPORT ASSOCIATION
BAGGAGE IDENTIFICATION LABEL

Bend Tab To Release

NAME

ADDRESS

CITY   STATE   ZIP

4.

Mary Lou Esqueda
8775 W. Tulare
Avenue
Visalia, California
93277-4811

AIR TRANSPORT ASSOCIATION
BAGGAGE IDENTIFICATION LABEL

Bend Tab To Release

NAME

ADDRESS

CITY   STATE   ZIP

EXERCISE 52c   On the next page, *print* the information in Column 1 on the change of address forms in Column 2. Use a capital letter followed by lowercase letters. Abbreviate the addresses where appropriate. Use the current year with the dates provided. Refer to Figures 3-1 and 3-2 for the proper size and shape of your letters.

1.

CHANGE OF ADDRESS FORM

NAME _____

☐ Permanent Move ☐ Temporary Move

Start Date: _____   End Date: _____

Address Change for: ☐ Individual ☐ Family ☐ Business

OLD ADDRESS:
_____
_____

NEW ADDRESS:
_____
_____

Email:_____ Phone: (_____) _____

Signature:_____ Date Signed:_____

Abby Martini
Permanent move starting
  May 8 for a family
Old address:
  9376 Bayside Drive
  San Francisco, California 94130
New address:
  197 Hemlock Street
  San Francisco, California 94109
Email: abscreations@fieldstone.com
Phone: (415) 555-1237
Signed by Abby Martini
  on April 19

2.

CHANGE OF ADDRESS FORM

NAME _____

☐ Permanent Move ☐ Temporary Move

Start Date: _____   End Date: _____

Address Change for: ☐ Individual ☐ Family ☐ Business

OLD ADDRESS:
_____
_____

NEW ADDRESS:
_____
_____

Email:_____ Phone: (_____) _____

Signature:_____ Date Signed:_____

Shang Industries
Permanent move starting
  October 20 for a business
Old address:
  753 Arabian Way
  Chichester, New Hampshire 03234
New address:
  487 Daphne Court, Suite 10A
  Concord, New Hampshire 03303
Email: Shangcorp@orchard.com
Phone: (603) 555-0141
Signed by James Shang
  on October 5

3.

CHANGE OF ADDRESS FORM

NAME _____

☐ Permanent Move ☐ Temporary Move

Start Date: _____   End Date: _____

Address Change for: ☐ Individual ☐ Family ☐ Business

OLD ADDRESS:
_____
_____

NEW ADDRESS:
_____
_____

Email:_____ Phone: (_____) _____

Signature:_____ Date Signed:_____

Ben Tsukamoto
Temporary move for an
  individual, March 17
  to September 17
Old address:
  492 Dale Circle
  Mesa, Arizona 85201
New address:
  3342 E. Marshall Street
  Tulsa, Oklahoma 74115
Email: BenTsu@abc.net
Phone: (602) 555-1132
Signed by Ben Tsukamoto
  on March 1

GOAL: Print information on business forms

In Exercise 52 you printed information on shipping labels in all capital letters. You also printed information on airline baggage forms and on change of address forms using capital and lowercase letters. As you complete the forms in this exercise, refer to Figures 3-1 and 3-2 in Exercise 52 and Figure 2-1 in Exercise 25 to review the proper size and shape of letters and numbers.

EXERCISE 53a   Complete the four time records using the information given for the forms. *Print* the information clearly within the spaces provided using a capital letter followed by lowercase letters. Write the figures slowly and legibly. Once you have entered the data, calculate the hours worked each day, then calculate the total weekly hours worked.

Form 1:   Prepare a time record for Barbara Dugan for the week ending 8/27. Her employee number is 847. She worked from 8:00 a.m. to 5:00 p.m. Monday through Thursday. She took a lunch hour from 12:30 to 1:30 each of these days. On Friday she worked from 10:00 a.m. to 6:30 p.m. with a lunch break from 1:00 to 1:30 p.m.

Form 2:   Prepare a time record for Adam Boswell for the week ending 8/27. His employee number is 623. Adam worked a split schedule. On Monday, Wednesday, and Friday he worked from 7:30 a.m. to 4:30 p.m. with a lunch break from 11:30 to 12:30. On Tuesday and Thursday he worked from 7:00 a.m. to 12:00 p.m. and again from 4:00 p.m. to 7:30 p.m. He also worked Saturday morning from 7:00 a.m. to 11:00 a.m.

Form 3:   Prepare a time record for LaKeisha Marcos for the week ending 9/16. Her employee number is 5490. On Monday she worked from 8:00 a.m. to 4:00 p.m. with a lunch break from 11:30 to 12:30. She worked from 8:30 a.m. to 5:30 p.m. Tuesday through Friday; she took a lunch hour from 12:00 to 1:00 each of these days. She also worked on Saturday from 9:30 a.m. to 1:00 p.m.

Form 4:   Prepare a time record for Myung Chu for the week ending 9/16. His employee number is 3372. He worked a split schedule. On Monday, Wednesday, and Friday he worked from 9:00 a.m. to 6:00 p.m. with a lunch break from 1:00 to 2:00. On Tuesday and Thursday he worked from 8:30 a.m. to 12:30 p.m. and again from 5:00 p.m. to 9:00 p.m.

Form 1

SAM'S WESTERN WEAR Time Record				Hours Worked
Name				
Employee No.				Hours Worked
Week Ending				
Mon	AM	In		
		Out		
	PM	In		
		Out		
Tues	AM	In		
		Out		
	PM	In		
		Out		
Wed	AM	In		
		Out		
	PM	In		
		Out		
Thurs	AM	In		
		Out		
	PM	In		
		Out		
Fri	AM	In		
		Out		
	PM	In		
		Out		
Sat	AM	In		
		Out		
	PM	In		
		Out		
Total Weekly Hours				

Form 2

SAM'S WESTERN WEAR Time Record				Hours Worked
Name				
Employee No.				Hours Worked
Week Ending				
Mon	AM	In		
		Out		
	PM	In		
		Out		
Tues	AM	In		
		Out		
	PM	In		
		Out		
Wed	AM	In		
		Out		
	PM	In		
		Out		
Thurs	AM	In		
		Out		
	PM	In		
		Out		
Fri	AM	In		
		Out		
	PM	In		
		Out		
Sat	AM	In		
		Out		
	PM	In		
		Out		
Total Weekly Hours				

Form 3

BEN'S BUFFET — Time Record				Hours Worked
Name				
Employee No.				
Week Ending				
Mon	AM	In		
		Out		
	PM	In		
		Out		
Tues	AM	In		
		Out		
	PM	In		
		Out		
Wed	AM	In		
		Out		
	PM	In		
		Out		
Thurs	AM	In		
		Out		
	PM	In		
		Out		
Fri	AM	In		
		Out		
	PM	In		
		Out		
Sat	AM	In		
		Out		
	PM	In		
		Out		
Total Weekly Hours				

Form 4

BEN'S BUFFET — Time Record				Hours Worked
Name				
Employee No.				
Week Ending				
Mon	AM	In		
		Out		
	PM	In		
		Out		
Tues	AM	In		
		Out		
	PM	In		
		Out		
Wed	AM	In		
		Out		
	PM	In		
		Out		
Thurs	AM	In		
		Out		
	PM	In		
		Out		
Fri	AM	In		
		Out		
	PM	In		
		Out		
Sat	AM	In		
		Out		
	PM	In		
		Out		
Total Weekly Hours				

Exercise 53

EXERCISE 53b Complete the two membership cards using the information given for the forms. *Print* the information using all capital letters. Try to abbreviate as many words as possible. For help with abbreviations, refer to the USPS Abbreviations pages in the *Reference Sources* section in the back of this book. Include punctuation where appropriate. *Write slowly and legibly.*

#19562935
Phone: (703) 555-0172
Janet M. Lund
Assistant Staff Manager
National Fine Arts Bureau
Winslow Plaza West, Building C-45, Suite 120
Arlington, Virginia 22202-6120

Form 1

MEMBER #		PHONE ( )
NAME		
TITLE		
COMPANY		
ADDRESS		
CITY	STATE	ZIP CODE

#02117538
Phone: (915) 555-0193
Mark B. Eddlemann
Director, Information Processing Center
Sage Electric Corporation
Southwest Utilities Plaza
El Paso, Texas 79921-6563

Form 2

MEMBER #		PHONE ( )
NAME		
TITLE		
COMPANY		
ADDRESS		
CITY	STATE	ZIP CODE

GOAL: Make decisions about printing
information on business forms

Completing forms is a necessary part of many job positions. Having experience in making decisions about filling out forms may give you an advantage when being considered for a position.

Complete the following insurance form using the information provided. Make your own decisions about correct printing, abbreviating, and placing of the information.

Form 1: On July 10 of the current year, Deborah M. Sweeney, who lives at 7492 Sun Dusk Lane, Apartment 2211, Las Vegas, Nevada 89134-1336, received Policy No. PRW7027549 from the Danna Company.

PRINT POLICY NO. BELOW	PRINT COMPANY NAME BELOW	MO.	DAY	YR.

PRINT LAST NAME BELOW	PRINT FIRST NAME BELOW	M.I.

PRINT STREET NO. BELOW	PRINT STREET NAME, ROUTE, OR P.O. BOX NO. BELOW	PRINT APT. NO. BELOW

PRINT CITY OR TOWN BELOW	STATE	ZIP CODE

Complete the following mailing labels using the information provided for each form. Make your own decisions about correct printing, abbreviating, and placing of the information.

Form 2:   Address a mailing label to Eric Johns who lives at 720 Hyatt Road, Leesville, Louisiana 71446-6746. The parcel is from Marjorie Legters who lives at 92 Lakeview Drive, Pell City, Alabama 35128-8016.

MAILING LABEL

FROM _____

_____

_____

TO _____

_____

_____

Form 3:   Address a mailing label to Charlotte Mathers who lives at 3016 Cousteau Court, Elk Grove, California 95758-4226. The parcel is from Dottie Hawk who lives at 79 Appleton Street, Providence, Rhode Island 02909-2730.

MAILING LABEL

FROM _____

_____

_____

TO _____

_____

_____

GOAL: Make decisions about printing information on business forms

_____ NAME

_____ CLASS

Marcus Bingham works in sales zone ALM037. He opens a new account (number 0029517328) for Ms. Sylvia R. Johannsen who lives at 3774 Heritage Springs Circle, Hattiesburg, Mississippi 39402-3386. Complete the form for new accounts below. Make your own decisions about correct printing, abbreviating, and placing of the information.

New Account 1

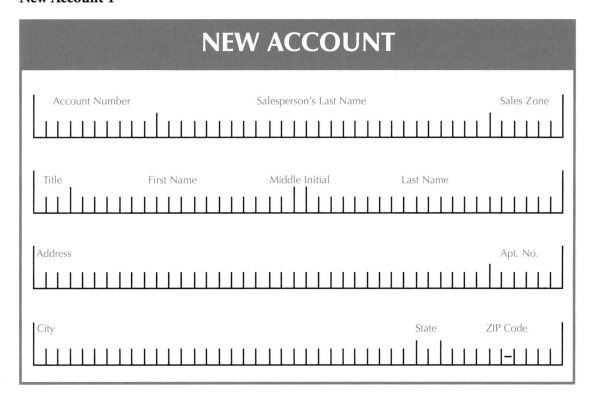

You are employed as a salesperson at the same company as Marcus Bingham. You work in sales zone RKQ449. Open two new accounts using the information provided for each account on the next page. In the Salesperson's Last Name space, use your own last name. Make your own decisions about correct printing, abbreviating, and placing of the information.

New Account 2

Open account number 4593657125 for Ms. Robin Byington who lives at 1985 Whittier Boulevard, Boulder, Colorado 80321-1144.

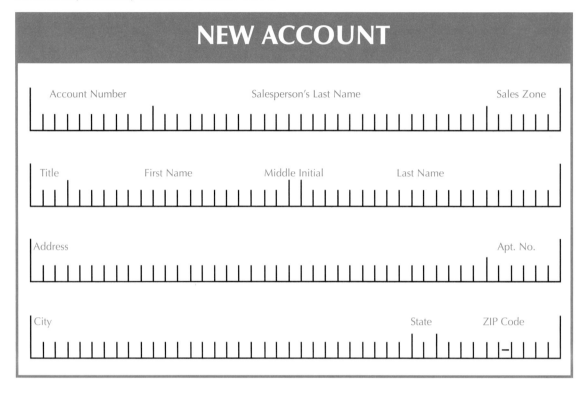

New Account 3

Open account number 4594756921 for Mr. Tucker Atteberry who resides at 3603 Riverside Drive, Apt. 12C, Loveland, Colorado 80538-1344.

GOAL: Complete telephone message forms

NAME _____

CLASS _____

In an office environment, you may be responsible for answering the telephone and taking messages for others. It is essential to be courteous to the callers and write down the messages accurately. Use the telephone message form in Figure 3-3 as a guide as you complete the forms in this exercise. As you read the instructions below the form, note that the numbered steps correspond with the circled numbers shown beside the form.

Figure 3-3   Telephone Message Form

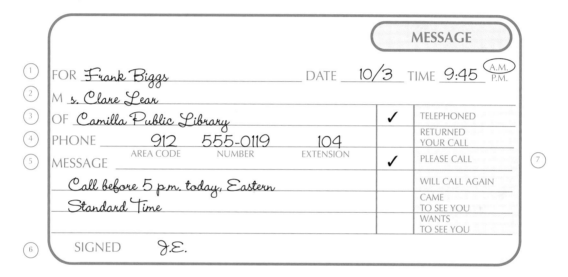

1. After *For,* write the name of the person to whom the call was made. The *Date* can be written in figures (10/3) or as Oct. 3. The *Time* of the call is written, and *A.M.* or *P.M.* is circled.

2. An *s* is written after the *M* to let Frank Biggs know Ms. Lear's title. It is important to obtain the caller's correct title. The title *Ms.* may be used for both married and unmarried women. The title *Miss* is used for an unmarried woman. *Mrs.* is used for a married woman. For a man, *Mr.* is used. Abbreviations are used for a doctor (Dr.), minister (Rev.), or other similar titles.

3. After *Of,* the name of the caller's place of employment is written. If the caller does not provide you with that information, or if the call was made from a home telephone, the line is left blank.

4. After *Phone,* the caller's telephone number is written. When applicable, the telephone extension is included. Always repeat the number back to the caller to make sure you have written the number correctly. You may say, "To confirm your number, I have 9-1-2-5-5-5-0-1-1-9, extension 1-0-4. Is that correct?"

5. The *Message* line may or may not be completed, depending on the information the caller gives you. In this example, Mr. Biggs is given a time by which to return the call, as well as the time zone. For long-distance calls, be sure to include the caller's time zone.

6. In this example the message was taken by a person with the initials *J.E.* You may write either your initials or your name on the *Signed* line.

7. The right side of the message form has spaces for checkmarks that give Mr. Biggs more information about the call. He can quickly determine that someone *Telephoned* and left a message to *Please Call*. He can then read the message to learn the details of the call.

Complete the telephone message forms that follow using the information given for the two calls. Write the information neatly on the forms.

Call 1: Use the current date and a time of 10:30 in the morning. Randy Foxwood received a call from Dr. Martha Johnson of Auburn University. She would like Randy to call her before noon today, Central Standard Time. Her telephone number is 205-555-0107, Extension 338.

```
┌──────────────────────────────────────────────────────────────┐
│                                          ╭──────────────────╮ │
│                                          │     MESSAGE       │ │
│                                          ╰──────────────────╯ │
│                                                         A.M.   │
│ FOR _____ DATE _____ TIME _____ P.M.     │
│ M _____ │
│ OF _____│ TELEPHONED          │
│ PHONE _____ │ RETURNED YOUR CALL   │
│        AREA CODE   NUMBER   EXTENSION   │ PLEASE CALL          │
│ MESSAGE _____│ WILL CALL AGAIN      │
│ _____│ CAME TO SEE YOU      │
│ _____│ WANTS TO SEE YOU     │
│    SIGNED                                                      │
└──────────────────────────────────────────────────────────────┘
```

Call 2: Use the current date and a time of 1:40 in the afternoon. Mandy Southworth received a call from Alex Westwood. He would like Mandy to call him at 555-0194, Extension 670. (The area code is not needed for a local call.) He wants her to speak at the monthly meeting of the Diabetes Support Group.

```
┌──────────────────────────────────────────────────────────────┐
│                                          ╭──────────────────╮ │
│                                          │     MESSAGE       │ │
│                                          ╰──────────────────╯ │
│                                                         A.M.   │
│ FOR _____ DATE _____ TIME _____ P.M.     │
│ M _____ │
│ OF _____│ TELEPHONED          │
│ PHONE _____ │ RETURNED YOUR CALL   │
│        AREA CODE   NUMBER   EXTENSION   │ PLEASE CALL          │
│ MESSAGE _____│ WILL CALL AGAIN      │
│ _____│ CAME TO SEE YOU      │
│ _____│ WANTS TO SEE YOU     │
│    SIGNED                                                      │
└──────────────────────────────────────────────────────────────┘
```

GOAL: Complete message forms

———————————————— NAME

———————————————— CLASS

You work for the Ohio Valley Insurance Agency as a clerk in the Claims Department. Clients often stop by the office to inquire about their claims, pay on their accounts, or ask questions regarding their insurance policies and rates. You are also responsible for taking messages for the agents in this department. Complete the message forms below. Write each message neatly and accurately. Use the current date for each form. Use your name or initials on each form.

Form 1: Mr. Bob Glamis of the Ohio Insurance Commission called for Alexis Smith at 10:18 a.m. He would like her to call him regarding new rate schedules. His phone number is (513) 555-0117.

OHIO VALLEY INSURANCE AGENCY
IMPORTANT MESSAGE

TO: ———————————————— TAKEN BY: ————————————

M ———————————————— DATE: ————————————

of ———————————————— TIME: ————————————

PHONE: (   ) ———————————— EXT.: ————————————

TELEPHONED		CAME TO SEE YOU
PLEASE PHONE		WOULD LIKE TO SEE YOU
WILL CALL AGAIN		WILL STOP BY LATER
RETURNED YOUR CALL		OTHER

MESSAGE/COMMENTS: ————————————————

————————————————————————

————————————————————————

Form 2:   Ms. Marabelle Johnson stopped by to see Frank Waller at 1:30 p.m. She wants Mr. Waller to call her regarding her recent automobile accident. Her claim no. is T403167. Her phone number is (513) 555-0146.

OHIO VALLEY INSURANCE AGENCY
IMPORTANT MESSAGE

TO: _____   TAKEN BY: _____

M _____   DATE: _____

of _____   TIME: _____

PHONE: (   ) _____   EXT.: _____

TELEPHONED		CAME TO SEE YOU
PLEASE PHONE		WOULD LIKE TO SEE YOU
WILL CALL AGAIN		WILL STOP BY LATER
RETURNED YOUR CALL		OTHER

MESSAGE/COMMENTS: _____

_____

_____

Form 3:   At 1:45 p.m. Xavier Lopez returned Isabelle Martin's call regarding his new homeowner's policy. He would like Ms. Martin to call him after 4:30 p.m. today at (513) 555-0161, Ext. 634.

OHIO VALLEY INSURANCE AGENCY
IMPORTANT MESSAGE

TO: _____   TAKEN BY: _____

M _____   DATE: _____

of _____   TIME: _____

PHONE: (   ) _____   EXT.: _____

TELEPHONED		CAME TO SEE YOU
PLEASE PHONE		WOULD LIKE TO SEE YOU
WILL CALL AGAIN		WILL STOP BY LATER
RETURNED YOUR CALL		OTHER

MESSAGE/COMMENTS: _____

_____

_____

GOAL: Complete property record forms

_____ NAME

_____ CLASS

Company property, such as employee identification cards or cellular telephones, may be issued to employees so they are able to do their jobs. They may use the items while employed in their positions, then return the items when they either change positions or leave the company.

You work for the City of Newton Falls in the Human Resources Department and are responsible for issuing city property to employees. Complete the property record forms that follow using the information provided for each form. At the bottom of the form, sign your name as the designee (someone chosen to perform a job or task).

Form 1: Deborah Mitchell, Employee No. 7416, is a recent hire in the Communications Department. Issue her the following items: entrance key card #0476, department key #C954, ID card #7416, and cellular telephone #ER279. Use the current date.

CITY OF NEWTON FALLS
PROPERTY RECORD

Employee Name: _____ Employee No.: _____

Department/Division: _____

The following city property has been issued to the above employee:

Item	Item No.	Date Issued	Date Returned
Bank Credit Card	_____	_____	_____
Camera, Digital	_____	_____	_____
Camera, Video	_____	_____	_____
Cellular Telephone	_____	_____	_____
Department Key	_____	_____	_____
Entrance Key (Card)	_____	_____	_____
ID Card	_____	_____	_____
Laptop Computer	_____	_____	_____
Pager	_____	_____	_____
Vehicle	_____	_____	_____
Other	_____	_____	_____

I understand that if I lose or damage the above equipment, I am responsible for the associated replacement costs. I understand that I have the option of making payments directly to the City of Newton Falls, or I may authorize payroll deductions in total or in payments not to exceed three (3) months.

_____   _____
Employee's Signature   Date

_____   _____
Supervisor/Designee's Signature   Date

Form 2: Guy Rutgers, Employee No. 5180, was promoted within the Finance Department. On April 19, 2009, he was issued the following items: entrance key card #0294, department key #F704, ID card #5180, cellular telephone #RM582, and bank credit card #CC098. Complete the form to log the items already in his possession.

Using the current date, issue these additional items Mr. Rutgers requires in his new position: vehicle #NFV287, laptop computer #LT9021, and pager #PG347Z.

CITY OF NEWTON FALLS
PROPERTY RECORD

Employee Name: _____ Employee No.: _____

Department/Division: _____

The following city property has been issued to the above employee:

Item	Item No.	Date Issued	Date Returned
Bank Credit Card	_____	_____	_____
Camera, Digital	_____	_____	_____
Camera, Video	_____	_____	_____
Cellular Telephone	_____	_____	_____
Department Key	_____	_____	_____
Entrance Key (Card)	_____	_____	_____
ID Card	_____	_____	_____
Laptop Computer	_____	_____	_____
Pager	_____	_____	_____
Vehicle	_____	_____	_____
Other	_____	_____	_____

I understand that if I lose or damage the above equipment, I am responsible for the associated replacement costs. I understand that I have the option of making payments directly to the City of Newton Falls, or I may authorize payroll deductions in total or in payments not to exceed three (3) months.

_____   _____
Employee's Signature   Date

_____   _____
Supervisor/Designee's Signature   Date

GOAL: Complete an order form

_____ NAME

_____ CLASS

You work for Shelby Medical Services, 7725 North Cedar Street, Wilmington, Delaware 19808-5703; phone (302) 555-0117; e-mail address YourName@sms.com. Your office is updating its storage equipment and you were assigned the task of determining the needs of the office and selecting the equipment. You have chosen the equipment and must now place the order.

Complete the order form on the following page using the information provided. Make your own decisions about correct printing, abbreviating, and placing of the information.

Item No.	Page No.	Description	Color	Qty.	Price Each
709642-4	63	Lateral File Cabinet, 4-drawer	Black	2	357.99
890756-3	75	Vertical File Cabinet, 3-drawer	Oak	1	247.99
890746-4	79	Wardrobe; steel, mobile	Gray	1	165.99
359076-5	37	Bookcase, 5-shelf	Oak	1	115.99

After calculating the subtotal for this order, calculate the tax at 7.50% (rounding up to the nearest cent). The shipping and insurance charge is $87.22; be sure to add this charge and the tax to the subtotal to calculate the total cost of the order.

The method of payment is the company's National Express card, number 8679-763-2890-51, expiration date 07/18. You are authorized to sign your name for the order.

WAYBORN OFFICE SUPPLIERS
764 Ash Street
Clifton, NJ 19711-2722
(862) 555-0131

Ordered by:

Company Name _____

Address _____

City _____ State _____ ZIP _____

Daytime Phone (____) _____

E-mail Address _____

Item No.	Page No.	Description	Color	Qty.	Price of Item	
					Each	Total
| | | | | |—|						
| | | | | |—|						
| | | | | |—|						
| | | | | |—|						
| | | | | |—|						
| | | | | |—|						
| | | | | |—|						
| | | | | |—|						

Subtotal	
Tax	
Shipping/Insurance	
Total	

Method of payment:

☐ Charge to my *(circle one):*

  AMERICARD

  NATIONAL EXPRESS

☐ Check or Money Order
  Enclosed

**Thank you
for your order!**

**Please include credit card number *and*
expiration date with charge orders.**

Expiration Date [Month / Year]

Signature _____
(required if using credit card)

**Call us toll-free 24 hours a day, 7 days a week
to charge your order: 1-800-555-0131**

GOAL: Complete work orders

_____ NAME

_____ CLASS

A **work order** is an order received by an organization from a customer or from a department within an organization for work to be completed. A work order is also called a job order, maintenance request, or repair request. It may provide the date the request was received and the location and nature of the service to be carried out. A completed work order may provide the date the service was performed and any labor or materials used. The completed work order then can be returned to the requesting customer or department as an invoice.

You work for the city of Grenville in the Public Works Department. Your responsibilities include keeping a record of when the citizens of Grenville notify the department with concerns. You must also determine whether the concern is urgent or not. Complete the work order forms that follow using the information provided for each form. Be concise and include only pertinent information. Indicate the urgency of the concern by circling _Yes_ or _No_. Sign each form with your name.

Form 1: Mrs. Nancy Carrier called on November 15 to report a fallen tree in the 400 block of Michigan Avenue. She states that it has fallen across the entire street and is blocking traffic. No one was injured. Her telephone number is (605) 555-1107.

CITY OF GRENVILLE
WORK ORDER

Date: _____ Phone Number: _____

Name: _____ Urgent: Yes   No

Description of concern: _____

_____

_____

Signed: _____

Form 2: David Forrester e-mailed on November 17 to report graffiti on High Street on the wall along the southeast corner of the Bishop Falls Shopping Center. His telephone number is (605) 555-0142.

CITY OF GRENVILLE WORK ORDER

Date: _____ Phone Number: _____

Name: _____ Urgent: Yes   No

Description of concern: _____

_____

_____

Signed: _____

Form 3: Paul Zaharis called on November 18 to report that the storm drain at North Avenue and Park Street is not draining. He is concerned because the current storm in the area is forecasted to continue through tomorrow. His telephone number is (605) 555-0416.

CITY OF GRENVILLE WORK ORDER

Date: _____ Phone Number: _____

Name: _____ Urgent: Yes   No

Description of concern: _____

_____

_____

Signed: _____

Well done! You have completed the exercises for Unit 3. Before your instructor administers the Unit 3 Test, review the exercises in this unit. Do not begin the Unit 4 exercises until your instructor has approved Unit 3.

Go Digital!

For additional activities visit www.cengage.com/school/bse

GOAL: Index names of persons

_____ NAME

_____ CLASS

To file names in **alphabetic order** means to put names in the same order as the letters of the alphabet, or in ABC order. Before you can put names in alphabetic order, you have to index them. **Indexing** is putting the name of a person or business in a certain order according to the rules of filing. In this unit you will study the rules of filing and complete exercises about those rules to help prepare you for a job in the business world.

RULE 1a   The name of a person is indexed in this way: (1) the last name (surname) is the key (or first) unit; (2) the first name (given name) or initial is the second unit; and (3) the middle name or initial is the third unit. Unusual or foreign names are indexed in the same way. When indexing foreign names, if you cannot tell which name is the surname, consider the last name written as the surname. (See Sergio Zapata in Table 4-1 below.)

A **cross-reference system** is used for indexing unusual names that might be easily confused or for records that might be filed in more than one place. **Cross-referencing** means that a card or sheet is put in a file folder in every place a person might look for a record. The cross-reference lets the filer know the storage location of the record. The card or sheet is usually a bright color that is easy to see in a file folder. For example, Sergio Zapata would be indexed with Zapata as the last name. All records for this person will be placed in the files under Zapata, Sergio. A cross-reference sheet will be placed in the files under Sergio, Zapata— Sergio as the last name. On the sheet in the Sergio, Zapata folder, a cross-reference note is written: _See Zapata, Sergio._ The filer then knows to look in the files under Zapata, Sergio for the records for this person.

Look at the examples in Table 4-1 to learn how to index names of persons for filing. The letter with a line under it shows the change from one letter in the alphabet to another letter that comes later in the alphabet. The names are placed in alphabetic order according to the underlined letters. On the second line, the H has a line under it. The H in Harley comes after the C in Cassara. The last names in the Key Unit column are in alphabetic order.

Table 4-1   Examples of Rule 1a

	INDEXING ORDER	
Name Before Indexing	**Key Unit** (Last Name)	**Unit 2** (First Name)
Theodora Cassara	Cassara	Theodora
Marjean Harley	Harley	Marjean
Rodney Marlowc	Marlowe	Rodney

INDEXING ORDER

Name Before Indexing	Key Unit (Last Name)	Unit 2 (First Name)
Sarah Suttles	<u>S</u>uttles	Sarah
Donald Upchurch	<u>U</u>pchurch	Donald
Margaret Yarbrough	<u>Y</u>arbrough	Margaret
*Sergio Zapata	<u>Z</u>apata	Sergio

*A file folder will also be set up labeled Sergio, Zapata (Sergio as the last name). Inside this file folder will be a cross-reference sheet with the notation: *See Zapata, Sergio.*

If two or more *last* names are exactly the same, look at the *first* names to see how they differ. Look at Table 4-2. For the first three names, Wilke is the last name. Look at the three first names to see how they are indexed and put in alphabetic order. A line is placed under the first letter in the name that is different than the one above it. The underlined letters determine the alphabetic order of the names. Each time you index last names that are identical, you will need to follow this procedure for the first names.

For the last three names in the table, Wilkes is the last name. Wilkes is indexed after Wilke because of the "s" in Wilkes. When indexing, always remember that *nothing comes before something.*

Table 4-2 Examples of Rule 1a

INDEXING ORDER

Name Before Indexing	Key Unit (Last Name)	Unit 2 (First Name)
Robert Wilke	Wilke	Robert
Roberta Wilke	Wilke	Robert<u>a</u>
Robin Wilke	Wilke	Rob<u>i</u>n
Robateen Wilkes	Wilke<u>s</u>	Robateen
Robert Wilkes	Wilkes	Rob<u>e</u>rt
Robinette Wilkes	Wilkes	Rob<u>i</u>nette

EXERCISE 61a Read carefully each sentence in Column 1. If the sentence is *true*, circle the *T* in Column 2. If the sentence is *false*, circle the *F* in Column 2. An example is shown.

COLUMN 1	COLUMN 2
Ex. Marla Marie Jeans comes before Marla Jane Jeans.	Ex. T (F)
1. Kent Bryant Galina comes before Kent Bryan Galina.	1. T F
2. Regina Wells Nitka comes before Regis Walter Nitka.	2. T F

COLUMN 1	COLUMN 2

3. Felecia Bevis comes after Felesia Bevis.   3.   T   F

4. Erik Earl Plemmons comes before Eva Edwanda Plemmens.   4.   T   F

5. Helen Farris Hardy comes after Helena Ferris Hardy.   5.   T   F

6. Mathew Allen Knowlas comes after Matthew Allan Knowles.   6.   T   F

7. Rosalin Lee Waymon comes before Rosalyn Lee Wayman.   7.   T   F

8. Conrad Elvin Knopf comes after Conrad Elvane Knopf.   8.   T   F

9. Stephen Folle and Stanley Grimes come after Marla Hester.   9.   T   F

10. Paula Routh comes after Barbara Martz and Alton Thorpe.   10.   T   F

11. Michael Jorgenson and Jim Morrow come after Jennifer Klaas.   11.   T   F

12. Denny Jacobs comes after Mabel Bomar and Andrea Draper.   12.   T   F

13. Syble Hubbard and Cecile Jacoby come after Harry Lyndell.   13.   T   F

14. Willa Beatrice Leonard and William Beetrose Leonerd come after Wylla Beatrise Leenard.   14.   T   F

15. Ronald Odel Hervey comes before Ronalla Odelle Harvey and Ronell Odella Hervay.   15.   T   F

EXERCISE 61b Look at the names listed below and study them carefully to see which names should be indexed first. After you have studied the names, write them *in alphabetic order* on the lines provided. Write the names in indexing order. *Underline the letter in each name that determines the alphabetic order.* The first two names to be indexed (Coleman, Derek and Collinge, Gail) are given as a guide.

Jamie Cusick	Derek Coleman	Franc Darnell
Nolan Davidson	Margaret Darling	Garth Collins
Hellena Davies	Maurice Davis	Kathy Colson
Gail Collinge	Noel Davidson	Rita Darwood
James Darling	Sissy Durwood	Midge Daewong
Betsy Cook	Warren Colson	

INDEXING ORDER

	Key Unit (Last Name)	Unit 2 (First Name)
Ex.	Coleman	Derek
Ex.	Collinge	Gail
1.		
2.		

Key Unit (Last Name)	Unit 2 (First Name)
3. _____	_____
4. _____	_____
5. _____	_____
6. _____	_____
7. _____	_____
8. _____	_____
9. _____	_____
10. _____	_____
11. _____	_____
12. _____	_____
13. _____	_____
14. _____	_____
15. _____	_____

GOAL: Index names of businesses

_____ NAME

_____ CLASS

In Exercise 61 you learned to index the names of persons for filing. In this exercise you will learn the indexing order for filing the names of businesses.

RULE 1b Business names are indexed and filed the way they are written using letterheads or trademarks as guides. Each word of a business name is indexed as a separate filing unit. Types of businesses and organizations include banks, stores, motels, churches, schools, newspapers, and magazines. Business names containing personal names are indexed as written. For newspapers that have the same name but are in different cities, the city name is indexed as the last unit. If the city names are the same, the state name is indexed after the city name.

Look at the examples in Table 4-3 to learn how to index the names of businesses for filing. Look carefully at the underlined letters in the table. These underlines show where the words differ from those directly above them. By matching the letters of the words from left to right and by underlining the first difference, you will be able to put lists of words or names in alphabetic order.

Table 4-3   Examples of Rule 1b

	INDEXING ORDER			
Name Before Indexing	Key Unit	Unit 2	Unit 3	Unit 4
Harris Wholesale Grocers	Harris	Wholesale	Grocers	
Harrisburg National Bank	Harrisburg	National	Bank	
Hawthorne Christian Church	Hawthorne	Christian	Church	
Health Hints Magazine	Health	Hints	Magazine	
Helen Hull Landscaping Service	Helen	Hull	Landscaping	Service
Helena Advertising Agency	Helena	Advertising	Agency	
Hilltop Dancing Academy	Hilltop	Dancing	Academy	
Hilton Head Gift Shop	Hilton	Head	Gift	Shop
Hometown News (Selma)	Hometown	News	Selma	
Hometown News (Tupelo)	Hometown	News	Tupelo	
Horton Harley Furniture Store	Horton	Harley	Furniture	Store
Houston Electronics Company	Houston	Electronics	Company	

EXERCISE 62a The letter *A, B, C,* or *D* appears before each of the four names in each group of business names in Column 1. In the space provided in Column 2, write the *A, B, C,* and *D* in the order that indicates the alphabetic order of the four names. An example is shown.

COLUMN 1   COLUMN 2

Ex. A. Wood Office Supply Company   Ex. _____A, C, D, B_____

     B. Woody Citrus Shippers

     C. Woodlawn National Bank

     D. Woodroe Woods Kennel

1.   A. *Weekly Neighbor News* (Roanoke, IL)   1. _____

     B. *Weekly Neighbor News* (Rockvale, CO)

     C. *Weekly Neighbor News* (Rocksprings, TX)

     D. *Weekly Neighbor News* (Rolling Hills, WY)

2.   A. Davis Auto Parts   2. _____

     B. Davidson Plumbing Supplies

     C. Davison House of Fashion

     D. Davies Day Care Center

3.   A. Gracely Automatic Washers   3. _____

     B. Graceland Music Museum

     C. Grace Christian Church

     D. Gracalene Beauty Shop

4.   A. Howard Animal Motel   4. _____

     B. Howard Counseling Clinic

     C. Howard Hynes Transmission Repairs

     D. Howard National Life Insurance Company

5.   A. James River Travel Agency   5. _____

     B. James Rivers Cattle Breeders

     C. James Rivera Roofing Company

     D. James Rives Furniture Finishers

6.   A. Massonry Building Supplies   6. _____

     B. Mason Boat Builders

     C. Masson Beauty Spot

     D. Mason Bars and Stools

EXERCISE 62b   Look carefully at each group of business names in Column 1 to determine which name should come first alphabetically. Write that name on the first line in Column 2. Determine which name comes next alphabetically. Write that name on the second line. Continue until all four names in each group are written in alphabetical order in Column 2. *Be sure to underline the letter that determines the alphabetic order.* An example is shown.

<table>
<tr><td colspan="2" align="center">COLUMN 1</td><td colspan="2" align="center">COLUMN 2</td></tr>
<tr><td>Ex.</td><td>Pauley Pilzin Printing Company</td><td>Ex.</td><td><u>Paul </u>Chamberlain Garden Shop</td></tr>
<tr><td></td><td>Paulette Art Supplies</td><td></td><td><u>Paula</u> Porcet Dance Studio</td></tr>
<tr><td></td><td>Paula Porcet Dance Studio</td><td></td><td><u>Paule</u>tte Art Supplies</td></tr>
<tr><td></td><td>Paul Chamberlain Garden Shop</td><td></td><td><u>Pauley</u> Pilzin Printing Company</td></tr>
<tr><td>1.</td><td>Murata Paint Contractors</td><td>1.</td><td></td></tr>
<tr><td></td><td>Minute Markets of Madison</td><td></td><td></td></tr>
<tr><td></td><td>Morrisey Optical Company</td><td></td><td></td></tr>
<tr><td></td><td>Metro Industrial Clinic</td><td></td><td></td></tr>
<tr><td>2.</td><td>Torrida Stamp Trading Center</td><td>2.</td><td></td></tr>
<tr><td></td><td>Tutschek Outdoor Advertising</td><td></td><td></td></tr>
<tr><td></td><td>Topware Home Parties</td><td></td><td></td></tr>
<tr><td></td><td>Treadway Pawn Shop</td><td></td><td></td></tr>
<tr><td>3.</td><td>Eastridge Tree Trimmers</td><td>3.</td><td></td></tr>
<tr><td></td><td>Eskridge Upholstery Center</td><td></td><td></td></tr>
<tr><td></td><td>Eldredge Marketing Research</td><td></td><td></td></tr>
<tr><td></td><td>Etheridge Animal Hospital</td><td></td><td></td></tr>
<tr><td>4.</td><td>Larette Marlin Art Studio</td><td>4.</td><td></td></tr>
<tr><td></td><td>Laramore Marlon Enterprises</td><td></td><td></td></tr>
<tr><td></td><td>Larry Marlon Chemical Co.</td><td></td><td></td></tr>
<tr><td></td><td>Larrue Marlen Fashion Nook</td><td></td><td></td></tr>
<tr><td>5.</td><td>Universe Tennis Center</td><td>5.</td><td></td></tr>
<tr><td></td><td>Unique Hair Styles</td><td></td><td></td></tr>
<tr><td></td><td>United Camper Sales</td><td></td><td></td></tr>
<tr><td></td><td>Unlimited Auto Parts</td><td></td><td></td></tr>
</table>

COLUMN 1	COLUMN 2

COLUMN 1 **COLUMN 2**

6. Davis Employment Agency

6. _____

Daves Distributors

_____

Davies Computer Supplies

_____

Davis Alterations

_____

7. Andreas Blair Carpet Repairs

7. _____

Andrew Blane Exterminators

_____

Andrews Blarr Upholstery Shop

_____

Andrea Blain Import Center

_____

8. Geoffroy Factory Outlet

8. _____

Geffen Properties

_____

Geffga Financial Group

_____

Geiger Aluminum Products

_____

9. Allbert Refrigeration Service

9. _____

Allen Telephone Repair

_____

Always Travel Planners

_____

Aldon Book Binders

_____

10. Flintridge Cleaning Service

10. _____

Frasher Quality Comics

_____

Flueman Importers

_____

Flubbs Toy Outlet

_____

GOAL: Index business names with minor words and symbols

_____ NAME

_____ CLASS

RULE 2   Prepositions, conjunctions, articles, and symbols are parts of some business names and are considered separate indexing units. Index prepositions (*in, out, to, at, with, on, off, for, of, over, by*); conjunctions (*and, but, or, nor*); and articles (*a, an, the*) as they appear in the name. Symbols (&, ¢, #, $, %, etc.) are spelled out in full when indexing (*and, cent/cents, number/pound, dollar/dollars, percent,* etcetera). When "The" is the first word in a business name, it is considered the *last* indexing unit.

Look at the examples in Table 4-4 to learn how to index business names containing minor words and symbols. The letter with a line under it shows the change from one letter in the alphabet to another letter that comes later in the alphabet. The names are placed in alphabetic order according to the underlined letters.

Table 4-4   Examples of Rule 2

	INDEXING ORDER				
Name Before Indexing	Key Unit	Unit 2	Unit 3	Unit 4	Unit 5
On Guard Alarm Systems	On	Guard	Alarm	Systems	
The On Time Delivery Service	On	Time	Delivery	Service	The
Out of This World Bakery	Out	of	This	World	Bakery
Out of Town Newspaper Center	Out	of	Town	Newspaper	Center
The Outer Banks Garage	Outer	Banks	Garage	The	
Outside & Inside Decorators	Outside	and	Inside	Decorators	
Outside and Inside Home Repairs	Outside	and	Inside	Home	Repairs
Outside the City Motel	Outside	the	City	Motel	
The Pay Less $ Store	Pay	Less	Dollars	Store	The
Pedro Ruiz # One Outfitters	Pedro	Ruiz	Number	One	Outfitters
Pedros and Ruiz Building	Pedros	and	Ruiz	Building	
Place in the Sun Resort	Place	in	the	Sun	Resort
Place on the Bay Villas	Place	on	the	Bay	Villas

The number in Column 1 (first, second, third, fourth, or fifth) indicates the *indexing unit* you are to find in the business name in Column 2. Write the correct word in the space provided in Column 3. An example is shown.

COLUMN 1	COLUMN 2	COLUMN 3
Ex. third	Ex. By the # Weightlifting Center	Ex. _____Pound_____
1. fourth	1. Over the Rainbow Nursery School	1. _____
2. second	2. Around Town Delivery Service	2. _____
3. first	3. Between Two Cities Animal Hospital	3. _____
4. fifth	4. End of the Pier Cafe	4. _____
5. second	5. More $ Savings Bargain Barn	5. _____
6. third	6. The Prado Mall Administrative Center	6. _____
7. second	7. Ten % Discounters	7. _____
8. first	8. Away from the Crowd Boutique	8. _____
9. fourth	9. Tomas the Chef Cooking School	9. _____
10. third	10. By the Sea Party Supplies	10. _____
11. third	11. Save Many ¢ Shop	11. _____
12. fifth	12. The Ramirez Family Sports Center	12. _____
13. second	13. Drummond & Lasky Marketing Group	13. _____
14. first	14. Citadel School of Broadcasting	14. _____
15. fourth	15. Off the Beaten Path Antiques	15. _____
16. fifth	16. A View from the Top Motel	16. _____
17. first	17. The University of Selma	17. _____
18. first	18. # One Dance Studios	18. _____
19. third	19. Pacific Carpet & Interior	19. _____
20. fourth	20. An Amazing House of Wares	20. _____

GOAL: Index names with punctuation and possessives

_____ NAME

_____ CLASS

RULE 3   All punctuation and possessives—including commas, colons, periods, hyphens, apostrophes, dashes, exclamation points, question marks, quotation marks, diagonals, and parentheses—are _disregarded_ when indexing personal and business names. Remove the punctuation or possessive, close up the word(s), and index as one unit.

Look at the examples in Table 4-5 to learn how to index names containing punctuation and possessives. The letter with a line under it shows the change from one letter in the alphabet to another letter that comes later in the alphabet. The names are placed in alphabetic order according to the underlined letters.

Table 4-5   Examples of Rule 3

	INDEXING ORDER				
Name Before Indexing	**Key Unit**	**Unit 2**	**Unit 3**	**Unit 4**	**Unit 5**
Ari, Blau, & Chay Imports	Ari	Blau	and	Chay	Imports
Carol Marie Bank	Bank	Carol	Marie		
Bank of Augusta—South	Bank	of	AugustaSouth		
Banks & Hewitt, Roofers	Banks	and	Hewitt	Roofers	
Anniesue Lynn Banks	Banks	Anniesue	Lynn		
Bank's "Cut-Rate" Drugs	Banks	CutRate	Drugs		
Banks' Dry Cleaners	Banks	Dry	Cleaners		
Andrea Bank-Valdez	BankValdez	Andrea			
Bankville Fix-It-Shop	Bankville	FixItShop			
Beale's $ Stretcher Stores	Beales	Dollar	Stretcher	Stores	
The Can We Bargain? Market	Can	We	Bargain	Market	The
China-Tone Music Shop	ChinaTone	Music	Shop		
Chinatown Inside/Outside Tours	Chinatown	InsideOutside	Tours		
Barney Joseph Cholton	Cholton	Barney	Joseph		
Chow Time! Restaurants	Chow	Time	Restaurants		

EXERCISE 64a   Look at each name below and write each unit in indexing order. An example is shown.

INDEXING ORDER

Name Before Indexing	Key Unit	Unit 2	Unit 3	Unit 4
Ex. By-the-Book Used Books	BytheBook	Used	Books	
1. Phil's Carpet/Rug Service				
2. Motor-Inn Lodge				
3. The Do-it-Over Pottery				
4. Manny's Auto Body Shop				
5. "Top-Vids" Video Store				
6. Barbie's Beauty Salon—West				
7. Hugo's Flip-It! Pancake House				
8. Daring Dives (Bungee Jumps)				

EXERCISE 64b   *Mentally* put the four names in each group in Column 1 in alphabetic order. (You may find it helpful to underline the letter that determines the alphabetic order of each name.) Then, in the space provided in Column 2, write *first, second, third,* or *fourth* to indicate where the underlined name would be in the alphabetic order. An example is shown.

COLUMN 1

COLUMN 2

Ex. Charles and Cowan Freight Lines

Ex. _____third_____

Charles-Town Shopping Mall

Charlesy Coffee Quick-Stop

Charleston's Commercial Bank

1. Belle-of-the-Ball Studios

1. _____

Bell's Baby Products

Baal-Port Motorcycle Sales & Service

Bells' Supermarkets

2. Offen, Scott, and Lane Department Stores

2. _____

Off-the-Square Flower Mart

Office Mates' Employment Agency

Leola Rita Offii

3. Fair Hills' Convalescent Center

3. _____

"Fairies & Clowns" Day Care Circus

Michelle Gina Fair-Blaine

Fairfax-South Mobile Home Park

COLUMN 1	COLUMN 2
4. <u>Middleburg/Ashton Historical Society</u>	4. _____
Mid-Town Garden Apartments	
Middy & Mike: Chimney Sweeps	
Middleton "Fail Safe!" Brake Repair	
5. Millie Myric Antiques & Collectibles	5. _____
Milne Paint and Body Shop	
<u>Mills/Afton Commercial Land Developers</u>	
Milano, Dewey, and Ogle Associates	
6. <u>Horsell's "Discount-Plus" Pharmacy</u>	6. _____
Horsley's Formal Rental Shop	
Horse-Town Trading Post	
Horseshoe Bend Camera Cove	
7. Carol's "Baby Duds" Thrift Shop	7. _____
Custom Rods (by Rodney)	
Cooking—for Your Health	
<u>Carpentry Wizards!</u>	
8. Selma Jessica Perkins	8. _____
Perkins' Painting & Repair	
<u>Selma Parkins' Home Decorating</u>	
Parking/Towing/Storage Services	

EXERCISE 64c Look at each group of names in Column 1 to determine the alphabetic order. After studying each group of names, write the names in *alphabetic order* on the lines in Column 2. Write the names in indexing order. *Underline the letter that determines the alphabetic order of each name.* An example is shown.

COLUMN 1	COLUMN 2
Ex. The Travelers' Choice Inn	Ex. <u>Travel Club of AustinFt Worth</u>
Travel Treads Footwear	<u>Travel T</u>reads Footwear
Travel-with-Us Tours	<u>Travele</u>rs Choice Inn The
Travel Club of Austin/Ft. Worth	<u>Travelw</u>ith Us Tours
1. Pearson's Car Rental Agency	1. _____
Parson Party-Paper Company	_____
Parreson "Fresh Produce" Market	_____
Parson/Persion Sandwich Company	_____

COLUMN 1	COLUMN 2
2. Glen-Dale Broadcasting Systems	2. _____
Eudella Cynthia Glenn-Hubbel	_____
Glenoaks Cabinet/Furniture Works	_____
Glenridge, Burbridge, & Beal Office Park	_____
3. Lillian Lea—Body Builder Centers	3. _____
Lil'/Lee's Fantastic Photography	_____
Lilly Linn's Animal Shelter	_____
Lil Lee Chocolatiers/Flowers (& More)	_____
4. Top-of-the-World Inn	4. _____
Top $ "Made to Order" Meals	_____
Top-Notch Cleaners	_____
Top-Flight Chimney Sweep	_____
5. "Jay and Faye" General Store	5. _____
Jason, Massey, and Scott: Gem Labs	_____
Jack and Jill's Playskool	_____
The Jason-Mack Marketing Service	_____
6. Crossed Blades! Sport of Fencing	6. _____
Cross-Rhodes Wrecker Service	_____
Crossroads Carpeting/Tile/Flooring	_____
Custom Neon—The Real Thing!	_____
7. The Summit Recreation-Equestrian Center	7. _____
Summit Hills' Stables & Boarding	_____
Summers-Cook Dental Lab	_____
Summertime "Outdoor Theatre"	_____
8. Tore's Technical Institute	8. _____
Torras-Farrand Auto Paints	_____
Toras' B/W & Color Copies	_____
The Toras' Italian Restaurant	_____

GOAL: Index names with single letters and
abbreviations

_____ NAME

_____ CLASS

RULE 4a Initials in _personal_ names (W. C. Yates, D. Marie Cully, Gena K. Law) are indexed as separate units. Abbreviations of personal names (Wm., Geo., Thos.) and nicknames (Liz, Theo, Bob) are indexed as written. Do not attempt to spell out abbreviated or shortened names.

RULE 4b Single letters in _business_ names are indexed as written. If single letters are separated by spaces, index each letter as a separate unit.

An **acronym** is a word formed from the first letters of several words. WHO (**W**orld **H**ealth **O**rganization) and VISTA (**V**olunteers **i**n **S**ervice **t**o **A**merica) are examples of acronyms. Index an acronym as one unit regardless of punctuation or spacing.

Abbreviated words (Mfg., Inc., Corp., Co.) and names (AA, YMCA, Y.W.C.A.) are indexed as one unit regardless of punctuation or spacing. Radio and television station call letters (WLW, WQXI, K N E N) are indexed as one unit regardless of spacing.

Table 4-6 Examples of Rule 4

	INDEXING ORDER			
Name Before Indexing	**Key Unit**	**Unit 2**	**Unit 3**	**Unit 4**
M. Izaguirre	Izaguirre	M		
Liz Izzo	Izzo	Liz		
J & A Ceramics	J	and	A	Ceramics
J Beck Construction	J	Beck	Construction	
Chas. Jacobs	Jacobs	Chas		
Michelle R. Jacobson	Jacobson	Michelle	R	
KABC Radio Station	KABC	Radio	Station	
LA Sports Memorabilia	LA	Sports	Memorabilia	
L.B.I. Ricter, Inc.	LBI	Ricter	Inc	
Media One Corp.	Media	One	Corp	
B. Eric Medina	Medina	B	Eric	
USA Travel Service	USA	Travel	Service	
VISTA	VISTA			
Chas. E. Wengler	Wengler	Chas	E	
West Covina Mfg.	West	Covina	Mfg	

EXERCISE 65a   Look at the names listed below and study them carefully to determine which names should be indexed first. After you have studied the names, write them in *alphabetic order* on the lines provided. Write the names in indexing order. *Underline the letter in each name that determines the alphabetic order.* The first name to be indexed is shown as an example.

Bosley Mfg. Co.	Jon P. Madison	Richardson's Mortuary Co.
Madison Mining Co., Inc.	E. Lusk's Guide Service	Do U Have Dancing Feet?
Thos. H. Callinge	Richardson's Quilting Grp.	KHJI Radio Station
W. Willison Williams	Jivin' Joe Jackson Recordings	M. K. Eckstine
Calling U Communications	R B T Realtors, Inc.	R. J. Atteberry
Hyatt Lake Resort	Marge Mary Mason	Line & Line Transportation Co.
Donut Haus A.M.	Eckstine's Portable BBQ's	Atteberry Reading Workshop

INDEXING ORDER

		Key Unit	Unit 2	Unit 3	Unit 4	Unit 5
Ex.	Atteberry	R	J			
1.						
2.						
3.						
4.						
5.						
6.						
7.						
8.						
9.						
10.						
11.						
12.						
13.						
14.						
15.						
16.						
17.						
18.						
19.						
20.						

EXERCISE 65b On the front of each group of cards that follow is a group number (*1, 2, 3,* etc.). In the upper-left corner of each card is a letter (*A, B, C, D,* or *E*). *Mentally* put the five cards in each group in alphabetic order according to the name on each card. (You may find it helpful to underline the letter that determines the alphabetic order of each name.) Then in the *Answers* column below, write the letters (*A, B, C, D, E*) to indicate the alphabetic order of the cards.

In the example shown below, card C (O & L Drywall & Roofing) is first in alphabetic order. Card D (Oberlin Mt. Inn) is second. Card A (Old Tyme Card & Gift Shop) is third. Cards B and E are fourth and fifth. In the *Answers* column, the letters indicate the alphabetic order of the cards: *C, D, A, B, E.*

ANSWERS

Example	C, D, A, B, E
Group 1.	_____
Group 2.	_____
Group 3.	_____
Group 4.	_____
Group 5.	_____
Group 6.	_____
Group 7.	_____
Group 8.	_____

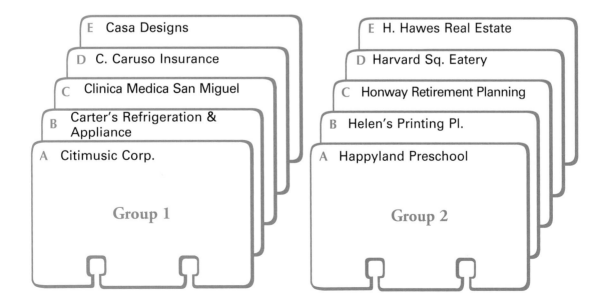

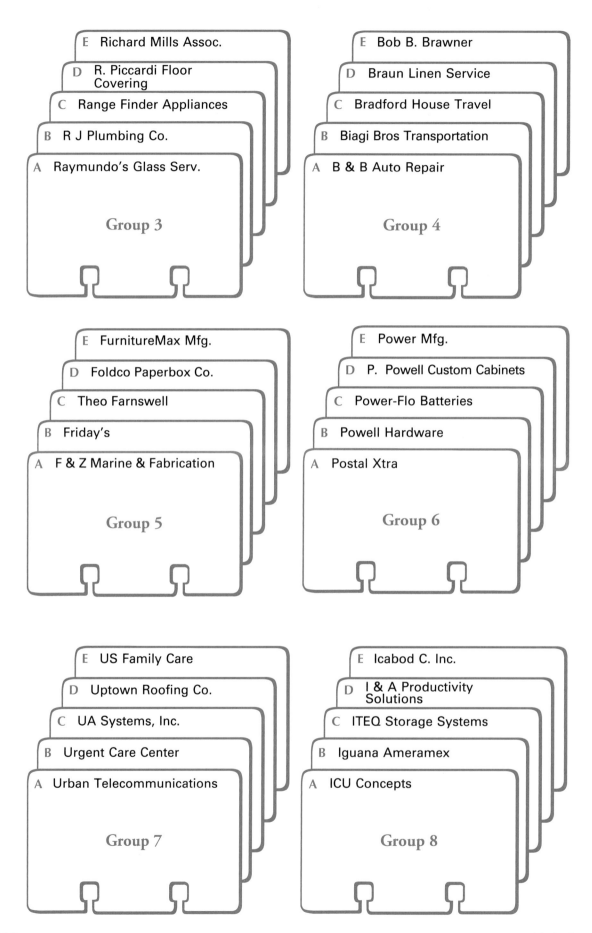

Group 3

E Richard Mills Assoc.
D R. Piccardi Floor Covering
C Range Finder Appliances
B R J Plumbing Co.
A Raymundo's Glass Serv.

Group 4

E Bob B. Brawner
D Braun Linen Service
C Bradford House Travel
B Biagi Bros Transportation
A B & B Auto Repair

Group 5

E FurnitureMax Mfg.
D Foldco Paperbox Co.
C Theo Farnswell
B Friday's
A F & Z Marine & Fabrication

Group 6

E Power Mfg.
D P. Powell Custom Cabinets
C Power-Flo Batteries
B Powell Hardware
A Postal Xtra

Group 7

E US Family Care
D Uptown Roofing Co.
C UA Systems, Inc.
B Urgent Care Center
A Urban Telecommunications

Group 8

E Icabod C. Inc.
D I & A Productivity Solutions
C ITEQ Storage Systems
B Iguana Ameramex
A ICU Concepts

GOAL: Index names with suffixes and titles

_____ NAME

_____ CLASS

RULE 5a When a suffix or title in a *personal* name is needed to distinguish between or among identical names, the suffix or title is indexed as the last unit. Examples of suffixes and titles are: seniority suffixes (II, III, Jr., Sr.); professional suffixes (CPA, Ph.D., R.N.); and titles (Dean, Dr., Governor, Mr., Mrs., Miss, Ms., Professor, Sergeant). A professional title appearing after a name is considered a suffix (Dean, Mayor, Senator).

Numeric suffixes (II, III) are filed before alphabetic suffixes (Jr., Mayor, Sr.). If a name contains both a title and a suffix, the title is the last indexing unit. Royal and religious titles followed only by a given name or a surname (Queen Anne, Father Tampico) are indexed as written.

Table 4-7   Examples of Rule 5a

	INDEXING ORDER			
Name Before Indexing	Key Unit	Unit 2	Unit 3	Unit 4 (Suffixes & Titles)
Brother Paul	Brother	Paul		
Senator Paula M. Brother	Brother	Paula	M	Senator
Paul Jas. Brotherton, Jr.	Brotherton	Paul	Jas	Jr
Paul Jas. Brotherton, Sr.	Brotherton	Paul	Jas	Sr
Mrs. Carrie L. Dowd	Dowd	Carrie	L	Mrs
Major Compton W. Dowd	Dowd	Compton	W	Major
Rev. Constance K. Dowd	Dowd	Constance	K	Rev
Father Thomas	Father	Thomas		
G. Paul Fatherton	Fatherton	G	Paul	
G. Paul Fatherton, II	Fatherton	G	Paul	II
G. Paul Fatherton, III	Fatherton	G	Paul	III
T. Cederick Fatherz, Ph.D.	Fatherz	T	Cederick	PhD
Brother Paul Luke Flanders	Flanders	Paul	Luke	Brother
Ms. Pauline Jane Flanders	Flanders	Pauline	Jane	Ms
Jan Barnes Flint, Mayor	Flint	Jan	Barnes	Mayor
Father Thomas J. Forbes	Forbes	Thomas	J	Father
Terry R. Foster, D.D.S.	Foster	Terry	R	DDS
Miss Terri G. Fosterly	Fosterly	Terri	G	Miss
Rabbi Isaac P. Greenberg	Greenberg	Isaac	P	Rabbi
Colonel Thos. O. Greenburg	Greenburg	Thos	O	Colonel
Wallace C. Gunnells, M.D.	Gunnells	Wallace	C	MD

RULE 5b Businesses use titles in their names to make the names unique. Titles in *business* names are indexed as written.

Table 4-8   Examples of Rule 5b

Name Before Indexing	Key Unit	Unit 2	Unit 3	Unit 4
		INDEXING ORDER		
Doctor Locke's Tutorial Service	Doctor	Lockes	Tutorial	Service
Dr. Dino Health Spa	Dr	Dino	Health	Spa
Mister Mighty Shock Absorbers	Mister	Mighty	Shock	Absorbers
Mr. Music Specialty Store	Mr	Music	Specialty	Store
Mrs. Joleen's Beauty Balm	Mrs	Joleens	Beauty	Balm
Ms. Lily Langtree's Salon	Ms	Lily	Langtrees	Salon
Professor Loo Lotions	Professor	Loo	Lotions	
Professors' School of Knowledge	Professors	School	of	Knowledge
Senator Walter's Golfwear	Senator	Walters	Golfwear	
Senator's Choice Campers	Senators	Choice	Campers	

Complete this exercise using the same procedure that you used in Exercise 65b. On the front of each group of cards is a group number. In the upper-left corner of each card is a letter. *Mentally* put the five cards in each group in alphabetic order according to the name on each card. (You may find it helpful to underline the letter that determines the alphabetic order of each name.) Then in the *Answers* column, write the letters (*A, B, C, D, E*) to indicate the alphabetic order of the cards. An example is shown.

ANSWERS

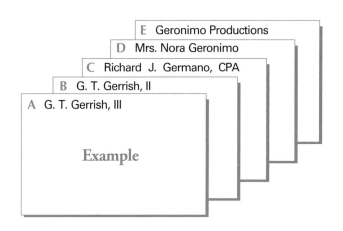

E Geronimo Productions

D Mrs. Nora Geronimo

C Richard J. Germano, CPA

B G. T. Gerrish, II

A G. T. Gerrish, III

Example

Example ___C, D, E, B, A___

Group 1. _____

Group 2. _____

Group 3. _____

Group 4. _____

Group 5. _____

Group 6. _____

Group 7. _____

Group 8. _____

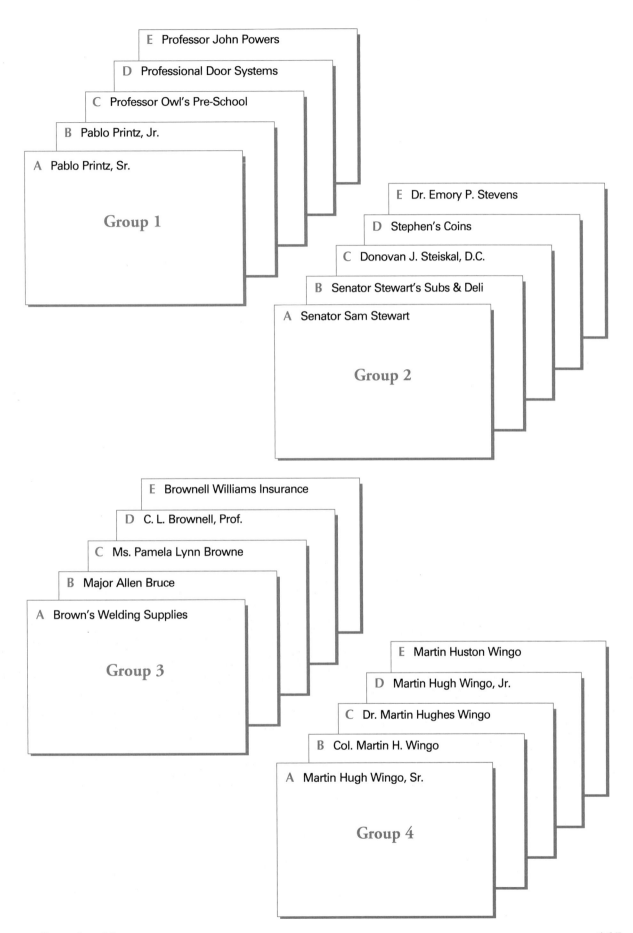

Group 1

- E Professor John Powers
- D Professional Door Systems
- C Professor Owl's Pre-School
- B Pablo Printz, Jr.
- A Pablo Printz, Sr.

Group 2

- E Dr. Emory P. Stevens
- D Stephen's Coins
- C Donovan J. Steiskal, D.C.
- B Senator Stewart's Subs & Deli
- A Senator Sam Stewart

Group 3

- E Brownell Williams Insurance
- D C. L. Brownell, Prof.
- C Ms. Pamela Lynn Browne
- B Major Allen Bruce
- A Brown's Welding Supplies

Group 4

- E Martin Huston Wingo
- D Martin Hugh Wingo, Jr.
- C Dr. Martin Hughes Wingo
- B Col. Martin H. Wingo
- A Martin Hugh Wingo, Sr.

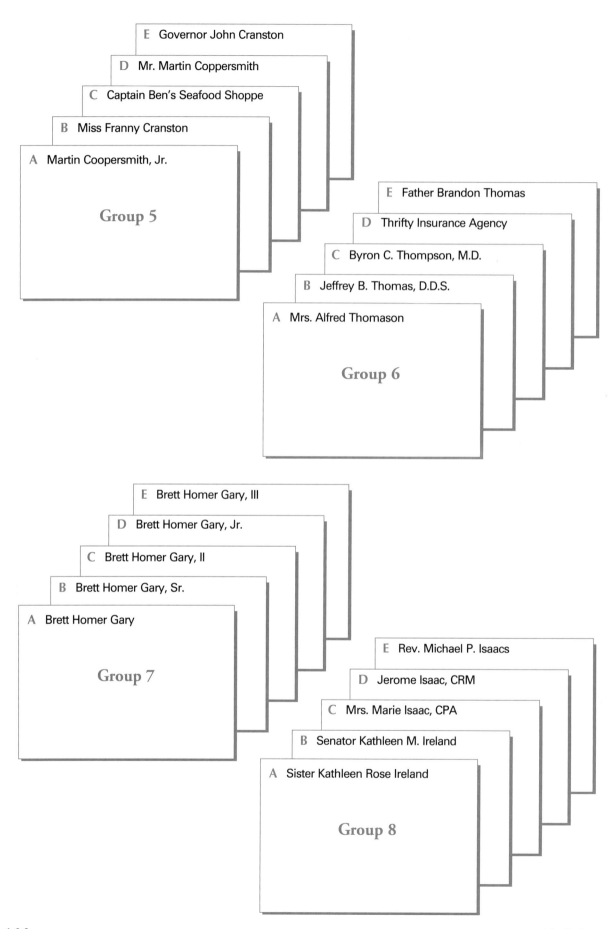

Group 5

E Governor John Cranston

D Mr. Martin Coppersmith

C Captain Ben's Seafood Shoppe

B Miss Franny Cranston

A Martin Coopersmith, Jr.

Group 6

E Father Brandon Thomas

D Thrifty Insurance Agency

C Byron C. Thompson, M.D.

B Jeffrey B. Thomas, D.D.S.

A Mrs. Alfred Thomason

Group 7

E Brett Homer Gary, III

D Brett Homer Gary, Jr.

C Brett Homer Gary, II

B Brett Homer Gary, Sr.

A Brett Homer Gary

Group 8

E Rev. Michael P. Isaacs

D Jerome Isaac, CRM

C Mrs. Marie Isaac, CPA

B Senator Kathleen M. Ireland

A Sister Kathleen Rose Ireland

GOAL: Index names with prefixes, articles, and particles

_____ NAME

_____ CLASS

RULE 6 A foreign article or particle in a personal or business name is joined with the part of the name following it to form one indexing unit. A space or punctuation between a prefix and the rest of the name is disregarded when indexing. For example, the last name De La Rue is indexed DeLaRue and the last name St. James is indexed StJames.

Examples of articles and particles are: a la, D', Da, De, Del, De la, Della, Den, Des, Di, Dos, Du, E', El, Fitz, Il, L', La, Las, Le, Les, Lo, Los, M', Mac, Mc, O', Per, Saint, San, Santa, Santo, St., Ste., Te, Ten, Ter, Van, Van de, Van der, Von, Von der.

Table 4-9 Examples of Rule 6

	INDEXING ORDER			
Name Before Indexing	Key Unit	Unit 2	Unit 3	Unit 4
Professor Louisa M. D'ando	Dando	Louisa	M	Professor
Louis Edwin D'Andrea	DAndrea	Louis	Edwin	
Dandria Lawncare Products	Dandria	Lawncare	Products	
Dr. Christiana J. De la Cruz	DelaCruz	Christiana	J	Dr
Delamar Electric Corp.	Delamar	Electric	Corp	
Del la Mar Printers, Inc.	DellaMar	Printers	Inc	
Ms. Charlotte Del la Rosa	DellaRosa	Charlotte	Ms	
Prof. C. Marvin DeNio	DeNio	C	Marvin	Prof
Glenna Mae D'Hollosey	DHollosey	Glenna	Mae	
Gregorio Diaz, D.D.S.	Diaz	Gregorio	DDS	
Sister Anna Maria du Pont	duPont	Anna	Maria	Sister
Charles W. MacFarland	MacFarland	Charles	W	
Rev. Josefina C. Martinez	Martinez	Josefina	C	Rev
McCue Nurseries, Inc.	McCue	Nurseries	Inc	
Miss Paula Gayle Mimms	Mimms	Paula	Gayle	Miss
Nina J. O'Day	ODay	Nina	J	
Alex W. Saints	Saints	Alex	W	
Andrea Elaine San Angelo	SanAngelo	Andrea	Elaine	
Joanna Cloe St. Amour	StAmour	Joanna	Cloe	
Vernon T. Ste. John	SteJohn	Vernon	T	
Van Allyn Florists	VanAllyn	Florists		
T. Oliver van Dyke	vanDyke	T	Oliver	
Brother Julio Velez	Velez	Julio	Brother	
Ouida J. von Borg, Ph.D.	vonBorg	Ouida	J	PhD

In Column 1 below and on the following pages are names *to be* indexed and filed. In Column 2 the same names *have been* indexed and filed. Follow these steps to complete the exercise:

1. Look at the group of five folders in Column 2 and determine the *one* folder that is out of order.

2. In the *Answers* column, write the corresponding letter (*A, B, C, D,* or *E*) of the folder that is out of order.

3. Repeat these steps for each of the nine groups of names.

In the example shown, the folder with Miss Alice B. Adam's name is out of order. The letter *B* is written in the *Answers* column.

ANSWERS

Example ___B___	Group 5. _____
Group 1. _____	Group 6. _____
Group 2. _____	Group 7. _____
Group 3. _____	Group 8. _____
Group 4. _____	Group 9. _____

COLUMN 1   COLUMN 2

Ms. Angela B. Adams
Mrs. A. Bonnie Adams
Mrs. Arlene Boone Addams
Miss Alice B. Adam
Ms. Arlisa Bea Adams

Kwik Kleen
Mrs. Connie Kwan
Mrs. Kramer's Cabinet Shop
Kwik-Stop Shop
Kwon Auto Accessories

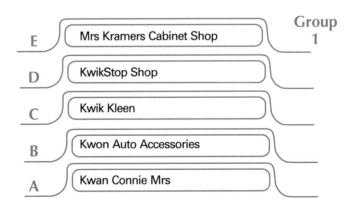

COLUMN 1	COLUMN 2

COLUMN 1

Mrs. Opal Anne De Moss
Orville Frank Delamor
Prof. Otto Karl Del Motte
Olivia Camille De La Mor
Otha Paul Delamore

E — DelMotte Otto Karl Prof
D — DeMoss Opal Anne Mrs
C — Delamore Otha Paul
B — Delamor Orville Frank
A — DeLaMor Olivia Camille

Group 2

Garry Franc St. Cyr
Glenda Faye Saint Louis
Gregory F. Saine
Gary Floy Saint
Gigi Faith St. Pierre, M.D.

E — StCyr Garry Franc
D — StPierre Gigi Faith MD
C — SaintLouis Glenda Faye
B — Saint Gary Floy
A — Saine Gregory F

Group 3

LaPlebe Bakery
Father Karroll La Presta
Richard John La Pierre
La Piccoletta Restaurant
Ricardo J. La Pierre

E — LaPresta Karroll Father
D — LaPlebe Bakery
C — LaPierre Ricardo J
B — LaPierre Richard John
A — LaPiccoletta Restaurant

Group 4

Mrs. Hortense D. Holley
Mrs. Holly Kaye Hollen
Miss Hallie Kate House
Hopson's House of Flowers
Miss Heather K. Hollar

E — Hopsons House of Flowers
D — House Hallie Kate Miss
C — Holley Hortense D Mrs
B — Hollen Holly Kaye Mrs
A — Hollar Heather K Miss

Group 5

Exercise 67

169

COLUMN 1   **COLUMN 2**

Jeff K. De Shazo
Jules Keyes Dos Pappas
Joy Kim De Savieu
Janelle Kane Des Jardins
Joshua Kevin De Santose

E	DosPappas Jules Keyes	**Group 6**
D	DesJardins Janelle Kane	
C	DeSavieu Joy Kim	
B	DeSantose Joshua Kevin	
A	DeShazo Jeff K	

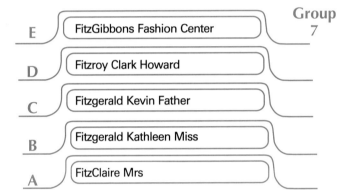

Mrs. Claire Fitz
Clark Howard Fitzroy
Father Kevin Fitzgerald
Fitz Gibbons Fashion Center
Miss Kathleen Fitzgerald

E	FitzGibbons Fashion Center	**Group 7**
D	Fitzroy Clark Howard	
C	Fitzgerald Kevin Father	
B	Fitzgerald Kathleen Miss	
A	FitzClaire Mrs	

Almira Lois Van de Veer
Allie Lee Von der Lynn
Alvin Louis Van der Griffe
Alston Lowe Vande Berg
Alf Loye Von Derlage

E	VonderLynn Allie Lee	**Group 8**
D	VonDerlage Alf Loye	
C	VanderGriffe Alvin Louis	
B	VandeBerg Alston Lowe	
A	VandeVeer Almira Lois	

Dos Com Computer Supplies
Mr. Paul Francis Dostalek
Peter Michael Dossey
Doskow Studios
Sanjay Doshi D.D.S.

E	Dostalek Paul Francis Mr	**Group 9**
D	Dossey Peter Michael	
C	Doshi Sanjay DDS	
B	Doskow Studios	
A	DosCom Computer Supplies	

GOAL: Index numbers in business names

NAME

CLASS

RULE 7   Numbers spelled out in business names (Fifty Yard Line Sporting Goods) are indexed as written and filed alphabetically. Numbers written in digits are filed before alphabetic letters or words (A-1 Electronics comes before A-One Advertising). Names with numbers written in digits in the first units are filed in ascending order (lowest to highest) before alphabetic names (337 Shop, 521 Café, Betty's Boutique). Arabic numerals are filed before Roman numerals (4 and 5 come before IV and V). Names with inclusive numbers (55-59) are indexed by the first digit(s) only (55). Names with numbers appearing in other than the first position are filed alphabetically and immediately before a similar name without a number (Route 55 Theater, Route Planners Tours).

Note: When indexing numbers written in digit form that contain *st*, *d*, and *th* (1st, 2d, 3d, 4th, 5th), ignore the letter endings and consider only the digits (1, 2, 3, 4, 5).

Table 4-10   Examples of Rule 7

	INDEXING ORDER			
Name Before Indexing	**Key Unit**	**Unit 2**	**Unit 3**	**Unit 4**
6th & Elm Warehouse	6	and	Elm	Warehouse
6th & Harmes Washerette	6	and	Harmes	Washerette
6 Hour Photo Developers	6	Hour	Photo	Developers
6 Pence Cafe	6	Pence	Cafe	
6th Quarter Hotel	6	Quarter	Hotel	
650-675 Bartels Blvd.	650	Bartels	Blvd	
The 650 Bartels Boutique	650	Bartels	Boutique	The
1667 Realty Company	1667	Realty	Company	
The 16000 Condominiums	16000	Condominiums	The	
IV Ever Jewelers	IV	Ever	Jewelers	
Six Zero Six Motel	Six	Zero	Six	Motel
The Sixth State Resort	Sixth	State	Resort	The
Six-Thousand Toy Museum	SixThousand	Toy	Museum	
Sixty Minutes Cleaners	Sixty	Minutes	Cleaners	
Trail 15 Nature Club	Trail	15	Nature	Club
Trail 28 Nature Society	Trail	28	Nature	Society
Trail Blazers Hiking Club	Trail	Blazers	Hiking	Club

In Column 1 are business names with a letter (*A, B, C, D*, etc.) before them. In Column 2 is a file drawer. Five of the names in Column 1 have already been printed in correct filing format on cards and filed in the drawer. In Column 3 are the corresponding letters of the names in Column 1. For example, the first card in the file drawer is *4 and Barnes Apothecary*. The corresponding letter of *4th & Barnes Apothecary* in Column 1 is *J*, the letter written on line 1 in Column 3.

Follow these steps to complete the exercise:

1. Determine which name should be filed after *4 and Barnes Apothecary*.

2. Print the name in correct filing format on the card in the file drawer.

3. Write the corresponding letter of the name in Column 3.

4. Repeat steps 1-3 until all the names have been filed in order in the drawer and all the letters have been written in Column 3.

COLUMN 1	COLUMN 2	COLUMN 3
	Highway ByWay Seafood	-- 15. ___D___
A. 4th Precinct Bug Specialists		-- 14. _____
B. Four Seasons Travel Service		-- 13. _____
C. 4 Maids Tearoom	Fourth Street Framer The	-- 12. ___G___
D. Highway By-Way Seafood		-- 11. _____
E. 1492 Americana Museum		-- 10. _____
F. 4th and Sorrento Market		
G. The Fourth Street Framer	14000 Office Park The	-- 9. ___N___
H. Highway 45 Buggyworks		-- 8. _____
I. 400-425 Harris Plaza		-- 7. _____
J. 4th & Barnes Apothecary		-- 6. _____
K. The Four Sons Dairy		
L. Highway 7 Radio & TV Doctor	4 Precinct Bug Specialists	-- 5. ___A___
M. 4 Minutes Heel Repair		-- 4. _____
N. The 14000 Office Park		-- 3. _____
O. The 400 Fruit & Vegetable Bin		-- 2. _____
	4 and Barnes Apothecary	-- 1. ___J___

GOAL: Index names of organizations and institutions

_____ NAME

_____ CLASS

RULE 8 Names of organizations and institutions are indexed and filed as the name appears on the company's letterhead. When "The" is the first word of the name, it is considered the last indexing unit. Examples of organizations and institutions are banks and other financial institutions, clubs, colleges, hospitals, hotels, lodges, magazines, motels, museums, newspapers, religious institutions, schools, unions, and universities.

Table 4-11 Examples of Rule 8

	INDEXING ORDER			
Name Before Indexing	Key Unit	Unit 2	Unit 3	Unit 4
Assembly of Truth Tabernacle	Assembly	of	Truth	Tabernacle
The Association for Beekeepers	Association	for	Beekeepers	The
Atlanta Pet Hospital	Atlanta	Pet	Hospital	
Atlantic Antiques Exchange	Atlantic	Antiques	Exchange	
Atlantic Shell Collectors Club	Atlantic	Shell	Collectors	Club
Bacon County Academy	Bacon	County	Academy	
Bank of Bakersfield	Bank	of	Bakersfield	
Bismarck Weavers Union	Bismarck	Weavers	Union	
Carolton Museum of Art	Carolton	Museum	of	Art
Church of Deliverance	Church	of	Deliverance	
Danville Mental Health Association	Danville	Mental	Health	Association
Denver Hearing Impaired Academy	Denver	Hearing	Impaired	Academy
Eagan Allergy Clinic	Eagan	Allergy	Clinic	
Ebsen Board of Realtors	Ebsen	Board	of	Realtors
Fairview Public Speaking Institute	Fairview	Public	Speaking	Institute
Fargo Motor Hotel	Fargo	Motor	Hotel	
Galveston Commission on Pollution	Galveston	Commission	on	Pollution
Georgetown Community College	Georgetown	Community	College	
Helen Hayes Middle School	Helen	Hayes	Middle	School
Hotel Gatlinburg	Hotel	Gatlinburg		
Midwest Order of Police	Midwest	Order	of	Police
Motel Miami Palms	Motel	Miami	Palms	
National Federation for Diabetes	National	Federation	for	Diabetes
National Music Lovers Society	National	Music	Lovers	Society
University of Hawaii	University	of	Hawaii	

Follow these steps to complete the exercise:

1. Determine which name should be filed after *AKRON LIBRARY FOR THE BLIND* in Column 2.

2. Print the name in ALL CAPITAL LETTERS on the card in the file drawer in Column 2. Go from the front of the file drawer to the back of the drawer as you print the names on the cards.

3. Write the corresponding letter of the name in Column 3.

4. Repeat steps 1-3 until all the names have been filed in alphabetic order in the drawer and all the letters have been written in Column 3.

COLUMN 1	COLUMN 2	COLUMN 3
A. Alamo Clinic of Chiropractors		-- 20. _____
B. Atlantic Quilters Group		-- 19. _____
C. Association of Legal Secretaries		-- 18. _____
D. The Allegheny Railroad Museum		-- 17. _____
E. Albany Hot Rod Club		-- 16. _____
F. Assembly of Holiness Church		-- 15. _____
G. All Journal of Family Wellness		-- 14. _____
H. American Alliance on Patriotism		-- 13. _____
I. Alamo Library Foundation		-- 12. _____
J. Almanor Lake Residents' Assoc.		-- 11. _____
K. All Around Austin Courier		-- 10. _____
L. Ashcroft Citizens' Bank		-- 9. _____
M. All Counties Mental Health Group		-- 8. _____
N. Allentown Alliance Against Hunger		-- 7. _____
O. The Albany County ASPCA		-- 6. _____
P. Albany Commission for Clean Air		-- 5. _____
Q. Alamos City Hospital		-- 4. _____
R. American Motor Lodge		-- 3. _____
S. Akron Library for the Blind		-- 2. _____
T. Alameda Unified School District	AKRON LIBRARY FOR THE BLIND	-- 1. __S__

A

GOAL: Index identical names

_____ NAME

_____ CLASS

RULE 9   Addresses determine the filing order when indexing identical (alike) names of persons, businesses, institutions, and organizations. Index addresses in this order: (1) city names, (2) state or province names, (3) street names, then (4) house or building numbers.

Note 1: When the first units of street names are written in digits (such as 12th Street), the names are indexed in ascending order (lowest number to highest number) and placed before alphabetic street names (such as Arnold Street). For example, the following street names would be filed in this order: 12th Street, 18th Street, Alamo Street, Alexander Street, Barnes Street.

Note 2: Street names with compass directions (North, South, East, West) are indexed as written. Street numbers written in digits after compass directions are placed before alphabetic street names. For example, NE Fourth, North 4th, North Main, Northeast Fourth.

Note 3: House and building numbers written as digits are indexed in ascending order (lowest number to highest number) and placed before alphabetic building names. For example, 29 Maxwell Building, 704 Maxwell Building, The Maxwell Building. If a street address _and_ a building name are shown in an address, disregard the building name. ZIP Codes are not considered in determining filing order.

Note 4: Titles and suffixes in names as explained in Rule 5 are considered _before_ addresses when determining filing order.

Table 4-12   Examples of Rule 9

	INDEXING ORDER				
Name Before Indexing	Key Unit	Unit 2	Unit 3	Unit 4	Address
(Names of Cities Used to Determine Filing Order)					
Ace Automation Center Des Moines, Iowa	Ace	Automation	Center		Des Moines Iowa
Ace Automation Center Waterloo, Iowa	Ace	Automation	Center		Waterloo Iowa
(Names of States and Provinces Used to Determine Filing Order)					
Bayshore Country Club Brunswick, Georgia	Bayshore	Country	Club		Brunswick Georgia
Bayshore Country Club Brunswick, Maine	Bayshore	Country	Club		Brunswick Maine
Cloudland Ranch Victoria, Arkansas	Cloudland	Ranch			Victoria Arkansas
Cloudland Ranch Victoria, British Columbia	Cloudland	Ranch			Victoria British Columbia

Name Before Indexing	Key Unit	Unit 2	Unit 3	Unit 4	Address
(Names of Streets and Building Numbers Used to Determine Filing Order)					
Discount Pharmacy 6500 - 15 Street Boise, Idaho	<u>D</u>iscount	Pharmacy			6500 - 15 Street
Discount Pharmacy 379 Amboy Street Boise, Idaho	Discount	Pharmacy			379 <u>A</u>mboy Street
Discount Pharmacy 636 Amboy Street Boise, Idaho	Discount	Pharmacy			<u>636</u> Amboy Street
Discount Pharmacy 825 SE 22 Street Boise, Idaho	Discount	Pharmacy			825 <u>SE</u> 22 Street
Discount Pharmacy 18 SE Ninth Street Boise, Idaho	Discount	Pharmacy			18 SE <u>N</u>inth Street
(Titles and Suffixes Used to Determine Filing Order Before Addresses)					
Henry G. Evans, II 701 Alma Circle Dallas, Texas	<u>E</u>vans	Henry	G	II	
Henry G. Evans, III 194 Victory Place Dallas, Texas	Evans	Henry	G	<u>III</u>	
Henry G. Evans, Jr. 220 Herman Court Arvada, Colorado	Evans	Henry	G	<u>J</u>r	<u>A</u>rvada Colorado
Henry G. Evans, Jr. 550 Lyric Lane Durham, North Carolina	Evans	Henry	G	Jr	<u>D</u>urham North Carolina
Henry G. Evans, M.D. 680 Moffit Road Durham, North Carolina	Evans	Henry	G	<u>MD</u>	
Mr. Henry G. Evans 398 Barley Drive Topeka, Kansas	Evans	Henry	G	M<u>r</u>	

EXERCISE 70a Write the following names and addresses in alphabetic order on the lines provided. Write the names—and addresses as needed—in indexing order. *Underline the letter or number that determines the alphabetic order.* Remember: The filing order for identical names is city, state, street, and number.

Johnston Marine Supplies
   White City, Oregon

Alpha-Omega Center
   Leadville, California

Steven Lindhorst
   3603 Riverside Dr., Chino, California

Tacos-2-Go
   4600 Hwy. 31, Gallup, New Mexico

Alpha-Omega Center
   Leadville, Arkansas

Steven Lindhorst, III
   846 Market Row, St. Louis, Missouri

Alpha-Omega Center
   Leadville, Colorado

Steven Lindhorst, Ph.D.
   9050 SW Eighth St., Houston, Texas

Robert Jones
   761 Mason St., Plymouth, Maine

Mr. Steven Lindhorst
   467 Wyoming Way, Houston, Texas

Robert Jones
  835 Mason St., Plymouth, Maine
Steven Lindhorst, Jr.
  550 Lyric Lane, Durham, North Carolina
Alpha-Omega Center
  73 Marigold St., Leadville, Colorado
Steven Lindhorst, II
  1243 Center St., Dallas, Texas
Johnston Marine Supplies
  Medford, Oregon

Robert Jones, Jr.
  467 Victoria Circle, Amherst, Massachusetts
Tacos-2-Go
  90 Hwy. 31, Gallup, New Mexico
Prof. Robert Jones
  678 Olive Pl., Walnut, California
Alpha-Omega Center
  972 Gold Dust Ave., Leadville, Colorado
Steven Lindhorst, II
  112 Drycreek Rd., Phoenix, Arizona

INDEXING ORDER

	Key Unit	Unit 2	Unit 3	Unit 4	Unit 5	Unit 6
1.						
2.						
3.						
4.						
5.						
6.						
7.						
8.						
9.						
10.						
11.						
12.						
13.						
14.						
15.						
16.						
17.						
18.						
19.						
20.						

Exercise 70

EXERCISE 70b Index the following cards in the correct order. (You may find it helpful to underline the letter or number that determines the indexing order.) Beginning at the *bottom* of the *Answers* column, write the letter from the upper-left corner of each card to indicate the correct order of the cards.

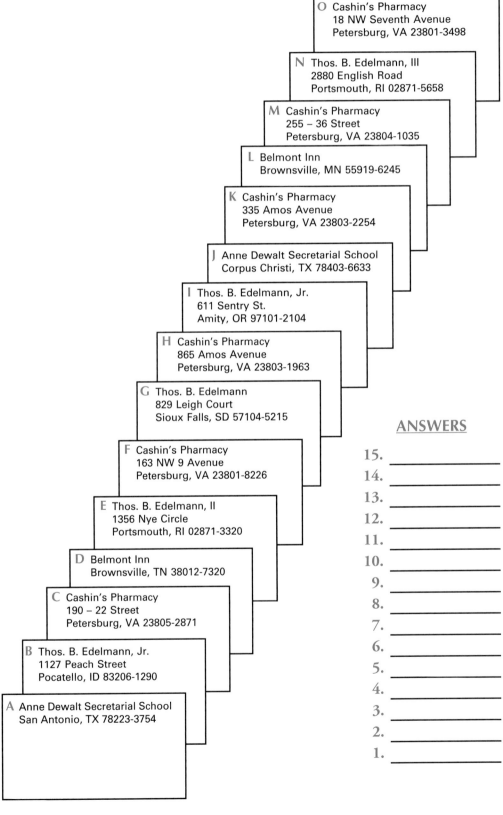

O Cashin's Pharmacy
18 NW Seventh Avenue
Petersburg, VA 23801-3498

N Thos. B. Edelmann, III
2880 English Road
Portsmouth, RI 02871-5658

M Cashin's Pharmacy
255 – 36 Street
Petersburg, VA 23804-1035

L Belmont Inn
Brownsville, MN 55919-6245

K Cashin's Pharmacy
335 Amos Avenue
Petersburg, VA 23803-2254

J Anne Dewalt Secretarial School
Corpus Christi, TX 78403-6633

I Thos. B. Edelmann, Jr.
611 Sentry St.
Amity, OR 97101-2104

H Cashin's Pharmacy
865 Amos Avenue
Petersburg, VA 23803-1963

G Thos. B. Edelmann
829 Leigh Court
Sioux Falls, SD 57104-5215

F Cashin's Pharmacy
163 NW 9 Avenue
Petersburg, VA 23801-8226

E Thos. B. Edelmann, II
1356 Nye Circle
Portsmouth, RI 02871-3320

D Belmont Inn
Brownsville, TN 38012-7320

C Cashin's Pharmacy
190 – 22 Street
Petersburg, VA 23805-2871

B Thos. B. Edelmann, Jr.
1127 Peach Street
Pocatello, ID 83206-1290

A Anne Dewalt Secretarial School
San Antonio, TX 78223-3754

ANSWERS

15. _____
14. _____
13. _____
12. _____
11. _____
10. _____
9. _____
8. _____
7. _____
6. _____
5. _____
4. _____
3. _____
2. _____
1. _____

GOAL: Index government names

_____ NAME

_____ CLASS

RULE 10   Government names are indexed first by the name of the governmental unit—city, county, state, or country. The distinctive name of the department, bureau, board, or office is indexed next. The words "Department of," "Office of," "Bureau of," etc., are separate indexing units when they are part of the official name.

Note: If "of" is not part of the official name as written, it is not added.

Rule 10a   Local and Regional Government Names   The first indexing unit is the name of the city, town, township, village, or county. For example, in the government name _Atlanta Parks and Recreation Department_, the city name _Atlanta_ is the first indexing unit. The most distinctive name of the department, board, bureau, or office is indexed next. If the words "City of," "County of," "Department of," etc., are in the names, each word is considered a separate indexing unit.

Table 4-13   Examples of Rule 10a—Local and Regional Government Names

			INDEXING ORDER			
Name Before Indexing	Key Unit	Unit 2	Unit 3	Unit 4	Unit 5	Unit 6
Chico Trash Collection Department	Chico	Trash	Collection	Department		
Marshall County Sheriff's Department	Marshall	County	Sheriffs	Department		
Merced County Department of Elections	Merced	County	Elections	Department	of	
City of Ontario City Clerk's Office	Ontario	City	of	City	Clerks	Office
City of Ontario Public Library	Ontario	City	of	Public	Library	
City of Pomona Water Works Department	Pomona	City	of	Water	Works	Department
County of San Bernardino Probation Department	SanBernardino	County	of	Probation	Department	
Sangamon County Department of Public Health	Sangamon	County	Public	Health	Department	of

EXERCISE 71a   Write the following local and regional government names in alphabetic order on the lines provided. Write the names in indexing order. _Underline the letter in each name that determines the alphabetic order._

North Platte County Fire Department

City of Selena Public Works

City of Selena Parks and Recreation

Marin County Department of Elections

Flood Control District, Yavapai County

City of Selena Animal Care/Control

San Bernardino County Tax Collector

City Manager, City of Selena

Cochise County Bureau of License Issuance

City of Redlands Senior Recreation Center

INDEXING ORDER

Key Unit	Unit 2	Unit 3	Unit 4	Unit 5	Unit 6
1.					
2.					
3.					
4.					
5.					
6.					
7.					
8.					
9.					
10.					

Rule 10b   State Government Names The first indexing unit is the name of the state or province. The most distinctive name of the department, board, bureau, office, or government/political division is indexed next. If the words "State of," "Province of," "Department of," etc., are in the names, each word is considered a separate indexing unit.

Table 4-14   Examples of Rule 10b—State Government Names

| Name Before Indexing | INDEXING ORDER | | | | |
	Key Unit	Unit 2	Unit 3	Unit 4	Unit 5
Department of Corrections Sacramento, California	California	Corrections	Department	of	
California Highway Patrol	California	Highway	Patrol		
California State Lottery Commission	California	State	Lottery	Commission	

INDEXING ORDER

Name Before Indexing	Key Unit	Unit 2	Unit 3	Unit 4	Unit 5
Banking Office Commerce Department St. Augustine, Florida	<u>F</u>lorida	Commerce	Department	Banking	Office
Department of Economic Development Atlanta, Georgia	<u>G</u>eorgia	Economic	Development	Department	of
Georgia Department of Revenue	Georgia	<u>R</u>evenue	Department	of	
Department of Labor Honolulu, Hawaii	<u>H</u>awaii	Labor	Department	of	
Bridge Maintenance Engineering Department Springfield, Illinois	<u>I</u>llinois	Engineering	Department	Bridge	Maintenance
Bureau of Labor Statistics Cleveland, Ohio	<u>O</u>hio	Labor	Statistics	Bureau	of
Bureau of Land Management Cincinnati, Ohio	Ohio	La<u>n</u>d	Management	Bureau	of

EXERCISE 71b   Write the following state government names in alphabetic order on the lines provided. Write the names in indexing order. *Underline the letter in each name that determines the alphabetic order.*

Mississippi Bureau of Justice Assistance

Nebraska Office of Public Instruction

Tennessee Wildlife Resources Agency

Massachusetts Department of Commerce

Idaho Employment Development Department Disability Insurance

Massachusetts Civil Service Commission

Tennessee Valley Authority

Missouri Department of Food and Agriculture

Nebraska Employment Development Department

Wyoming Geologist & Geophysical Registration Department

INDEXING ORDER

Key Unit	Unit 2	Unit 3	Unit 4	Unit 5	Unit 6
1.					
2.					
3.					
4.					
5.					
6.					

Exercise 71

Key Unit	Unit 2	Unit 3	Unit 4	Unit 5	Unit 6

7._____

8._____

9._____

10._____

Rule 10c   Federal Government Names When indexing federal government names, use indexing "levels" rather than units. The first level is always *United States Government*. The second level is the name of the department indexed by the most distinctive part of the name; for example, *Justice Department (of)*. The third level is the next most distinctive name; for example, *Drug Enforcement Administration*. Do not consider the words *of* or *of the* when indexing federal government names.

> **Note:** Current lists of federal government agencies and offices are published annually in the *United States Government Manual* and the *Congressional Directory*. The *State Information Book* by Susan Lukowski includes a list of state departments and their addresses. A breakdown of U.S. government departments, bureaus, and offices can be found on the Internet through many sources, including the web site for the National Technology Transfer Center (http://www.nttc.edu/resources/governmentwebsites.asp).

Table 4-15   Examples of Rule 10c—Federal Government Names

Level 1

United States Government

Name	Level 2	Level 3
Farm Service Agency Department of Agriculture	Agriculture Department (of)	Farm Service Agency
Bureau of Economic Analysis Department of Commerce	Commerce Department (of)	Economic Analysis Bureau (of)
Economic Development Administration Department of Commerce	Commerce Department (of)	Economic Development Administration
Economics & Statistics Administration U.S. Department of Commerce	Commerce Department (of)	Economics and Statistics Administration
Air, Pesticides, and Toxic Management Division U.S. Environmental Protection Agency	Environmental Protection Agency	Air Pesticides and Toxic Management Division
Office of the Attorney General Department of Justice	Justice Department (of)	Attorney General Office (of the)

United States Government

Name	Level 2	Level 3
Employee Benefits Security Administration U.S. Labor Department	<u>L</u>abor Department	<u>E</u>mployee Benefits Security Administration
Bureau of International Labor Affairs Labor Department	<u>L</u>abor Department	<u>I</u>nternational Labor Affairs Bureau (of)

EXERCISE 71c   Write the following federal government names in alphabetic order on the lines provided. Write the names in indexing order by level. Level 1 has been indexed for you (United States Government). Index Levels 2 and 3 for each name. *Underline the letter in each name that determines the alphabetic order.*

Veterans Benefits Administration, Department of Veterans Affairs

Office of Legal Policy, Department of Justice

Bureau of the Public Debt, Department of the Treasury

Benefits Review Board, Labor Department

Veterans Health Administration, Department of Veterans Affairs

Federal Aviation Administration, Transportation Department

National Security Division, Department of Justice

National Cemetery Administration, Department of Veterans Affairs

Justice Management Division, Department of Justice

Internal Revenue Service, Department of the Treasury

Level 1

United States Government

Level 2	Level 3
1. _____	_____
2. _____	_____
3. _____	_____
4. _____	_____
5. _____	_____

Level 1

United States Government

Level 2	**Level 3**
6._____	_____
7._____	_____
8._____	_____
9._____	_____
10._____	_____

Rule 10d   Foreign Government Names   When indexing foreign government names, write the English translation of the name on the document. The distinctive English name is the first indexing unit for foreign government names. The rest of the formal name of the government is indexed next, if needed, and if it is part of the official name. Branches, departments, and divisions follow in order by their distinctive names. States, colonies, provinces, cities, and other divisions of foreign governments are filed by their distinctive or official names as spelled in English. If necessary, cross-reference the foreign spelling of the name to the English spelling.

> **Note:** The *World Almanac and Book of Facts* is updated annually and provides the English spellings of many foreign government names. Your local library should have these reference books. Information about foreign countries can be found on the Internet using a search engine such as Lycos infoplease.com (http://lycos.infoplease.com/countries.html).

Table 4-16   Examples of Rule 10d—Foreign Government Names

Name Before Indexing	Indexing Order

Bharat
   Rajya Sabha
	India
	   Council of States

Kazakh Respublikasi	Kazakhstan Republic of
Furstentum Liechtenstein	Liechtenstein Principality of
Dawlat Qatar	Qatar State of
Al Jumhuriyah at Tunisiyah	Tunisia Republic of

GOAL: Index numbers for filing

_____ NAME

_____ CLASS

In Exercise 61 you put names of persons in order for filing according to filing rules and the letters of the alphabet. In this exercise you will put numbers in order for filing.

In Figure 4-1 the numbers on the file folder tabs are in order with the smallest number at the bottom (or front) of the group of file folders. The largest number is at the top (or back). **Consecutive order** means numbers follow one after another from lowest to highest; for example, 1, 2, 3, and so on. In Figure 4-1 the numbers 1035, 1036, 1037, 1038, and 1039 are in consecutive order from the front of the file to the back of the file.

Figure 4-1   Numeric File

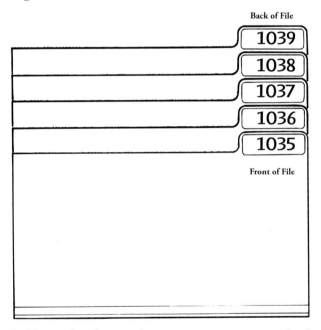

In Figure 4-2 the numbers are in consecutive order from the bottom to the top (or front to back): 1255, 1257, 1258, 1259, and 1260. Note that the 1256 file folder is not in the file. When this file folder is put back in the file, it will be placed in correct numeric order as shown by the arrow.

Figure 4-2   Numeric File with a Missing Folder

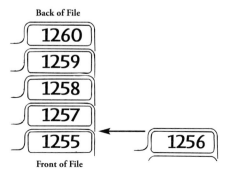

Exercise 72

The numbers on the file folder tabs in Column 1 are in consecutive order. The number at the front of the file (1647) is the lowest number. The rest of the numbers are filed from smallest to largest, or in consecutive order, behind this first number. On the file folder tabs in Column 2, write the numbers from Column 3 in the place where the file folders in Columns 2 will be in consecutive order with the file folders in Column 1. The first number (1658) is given as a guide. 1658 is larger than 1657 and smaller than 1659, so it is written on the file folder tab between these two numbers. As you read each number in Column 3, find the two numbers in Column 1 that it should be filed between.

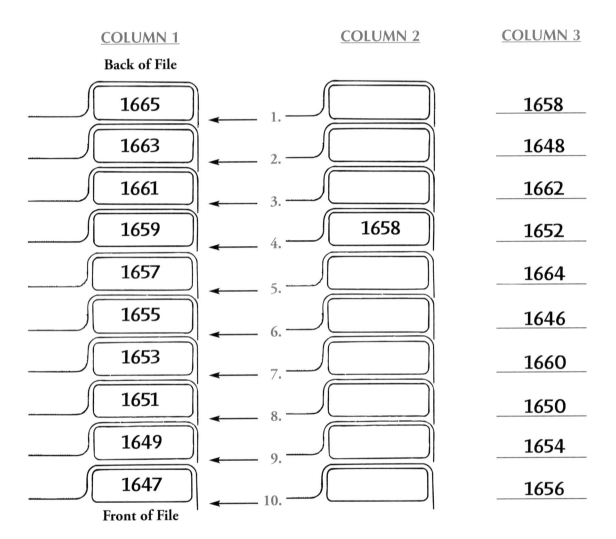

COLUMN 1	COLUMN 2	COLUMN 3
Back of File		
1665		1658
1663	1.	1648
1661	2.	1662
1659	3.	1652
1657	4. 1658	1664
1655	5.	1646
1653	6.	1660
1651	7.	1650
1649	8.	1654
1647	9.	1656
Front of File	10.	

GOAL: Prepare an accession log and alphabetic index

_____ NAME

_____ CLASS

Some businesses use numeric (number) filing rather than alphabetic filing. With a numeric filing system, records are indexed by number. An **accession log** is a list of the code numbers assigned to records in a numeric filing system. The log shows the numeric code for each name or subject and the date the code was assigned. The accession log also shows the next code number available in the numeric filing system. Names and subjects are entered into the log in indexed order. Computer-generated logs are simple to prepare and update and can be created to fit the needs of the business. A notebook, three-ring binder, or ruled paper also may be used for the accession log.

Figure 4-3 below shows a typical accession log. Notice that the names are not listed in alphabetic order but in numeric order by their assigned code numbers. The codes are assigned in **chronological order**, which means in order of time, using dates to determine placement. On April 10 code number 622 was assigned to Early Bird Cleaners. All correspondence with Early Bird Cleaners is filed in a folder numbered 622. Number 623 is the next code number available in the file for a new name. The _SEE_ column of the log is used for names that need to be cross-referenced. If necessary, refer to Exercise 61 to review cross-referencing.

Figure 4-3   Accession Log

ACCESSION LOG			
CODE NO.	NAME OR SUBJECT	DATE	SEE
622	Early Bird Cleaners	4/10/–	
623	Resource Assistance	4/10/–	
624	Ragland Charles M	4/13/–	
625	McVittie William S	4/15/–	
626	SouthWest Interiors Inc	4/18/–	
627	EZ Haulers and Movers	4/19/–	Easy Haulers and Movers
628	Quick Removal Pest Control	4/23/–	
629	MacNeil David	4/25/–	
630	Dans Furniture Refinishers	4/28/–	
631	Martinez Lopez	4/30/–	Lopez Martinez
632			

In addition to an accession log, a numeric filing system requires an alphabetic index. An **alphabetic index** is an alphabetic list of names or subjects and their assigned code numbers. Records are stored and retrieved by looking first at the alphabetic index to identify a name's numeric code. Figure 4-4 below shows the alphabetic index that accompanies the accession log in Figure 4-3. The X after a code number indicates a cross-referenced file.

Figure 4-4 Alphabetic Index for an Accession Log

ALPHABETIC INDEX		
NAME OR SUBJECT	CODE NO.	SEE
Dans Furniture Refinishers	630	
Early Bird Cleaners	622	
Easy Haulers and Movers	627X	EZ Haulers and Movers
EZ Haulers and Movers	627	Easy Haulers and Movers
Lopez Martinez	631X	Martinez Lopez
MacNeil David	629	
Martinez Lopez	631	Lopez Martinez
McVittie William S	625	
Quick Removal Pest Control	628	
Ragland Charles M	624	
Resource Assistance	623	
SouthWest Interiors Inc	626	

EXERCISE 73a   Write the following names and dates in *chronological order* on the accession log below. Use the current year. Write the names in indexing order. Assign code numbers as you log the names and dates. The first entry is given as a guide. Remember to complete the *SEE* column for names that need a cross-reference. If necessary, refer to the accession log shown in Figure 4-3 as a guide.

Board Certified Accountants, 11/18/–

Lily Camille, 11/17/–

Michael Callaway, 11/10/–

Joseph R. Banks, 11/20/–

The Apple Core Café, 11/21/–

Hugo Schaefer, 11/23/–

Sawgrass Entertainers, 11/25/–

Joseph Banks Clothiers, 11/15/–

Ling Chung, 11/19/–

Botsworth Investments, 11/18/–

CODE NO.	NAME OR SUBJECT	DATE	SEE
	ACCESSION LOG		
497	Callaway Michael	11/10/-	

EXERCISE 73b Using the information you entered in the accession log in Exercise 73a, complete the alphabetic index below. Include the information needed for any names that were cross-referenced. If necessary, refer to the alphabetic index shown in Figure 4-4 as a guide.

NAME OR SUBJECT	CODE NO.	SEE

ALPHABETIC INDEX

GOAL: File records using a numeric system

_____ NAME

_____ CLASS

A pharmacy may file prescriptions for medicine numerically. When a customer takes a prescription from their doctor to a pharmacy, the pharmacist assigns a code number to the prescription. All records and refill information pertaining to the customer's prescription are filed under the assigned numeric code.

Figure 4-5   File Cabinets for Numeric Filing

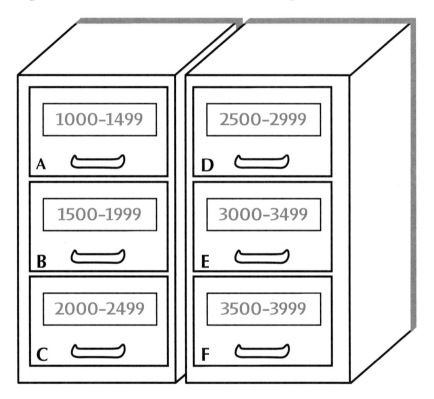

The two file cabinets in Figure 4-5 each have three drawers. In the lower-left corner of each drawer is a letter (_A, B, C, D, E,_ or _F_). Each drawer has a label indicating the file numbers of the prescriptions filed in the drawer. For example, prescriptions that have been assigned the numbers 1000–1499 are filed in Drawer A. Prescription numbers 1500–1999 are filed in Drawer B, etc. Refer to the letter of the alphabet and the numbers on each drawer label as you complete the following exercise.

Look at the number of the prescription file folder in Column 1. Determine the drawer (*A, B, C, D, E,* or *F*) where the folder would be filed. Write the letter of the file drawer in Column 2. An example is shown.

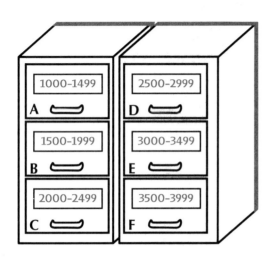

	COLUMN 1		COLUMN 2
Ex.	3291	Ex.	E
1.	2403	1.	
2.	1039	2.	
3.	3767	3.	
4.	3498	4.	
5.	1860	5.	
6.	2888	6.	
7.	3585	7.	
8.	1490	8.	
9.	2052	9.	
10.	2502	10.	
11.	3336	11.	
12.	1685	12.	
13.	2014	13.	
14.	3920	14.	
15.	1114	15.	

GOAL: File records by date

_____ NAME

_____ CLASS

Records are sometimes filed in chronological order by date. The two file cabinets in Figure 4-6 each have four drawers. In the lower-left corner of each drawer is a letter (*A, B, C, D, E, F, G,* or *H*). Each drawer has a label indicating the dates of the records filed in that drawer. For example, records dated between January 1, 2009 and April 30, 2009 are filed in Drawer A. Records dated between May 1, 2009 and August 31, 2009 are filed in Drawer B, etc. Refer to the letter of the alphabet and the dates on each drawer as you complete the following exercise.

Figure 4-6 File Cabinets for Chronological Filing

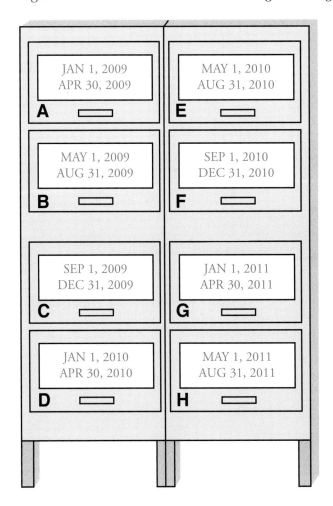

JAN 1, 2009
APR 30, 2009
A

MAY 1, 2010
AUG 31, 2010
E

MAY 1, 2009
AUG 31, 2009
B

SEP 1, 2010
DEC 31, 2010
F

SEP 1, 2009
DEC 31, 2009
C

JAN 1, 2011
APR 30, 2011
G

JAN 1, 2010
APR 30, 2010
D

MAY 1, 2011
AUG 31, 2011
H

Look at the date in Column 1. Determine the drawer (*A, B, C, D, E, F, G,* or *H*) where a record with this date would be filed. Write the letter of the file drawer in Column 2. An example is shown.

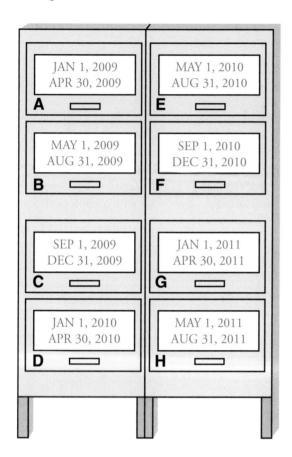

	COLUMN 1		COLUMN 2
Ex.	November 3, 2009	Ex.	C
1.	October 11, 2010	1.	_____
2.	March 3, 2011	2.	_____
3.	November 18, 2010	3.	_____
4.	May 19, 2009	4.	_____
5.	July 22, 2009	5.	_____
6.	February 12, 2009	6.	_____
7.	May 5, 2011	7.	_____
8.	April 1, 2010	8.	_____
9.	December 14, 2009	9.	_____
10.	August 30, 2009	10.	_____
11.	June 8, 2010	11.	_____
12.	July 24, 2011	12.	_____
13.	April 18, 2009	13.	_____
14.	January 3, 2010	14.	_____
15.	September 18, 2009	15.	_____
16.	January 1, 2011	16.	_____
17.	September 20, 2010	17.	_____
18.	February 5, 2011	18.	_____
19.	March 18, 2009	19.	_____
20.	April 17, 2010	20.	_____

The drawers pictured are labeled:

- A: JAN 1, 2009 – APR 30, 2009
- B: MAY 1, 2009 – AUG 31, 2009
- C: SEP 1, 2009 – DEC 31, 2009
- D: JAN 1, 2010 – APR 30, 2010
- E: MAY 1, 2010 – AUG 31, 2010
- F: SEP 1, 2010 – DEC 31, 2010
- G: JAN 1, 2011 – APR 30, 2011
- H: MAY 1, 2011 – AUG 31, 2011

GOAL: File discs using a numeric system

NAME

CLASS

CD-ROM is an abbreviation for **c**ompact **d**isc **r**ead-**o**nly **m**emory. **DVD-ROM** is an abbreviation for **d**igital **v**ersatile (or **v**ideo) **d**isc **r**ead-**o**nly **m**emory. These discs contain data that can be read by a computer. CD-ROM and DVD-ROM discs can be filed in subject, geographic, numeric, or alphabetic order. Two types of containers for filing CD-ROM and DVD-ROM discs are shown in Illustration 4-1. The correct disc can be retrieved and filed more efficiently using these types of storage containers.

Illustration 4-1   Containers for Filing CD-ROM and DVD-ROM Discs

Dja65/Shutterstock.com

aragami12345s/Shutterstock.com

The discs shown on the next page are not in correct numeric order. Put the discs in order so that the numbers are consecutive from the lowest number to the highest number. Beginning at the *bottom* of the *Answers* column, write the letter (*A, B, C, D,* etc.) shown beside each number to indicate the correct order of the discs. The letter for the disc with the lowest number is shown on line 1. The letter for the disc with the highest number will be on line 15.

O No. 13876	
N No. 12534	
M No. 13844	
L No. 13561	
K No. 12840	
J No. 12196	
I No. 12480	
H No. 13345	
G No. 12407	
F No. 12774	
E No. 13288	
D No. 12993	
C No. 13117	
B No. 12405	
A No. 13028	

DEPARTMENT: *LEGAL*

DATA: *VENDOR CONTRACTS*

DATES: *03/-- to 04/--*

15. _____
14. _____
13. _____
12. _____
11. _____
10. _____
9. _____
8. _____
7. _____
6. _____
5. _____
4. _____
3. _____
2. _____
1.   J

GOAL: File records using the terminal-digit method

_____ NAME

_____ CLASS

In previous exercises you put numbers in consecutive order. In this exercise you will learn terminal-digit filing. **Terminal-digit filing** is a method of numeric filing in which numbers are filed in consecutive order (lowest number to highest number); however, the numbers are divided into groups and are read from _right to left_.

A _digit_ is one number. Terminal-digit filing is used when numbers have five or more digits. In the number 412336, the digits could be separated into two groups of three digits each (412 336) or three groups of two digits each (41 23 36). The words **terminal digit** refer to the end digits of the number (41 23 <u>36</u>). The digits in the number may be divided into groups by spaces or hyphens (41-23-36). Reading from _right to left_, the groups of numbers are identified as **primary number** (first in rank or importance), **secondary number** (second in rank or importance), and **tertiary number** (third in rank or importance).

Tertiary	Secondary	Primary
41	23	36

Locate the folder labeled 41-23-36 in the file drawer in Figure 4-7 below. As you read the following instructions, note that the numbered steps correspond with the circled numbers shown in the figure.

1. Determine the terminal digit, or primary number, which in this example is 36. File drawers are usually labeled with the primary number. All files within this drawer have numbers ending in 36.

2. The file guides in the drawer are in consecutive order: 22, 23, 24, and 25. Locate the file guide with the secondary number, 23. All files behind this guide have secondary numbers of 23.

3. Locate the folder behind file guide 23 with the tertiary number, 41. Folders are arranged in consecutive order behind each guide according to the tertiary numbers, or the digits at the far left of the number.

Figure 4-7 Terminal-Digit Numeric File

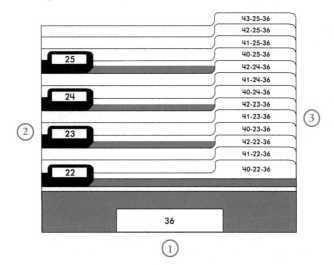

Some file folders are out of order in the file drawer below. Beginning at the front of the file drawer, place an *X* in the *Answers* column across from any file folder that is out of order. The first *X* is shown as an example. Refer to Figure 4-7 on the previous page if necessary.

ANSWERS

File Folder		Answer	
57-33-66		24.	
51-83-65		23.	
50-83-65		22.	
51-32-65		21.	
51-38-65		20.	
50-32-65		19.	
52-31-65		18.	
51-31-66		17.	
50-31-65		16.	
52-30-65		15.	
51-30-65		14.	
50-30-65		13.	
51-29-65		12.	
51-39-65		11.	
50-29-65		10.	
51-28-65		9.	
50-28-65		8.	
50-28-66		7.	X
52-27-65		6.	
51-27-65		5.	
50-27-65		4.	
52-26-65		3.	
51-26-65		2.	
50-26-65		1.	

33
32
31
30
29
28
27
26

65

Well done! You have completed the exercises for Unit 4. Before your instructor administers the Unit 4 Test, review the exercises in this unit. Do not begin the Unit 5 exercises until your instructor has approved Unit 4.

Go Digital!

For additional activities visit www.cengage.com/school/bse

GOAL: Use reference sources to find
    information

_____ NAME

_____ CLASS

When working in a business office, you will find information by referring to many different sources. Pages from common reference sources are provided in the *Reference Sources* section in the back of this text-workbook.

Use the *Reference Sources* on pages 245–274 to find the answers to the questions below. Write your answer in the space to the right of each question. Be sure to use your best handwriting or printing. To help you find the answers, the section of the *Reference Sources* pages that you will need to refer to is shown after the first question in each set of questions.

<u>ANSWERS</u>

1a. For which city is JFK the airport code?
    (Airlines—Airport Codes)

1a. _____

1b. What is the code for the Raleigh/Durham, NC, airport?

1b. _____

2a. In which time zone is Iowa?
    (Map—Area Codes and Time Zones)

2a. _____

2b. In which area code are the telephone numbers in Maine?

2b. _____

3a. For a $6.50 sale, what is the 7% sales tax?
    (Charts—Sales Tax)

3a. _____

3b. For a $21.70 sale, what is the 6.5% sales tax?

3b. _____

4a. What is the income tax withheld for a single person claiming two allowances with monthly wages of $1,160? *(Charts—Payroll, Monthly)*

4a. _____

4b. What is the income tax withheld for a married person claiming zero allowances with monthly wages of $2,225?

4b. _____

5a. What is the U.S. Postal Service abbreviation for Meadows? *(USPS—Abbreviations)*

5a. _____

5b. How is the state name of Louisiana abbreviated?

5b. _____

6a. What is the proofreaders' mark to move material to the right? *(Proofreaders' Marks)*

6a. _____

6b. What is the mark to use a lowercase letter?

6b. _____

7a. What is the maximum balance on the stock record card for stock number PE211? *(Inventory—Stock Record Cards)*

7a. _____

7b. What is the September 30 balance on the stock record card for stock number CD368?

7b. _____

8a. At the Postal Service, what is the telephone number for passport information? *(Telephone Directory)*

8a. _____

8b. If you needed to rent a car from NBS Car Rentals, what number would you call?

8b. _____

9a. What is the cost of two packs of Business Form VI58? *(Price Lists—Business Forms)*

9a. _____

9b. What is the cost of four packs of Business Form MM48?

9b. _____

10a. Who is the author of *Winning Job Interviews*? *(Bibliography)*

10a. _____

10b. Who is the author of *A Grammar Book for You and I…Oops, Me!*?

10b. _____

11a. What is the closing inventory of standard #10 envelopes? *(Inventory—Accounting Department)*

11a. _____

11b. What is the inventory value of the entire inventory?

11b. _____

12a. Washington is bordered on the south by which state? *(Map—United States with Capitals)*

12a. _____

12b. How many states border Arkansas?

12b. _____

13a. What is the number of driving miles between Philadelphia, PA, and Albuquerque, NM? *(Mileage Chart—Driving Distances)*

13a. _____

13b. What is the number of driving miles between Houston, TX, and Baltimore, MD?

13b. _____

14a. If you caught the Airport Express Shuttle at the Baymont Hotel at 0730A, at what time would you arrive at the airport? *(Airport Express Shuttle Schedule)*

14a. _____

14b. If you were staying at the Pacific Palms and needed to be at the airport by 1215P, at what time should you catch the shuttle?

14b. _____

15a. What is the numbered section of the *Daily News* for Antiques? *(Newspaper Business Section)*

15a. _____

15b. In which numbered section of the *Daily News* will you find Homes With Acreage?

15b. _____

GOAL: Use reference sources to find information

_____ NAME

_____ CLASS

To find the answers to the questions below, use the *Reference Sources* on pages 245–274. Write your answer in the space to the right of each question. To help you find the answers, the section of the *Reference Sources* pages that you will need to refer to is included after the first question in each set of questions.

ANSWERS

1a. What is the income tax withheld for a single person claiming zero allowances with monthly wages of $780? *(Charts—Payroll, Monthly)*

1a. _____

1b. What is the income tax withheld for a single person claiming three allowances with monthly wages of $950?

1b. _____

2a. What is the price of one Auto Part No. 11749505? *(Price Lists—Auto Parts)*

2a. _____

2b. Find the price of one Auto Part No. 43516653. What would be the cost for six of these parts?

2b. _____

3a. What is the price of one LS445 Sheet-Fed All-in-One machine? *(Price Lists—Office Equipment)*

3a. _____

3b. What is the price of one RJ605B Drum?

3b. _____

4a. What is the U.S. Postal Service fee for a 9-pound express mail package? *(USPS—Rates and Services)*

4a. _____

4b. What is the fee for insuring a package valued at $350?

4b. _____

5a. What is the number of driving miles between Washington, D.C., and Orlando, FL? *(Mileage Chart—Driving Distances)*

5a. _____

5b. What is the number of driving miles between Los Angeles, CA, and New York, NY?

5b. _____

6a. What type of aircraft is used for Flight 625? *(Airlines—Flight Information)*

6a. _____

6b. What is the flying time (hours, minutes) of Flight 435?

6b. _____

7a. In South Burlington, VT, what is the ZIP Code for Rural Routes 01 and 02? *(USPS—ZIP Codes)*

7a. _____

7b. What is the address for the Postmaster in Burlington, VT?

7b. _____

8a. On check stub 1317, what was the Balance Brought Forward? *(Checkbook Register)*

8a. _____

8b. Check 1325 was written to pay what bill?

8b. _____

9. In Indianapolis:

    a. on which day is the temperature forecast the lowest? *(Weather Forecasts)*

9a. _____

    b. what is the forecasted lowest temperature?

9b. _____

10a. What lake is directly north of Wisconsin? *(Map—Central States and Northwestern States)*

10a. _____

10b. What is the capital of Illinois?

10b. _____

11a. What is the September 15 balance on the stock record card for stock number EN211? *(Inventory—Stock Record Cards)*

11a. _____

11b. What is the September 30 balance on the stock record card for stock number EN211?

11b. _____

12a. How many incoming calls were received during April? *(Calls Register)*

12a. _____

12b. To what city and state was a call placed on 4-10?

12b. _____

13a. What is the area code for Vermont? *(Map—Area Codes and Time Zones)*

13a. _____

13b. What is the area code for New Brunswick?

13b. _____

14a. What is the income tax withheld for a married person claiming three allowances with weekly wages of $425? *(Charts—Payroll, Weekly)*

14a. _____

14b. What is the income tax withheld for a single person claiming zero allowances with weekly wages of $295?

14b. _____

15a. What does the proofreaders' mark QS mean? *(Proofreaders' Marks)*

15a. _____

15b. What mark would you use to correct *theproof*?

15b. _____

GOAL: Use reference sources to find
information

_____ NAME

_____ CLASS

To find the answers to the questions below, use the *Reference Sources* on pages 245–274.
Write your answer in the space to the right of each question. To help you find the answers,
the section of the *Reference Sources* pages that you will need to refer to is included after the
first question in each set of questions.

ANSWERS

1a. What body of water lies south of Texas, Louisiana,
Mississippi, Alabama, and Florida?
(Map—United States with Capitals)

1a. _____

1b. What is the capital of Pennsylvania?

1b. _____

2a. What is the unit size for Ruled Index Cards?
(Inventory—Accounting Department)

2a. _____

2b. What is the closing inventory for product
number ST629?

2b. _____

3a. For which city is MSY the airport code?
(Airlines—Airport Codes)

3a. _____

3b. ICT is the airport code for which city?

3b. _____

4a. What is the ZIP Code for Bridgewater,
Windsor County, VT? *(USPS—ZIP Codes)*

4a. _____

4b. East Burke, VT, is located in what county?

4b. _____

5a. At the Postal Service, what is the telephone
number for mail processing? *(Telephone Directory)*

5a. _____

5b. If you wanted to send flowers to a friend,
what number would you call?

5b. _____

6. What is the number of the section in *The Herald*
for each of the services listed below:
(Newspaper Business Section)

   a. Printing Services

6a. _____

   b. Daycare/Childcare Services

6b. _____

7a. One PC509 Color Inkjet Printer is priced
at how much? *(Price Lists—Office Equipment)*

7a. _____

7b. One FC692A Black Ink cartridge,
including 7% sales tax, costs how much?

7b. _____

8a. What is the proofreaders' mark to move material to the left? *(Proofreaders' Marks)*

8a. _____

8b. What mark would you use to show that material should be italicized?

8b. _____

9a. What is the income tax withheld for a single person claiming one allowance with weekly wages of $193? *(Charts—Payroll, Weekly)*

9a. _____

9b. What is the income tax withheld for a married person claiming four allowances with weekly wages of $355?

9b. _____

10a. Who is the author of *100 Fastest-Growing Careers*? *(Bibliography)*

10a. _____

10b. In what state is *The Anxiety Cure* published?

10b. _____

11a. In which area code are the telephone numbers in New Hampshire? *(Map—Area Codes and Time Zones)*

11a. _____

11b. In which time zone is New Mexico?

11b. _____

12a. In which state will you find the Great Salt Lake? *(Map—United States with Capitals)*

12a. _____

12b. What is the capital of Massachusetts?

12b. _____

13a. Who placed the incoming call on 4-15? *(Calls Register)*

13a. _____

13b. Who was the caller to Dover, DE, on 4-18?

13b. _____

14a. What is the USPS abbreviation for Canyon? *(USPS—Abbreviations)*

14a. _____

14b. What is the abbreviation for Plaza?

14b. _____

15a. If you must be at the shuttle pick-up location 20 minutes before the shuttle leaves for the airport, at what time should you be at the Lemon Tree Inn to catch the shuttle that arrives at the airport at 0525P? *(Airport Express Shuttle Schedule)*

15a. _____

15b. If you caught the shuttle at the Baymont Hotel at 0300P, at what time would you arrive at the airport?

15b. _____

GOAL: Use reference sources to find
information

_____ NAME

_____ CLASS

To find the answers to the questions below, use the *Reference Sources* on pages 245–274.
Write your answer in the space to the right of each question.

Note: In the previous exercises in this unit, you were told which section of the
Reference Sources pages to refer to for the information needed. Now YOU must decide
where to look for the information. You will find it helpful to use the Contents listing on
page 245.

ANSWERS

1a. Who is the author of *The Job Search Solution*? 1a. _____

1b. Who is the publisher of *Reinventing Yourself*? 1b. _____

2a. What is the income tax withheld for a married 2a. _____
person claiming two allowances with monthly
wages of $2,137?

2b. What is the income tax withheld for a single 2b. _____
person claiming one allowance with monthly
wages of $850?

3a. TPA is the airport code for which city? 3a. _____

3b. What is the airport code for Albuquerque? 3b. _____

4a. What is the ZIP Code for the federal building 4a. _____
in Burlington, VT?

4b. What is the general delivery ZIP Code for 4b. _____
Brattleboro, VT?

5a. What is the 8.25% sales tax on a $61.12 5a. _____
purchase?

5b. What is the 7 3/4% sales tax on a $35.40 5b. _____
purchase?

6a. What was the amount of the March 27 6a. _____
deposit in the checkbook?

6b. What was the Balance Brought Forward 6b. _____
on check stub 1322?

7. What is the number of the section in *The Herald* for each of the services listed below:

    a. Pet Grooming Services

    7a. _____

    b. Secretarial Services

    7b. _____

8a. What is the total cost of four Auto Part No. 00145571, including 6.5% sales tax?

    8a. _____

8b. What is the cost of eight Auto Part No. 00556328?

    8b. _____

9a. In which city is the temperature forecast lowest on Wednesday: Charleston, SC; Charlotte, NC; or Portland, ME?

    9a. _____

9b. Of the three cities Orlando, Memphis, and New York, which has the best weather forecast for Friday?

    9b. _____

10a. What is the total cost of two packs of Business Form BD81, including 7% sales tax?

    10a. _____

10b. What is the total cost of one pack of Business Form RB90, including 7 3/4% sales tax?

    10b. _____

11a. If you caught the Airport Express Shuttle at the Lemon Tree Inn at 1010A, at what time would you arrive at the airport?

    11a. _____

11b. If you were staying at the Pacific Palms and needed to be at the airport at 0825P, at what time should you catch the shuttle?

    11b. _____

12a. What is the cost of a large postcard?

    12a. _____

12b What is the cost of a domestic Large Flat Rate Box?

    12b. _____

13a. What is the inventory product number for jumbo paper clips?

    13a. _____

13b. What is the unit price of medium black ballpoint pens?

    13b. _____

14a. What country borders the United States to the north?

    14a. _____

14b. What body of water lies east of the Carolinas?

    14b. _____

15a. What is the number of driving miles between Denver, CO, and Los Angeles, CA?

    15a. _____

15b. What is the number of driving miles between Myrtle Beach, SC, and Milwaukee, WI?

    15b. _____

GOAL: Use reference sources to find
information

_____ NAME

_____ CLASS

To find the answers to the questions below, use the *Reference Sources* on pages 245–274.
Write your answer in the space to the right of each question.

ANSWERS

1a. What is the proofreaders' mark to capitalize a
letter or word?

1a. _____

1b. What is the mark to show that a correction
should be ignored?

1b. _____

2a. What is the capital of the United States?

2a. _____

2b. What river runs along the Texas–Mexico border?

2b. _____

3a. What is the income tax withheld for a married
person claiming five allowances with monthly
wages of $1,550?

3a. _____

3b. What is the income tax withheld for a
single person claiming one allowance with
monthly wages of $975?

3b. _____

4a. What is the inventory value of product number
RL308?

4a. _____

4b. What is the unit price of printer paper,
5,000/case?

4b. _____

5. What is the number of the section in *The Herald*
for each of the services listed below:

   a. Employment Services

5a. _____

   b. Solar Energy Services

5b. _____

6a. One SG478 Copier is priced at how much?

6a. _____

6b. A Toner cartridge for the SG478 Copier
is priced at how much?

6b. _____

7a. What lake lies between Wisconsin and Michigan?

7a. _____

7b. What river runs through the Central states?

7b. _____

8a. What two cities are served by Flight 355?
(List the city names, not the airport codes.)

8a. _____

8b. What type of aircraft is used for Flight 505?

8b. _____

9a. GU is the USPS abbreviation for what?   9a. _____

9b. What is the abbreviation for Office?   9b. _____

10a. The state of North Dakota has how many   10a. _____
time zones?

10b. In which time zone is Georgia?   10b. _____

11a. What is the total cost of six packs of Business   11a. _____
Form SE32, including 7 3/4% sales tax?

11b. Three packs of EF88, including 7% sales tax,   11b. _____
costs how much?

12a. What is the ZIP Code for Fairfax, Chittenden   12a. _____
County, VT?

12b. What is the ZIP Code for P.O. Box 198 in   12b. _____
Colchester, VT?

13a. If you wanted to research Personal and   13a. _____
Professional Development skills on the
Internet, what web site would be useful?

13b. In what state is *The Success Principles*   13b. _____
published?

14a. What is the maximum balance on the stock   14a. _____
record card for stock number PC600?

14b. What is the unit on the Staples stock   14b. _____
record card?

15a. For a $95.46 sale, what is the 8.25% sales tax?   15a. _____

15b. For a $15.00 sale, what is the 7% sales tax?   15b. _____

GOAL: Use reference sources to find information

_____ NAME

_____ CLASS

To find the answers to the questions below, use the *Reference Sources* on pages 245–274. Write your answer in the space to the right of each question.

<u>ANSWERS</u>

1a. To reach the airport at 0225P, at what time would you have to catch the shuttle from the Pacific Palms?

1a. _____

1b. If you board the shuttle at the Baymont Hotel at 0900P, how many minutes will it take to arrive at the airport?

1b. _____

2a. The state of Alaska is located between what two countries?

2a. _____

2b. The Hawaiian Islands are in what ocean?

2b. _____

3a. What is the airport code for Montgomery, AL?

3a. _____

3b. BHM is the airport code for which city?

3b. _____

4a. What is the street address of NBS Car Rentals?

4a. _____

4b. What is the profession of Thos. J. Native?

4b. _____

5a. What is the inventory value of DVD-R, 10/pack?

5a. _____

5b. What is the closing inventory of fax paper, 6/pack?

5b. _____

6a. What is the income tax withheld for a single person claiming two allowances with weekly wages of $265?

6a. _____

6b. What is the income tax withheld for a married person claiming one allowance with weekly wages of $377?

6b. _____

7a. What is the total cost of six Auto Part No. 00145573, including 7% sales tax?

7a. _____

7b. What is the cost of four Auto Part No. 00204836?

7b. _____

8a. What is the USPS abbreviation for the Marshall Islands?

8a. _____

8b. How would you abbreviate the word Hollow?

8b. _____

9a. What is the number of driving miles between Minneapolis, MN, and Chicago, IL?

9a. _____

9b. What is the number of driving miles between Portland, OR, and Houston, TX?

9b. _____

10a. What is the capital of Montana?

10a. _____

10b. What state is directly east of Mississippi?

10b. _____

11a. What is the proofreaders' mark to delete?

11a. _____

11b. What is the mark to insert an apostrophe?

11b. _____

12a. Cheyenne will have the highest temperature on which day?

12a. _____

12b. On which day is Lubbock forecast to have rain?

12b. _____

13a. For a $12.35 sale, what is the 6.5% sales tax?

13a. _____

13b. For a $102.08 sale, what is the 8.25% sales tax?

13b. _____

14a. What is the fee for certified mail?

14a. _____

14b. What is the fee for registered mail for a package valued at $1,500?

14b. _____

15a. What is the year of publication of *Garner's Modern American Usage*?

15a. _____

15b. Who is the author of *Eats, Shoots & Leaves: The Zero Tolerance Approach to Punctuation*?

15b. _____

GOAL: Use reference sources to find information

_____ NAME

_____ CLASS

To find the answers to the questions below, use the *Reference Sources* of this text-workbook. Write your answer in the space to the right of each question.

ANSWERS

1a. What is the income tax withheld for a single person claiming two allowances with monthly wages of $1,038?

1a. _____

1b. What is the income tax withheld for a married person claiming one allowance with monthly wages of $2,227?

1b. _____

2a. What type of aircraft is used for Flight 258?

2a. _____

2b. How many air miles are flown on Flight 185?

2b. _____

3a. What is the minimum balance on the stock record card for stock number ST722?

3a. _____

3b. What is the unit on the Pencils stock record card?

3b. _____

4a. If a business associate is expecting your call at 3:00 p.m. Eastern time and you are located in Nevada, at what time should you place the call?

4a. _____

4b. The Canadian provinces of Saskatchewan and Manitoba are in which time zone?

4b. _____

5a. What was the Balance before check 1315 was written?

5a. _____

5b. What was the amount of check 1321?

5b. _____

6a. What is the USPS abbreviation for Nova Scotia in Canada?

6a. _____

6b. What is the abbreviation for Rapids?

6b. _____

7a. What is the telephone number for federal workers' compensation at the Department of Labor?

7a. _____

7b. How many addresses are listed for Necco Sewing Center?

7b. _____

8a. Which state is the largest to be bordered with Canada?

8a. _____

8b. What is the capital of Missouri?

8b. _____

9a. What is the total cost of two packs of Business Form LQ38, including 6.5% sales tax?

9a. _____

9b. What is the price of one pack of Business Form HB22?

9b. _____

10a. How much does it cost to mail an 8-pound parcel post package?

10a. _____

10b. What is the fee for receiving delivery confirmation electronically?

10b. _____

11a. Who was the person called in Duluth, MN, on 4-8?

11a. _____

11b. What was the time of the call placed on 4-23 to West Chester, PA?

11b. _____

12a. On the Mileage Chart, which two cities are the farthest apart?

12a. _____

12b. What is the number of driving miles between the two farthest cities?

12b. _____

13a. What river runs from Wyoming to Washington?

13a. _____

13b. Minnesota is bordered on the south by which state?

13b. _____

14a. In Atlanta, on which day is the temperature forecast the highest?

14a. _____

14b. What is the forecasted highest temperature in Brownsville?

14b. _____

15a. Who is the publisher of *Cool Careers for Dummies*?

15a. _____

15b. Who is the publisher of *Monster Careers: How to Land the Job of Your Life*?

15b. _____

GOAL: Use reference sources to find
information

_____ NAME

_____ CLASS

To find the answers to the questions below, use the *Reference Sources* of this text-workbook.
Write your answer in the space to the right of each question.

ANSWERS

1a. What is the proofreaders' mark to close up
material?

1a. _____

1b. What is the mark for a new paragraph?

1b. _____

2. In Phoenix:

a. on which day is the temperature forecast
the highest?

2a. _____

b. what is the forecasted highest temperature?

2b. _____

3a. If you were staying at the Newport Outrigger
and needed to be at the airport by 0125P,
at what time should you catch the shuttle?

3a. _____

3b. How much time (hours, minutes) is required to
reach the airport from the Newport Outrigger?

3b. _____

4a. What is the income tax withheld for a married
person claiming two allowances with monthly
wages of $1,640?

4a. _____

4b. What is the income tax withheld for a married
person claiming zero allowances with monthly
wages of $2,190?

4b. _____

5a. In which area code are the telephone numbers
in South Dakota?

5a. _____

5b. Which Canadian province is in the Mountain
time zone?

5b. _____

6a. What is the unit size for Black Stamp Pad Ink?

6a. _____

6b. What is the inventory value of Standard
File Folders?

6b. _____

7a. In which numbered section of the *Daily News*
will you find Ticket Mart?

7a. _____

7b. What is the number of the section in
The Herald for Financial Services?

7b. _____

8a. What is the 7% sales tax on a $5.55 purchase?

8a. _____

8b. What is the 8.25% sales tax on a $104.50 purchase?

8b. _____

9a. What is the cost of two PC509A Black Ink cartridges?

9a. _____

9b. What is the total cost of two FC692C Magenta Ink cartridges, including 7 3/4% sales tax?

9b. _____

10a. CAE is the airport code for which city?

10a. _____

10b. For which city is MCI the airport code?

10b. _____

11. What are the Postal Service abbreviations for the following words:

   a. Junction

11a. _____

   b. Causeway

11b. _____

12a. What is the cost of three packs of Business Form PO80?

12a. _____

12b. If you have $60, how many packs of Business Form DE76 can you purchase?

12b. _____

13a. What is the telephone number of the regional commissioner at the Bureau of Labor Statistics?

13a. _____

13b. What is the telephone number of the public affairs office at the Department of Labor?

13b. _____

14a. Nebraska is bordered on the north by which state?

14a. _____

14b. Which state does Lake Ontario border?

14b. _____

15a. What is the cost of five Auto Part No. 32268357?

15a. _____

15b. What is the total cost of four Auto Part No. 48356685, including 7 3/4% sales tax?

15b. _____

GOAL: Use reference sources to find
information

_____ NAME

_____ CLASS

To find the answers to the questions below, use the *Reference Sources* of this text-workbook.
Write your answer in the space to the right of each question.

ANSWERS

1a. If you purchased one Auto Part No. 57717337
and the sales tax was 8.25%, what would
be the total cost?

1a. _____

1b. What is the price of one Auto Part
No. 77477947?

1b. _____

2a. How much time (hours, minutes) will you
be in the air on Flight 3100?

2a. _____

2b. What two cities are served by Flight 333?
(List the city names, not the airport codes.)

2b. _____

3a. If you lived on Benjamin Rd. in East Corinth,
VT, what would be your ZIP Code?

3a. _____

3b. In Essex Junction, VT, what is the ZIP Code
for most of the named street addresses?

3b. _____

4a. What is the income tax withheld for a single
person claiming two allowances with weekly
wages of $285?

4a. _____

4b. What is the income tax withheld for a married
person claiming three allowances with weekly
wages of $426?

4b. _____

5a. On the Mileage Chart, which two cities are
closest to each other?

5a. _____

5b. What is the number of driving miles between
the two closest cities?

5b. _____

6a. What is the September 1 balance on the stock
record card for stock number PE234?

6a. _____

6b. What is the minimum balance on the Index
Cards stock record card?

6b. _____

7a. What postal service should you use to mail a package containing books and CDs?

7a. _____

7b. How much does it cost to mail a one-ounce piece of first-class mail?

7b. _____

8a. Who is the author of *The One Thing Holding You Back*?

8a. _____

8b. In what state is *Grammatically Correct* published?

8b. _____

9a. Which of the 48 contiguous states is farthest south?

9a. _____

9b. Which of all 50 states is farthest south?

9b. _____

10a. What is the proofreaders' mark to transpose?

10a. _____

10b. What does the mark DS mean?

10b. _____

11a. To whom did Danny Lavant place a telephone call on 4-4?

11a. _____

11b. During April a call was placed to what telephone number in Abilene, TX?

11b. _____

12. Of the three cities Anchorage, Fairbanks, and Juneau:

   a. which city has the lowest temperature forecast for Friday's high?

12a. _____

   b. what is the forecasted temperature?

12b. _____

13a. To whom was check 1324 written?

13a. _____

13b. Check 1319 was written to pay what bill?

13b. _____

14a. What is the telephone number for the Navy Recruiting Station on Cobb Pkwy?

14a. _____

14b. What is the address for the National Youth Foundation?

14b. _____

15a. The Mississippi River empties into what body of water?

15a. _____

15b. Nevada is bordered on the west by which state?

15b. _____

GOAL: Use reference sources to find
    information

_____ NAME

_____ CLASS

To find the answers to the questions below, use the *Reference Sources* of this text-workbook.
Write your answer in the space to the right of each question.

<u>ANSWERS</u>

1. In which numbered section of the *Daily News* will
you find:

   a. Unfurnished Apartments

     1a. _____

   b. Computers, Needs

     1b. _____

2a. What is the 7 3/4% sales tax on a $20 purchase?

     2a. _____

2b. What is the 6.5% sales tax on a $3.57 purchase?

     2b. _____

3a. *Essentials of English Grammar* has had how
many editions?

     3a. _____

3b. If you wanted to job search on the Internet, what
web sites would be useful?

     3b. _____

4a. What is the USPS abbreviation for Pennsylvania?

     4a. _____

4b. What is the abbreviation for Missouri?

     4b. _____

5a. Who received a call on 4-25?

     5a. _____

5b. To whom did Juanita Ham place a call on 4-19?

     5b. _____

6a. What is the price of one FI376 Inkjet
Fax machine?

     6a. _____

6b. What is the cost of two PL647A Toner
cartridges?

     6b. _____

7a. What two cities are served by Flight 290?
(List the city names, not the airport codes.)

     7a. _____

7b. Flight 4624 has how many stops?

     7b. _____

8a. If you were driving from Chicago, IL, to
Portland, OR, and you drove 600 miles a day,
about how many days would it take you
to reach Portland?

     8a. _____

8b. If you drove 470 miles a day, about how many
days would it take you to drive from
Washington, DC, to Albuquerque, NM?

     8b. _____

9a. What business is located on Dogwood Highway?

9a. _____

9b. What is the telephone number for Nationwide Haulers?

9b. _____

10a. How many degrees is the temperature forecasted to fall (from high to low) in Seattle on Wednesday?

10a. _____

10b. What is the weather forecast for Dallas on Friday?

10b. _____

11a. What is the inventory value of product number TA821?

11a. _____

11b. What is the unit price of the desk appointment book?

11b. _____

12a. How would you abbreviate the word Basement?

12a. _____

12b. STRM is the USPS abbreviation for what word?

12b. _____

13a. How much does it cost to send a postal military money order?

13a. _____

13b. What is the cost of a return receipt that is requested at the time of mailing and is received by mail?

13b. _____

14a. What is the proofreaders' mark to insert a period?

14a. _____

14b. What is the mark to insert a hyphen?

14b. _____

15a. When it is 1 p.m. in Connecticut, what time is it in Oregon?

15a. _____

15b. If you left Miami, Florida, at 5 p.m., what time would it be in New Orleans, Louisiana, when you arrive after a 1-hour, 23-minute flight?

15b. _____

Well done! You have completed the exercises for Unit 5. Before your instructor administers the Unit 5 Test, review the exercises in this unit. You will need to refer to the *Reference Sources* section of this text-workbook to complete the test. Do not begin the Unit 6 exercises until your instructor has approved Unit 5.

Go Digital!

For additional activities visit www.cengage.com/school/bse

GOAL: Set personal priorities

_____ NAME

_____ CLASS

To manage your time effectively, you must set priorities. **Prioritizing** is the process of determining the order in which tasks should be completed. To select the tasks that should be priorities in your personal work plan, you must determine how important each task is and when it is due. Therefore, when setting priorities, you must consider each task's *importance* and *deadline*.

It is Friday afternoon, and you have a long list of tasks to complete before Monday. The weekend is your time to "recover" from the week, catch up on some chores at home, and get a head start on the next week. This weekend is especially full since you are a volunteer coach for your high school's basketball team, and your team has a weekend game as well as a tournament that starts Monday evening.

Read the list of weekend tasks below, noting any deadline information. On the form on the next page, list the tasks you would complete each day (Friday evening, Saturday, and Sunday). Be sure to write the tasks in the order you would complete them each day. If there are any tasks that you would postpone until after the weekend or cancel, write those tasks at the bottom of the form, then place a check mark in either the postpone or cancel box. Note: You may have blank lines left, but all tasks must be written on the form.

WEEKEND TASKS

Bathe the dog

Read materials for a training session scheduled for Tuesday at work

Wash the car

Coach the basketball game on Saturday

Arrange your CDs

Practice the piano for your next lesson on Thursday

Do laundry

Outline a report due on Wednesday

Attend a free concert on Sunday

Eat pizza with friends on Friday night

Iron your work clothes

Write thank-you notes to your grandparents for gifts you received three weeks ago

Make reservations at a local restaurant for a holiday dinner that will take place in three months

Go shopping at the mall on Saturday

Watch a favorite TV show on Sunday evening

WEEKEND TASKS—PRIORITIZED

Friday

1. _____
2. _____
3. _____
4. _____
5. _____

Saturday

1. _____
2. _____
3. _____
4. _____
5. _____
6. _____
7. _____

Sunday

1. _____
2. _____
3. _____
4. _____
5. _____
6. _____
7. _____

Postpone or Cancel

	Postpone	Cancel
1. _____	☐	☐
2. _____	☐	☐
3. _____	☐	☐

GOAL: Improve time and task management skills

_____ NAME

_____ CLASS

Understanding how you spend your time will help you identify ways in which you might be wasting time and will assist you in improving your time management skills. **Time management** is the process of controlling the amount of time spent on specific tasks in order to increase efficiency. Improving time management skills often requires analyzing how time is spent. Everyone has the same amount of time each day, of course, but people spend this time in different ways. To be an efficient manager of time, you must spend the right amount of time on each task.

EXERCISE 89a   Examine the activity categories on the time analysis chart on the next page. Fill out the chart for a typical weekday by assigning a category to each hour or half hour. The vertical dotted lines on the chart separate each hour into a half hour. For example, in the 7 a.m.–8 a.m. box, you might write "Sleep." Or you might write "Sleep" in the 7–7:30 a.m. space and "Grooming" in the 7:30–8 a.m. space.

When you have finished filling out the chart, add the number of hours spent on each activity and write the number in the space next to the category. Your total number of hours should equal 24.

EXERCISE 89b   When you have completed the chart on the next page and have totaled your hours, analyze the data. Consider what the activity has shown you about how you spend your time. Answer the following questions:

1. How do I spend the majority of my time each day? _____

    _____

2. On what activities do I spend the least amount of time? _____

    _____

3. Should I make any changes in my daily time use? If so, what are they, and why should I make these changes?

    _____

    _____

TIME ANALYSIS

_____ School

_____ Homework

_____ Chores

_____ Commuting

_____ Playing games
on computer/
phone/etc.

_____ Sleep

_____ Sports/exercise

_____ Grooming

_____ Doing nothing

_____ Other activity
(identify below)

_____ Watching TV

_____ Work

_____ Meals

_____ Entertainment

7 a.m.–8 a.m.	8 a.m.–9 a.m.	9 a.m.–10 a.m.
10 a.m.–11 a.m.	11 a.m.–12 noon	12 noon–1 p.m.
1 p.m.–2 p.m.	2 p.m.–3 p.m.	3 p.m.–4 p.m.
4 p.m.–5 p.m.	5 p.m.–6 p.m.	6 p.m.–7 p.m.
7 p.m.–8 p.m.	8 p.m.–9 p.m.	9 p.m.–10 p.m.
10 p.m.–11 p.m.	11 p.m.–12 midnight	12 midnight–1 a.m.
1 a.m.–2 a.m.	2 a.m.–3 a.m.	3 a.m.–4 a.m.
4 a.m.–5 a.m.	5 a.m.–6 a.m.	6 a.m.–7 a.m.

GOAL: Set priorities in a business setting

_____ NAME

_____ CLASS

In Exercise 88, you learned to set personal priorities. When you work in an office, it is important to prioritize office tasks that must be completed. Managing your time in a business setting is crucial to being an efficient and productive worker. You must be able to make wise choices about which activity should be completed first, second, third, etc.

In this exercise you will use the time of day to determine the priority of each activity listed below. Read the activities, then write them on the *Things To Do Today* form on the next page in the order they should be completed. *Read all ten activities before you complete the form.* Write only the necessary information about each activity on the form. You do not need to copy each activity word for word as it is shown in the list. Write the activity to be completed first on Line 1 of the form. The activity to be completed last should be written on Line 10. Use the current date. Office hours are 8 a.m. to 5 p.m.

1. Last thing before leaving office, remind night supervisor to set up conference room for meeting tomorrow.

2. Be at People's National Bank at 3 p.m. for closing of loan. Allow 30 minutes.

3. Just before lunch, call Carlos Fuentes of Del Rio Products at 555-0160.

4. After dental appointment, deliver the order to Daniels and Williams. Allow 25 minutes to drive.

5. Return to office by 4 p.m. to call Lillian Noble with the Visitors and Tourists Bureau at 555-0128.

6. First thing upon arrival at the office, call Sylvia Byrum of Wise Electronics in Winston-Salem, NC, at (704) 555-0123, extension 88.

7. At 1:45 p.m. meet Clare Leer to tour her new car dealership. Allow one hour.

8. At 6:30 this evening attend Desktop Publishing Seminar at Prescott Hotel.

9. Meet Captain Farrell of the Salvation Army at noon for United Way kick-off luncheon at Biltmore Plaza. Allow 1½ hours.

10. Be at dentist at 9:30 a.m. for a one-hour appointment.

THINGS TO DO
TODAY

DATE: _____

1. _____

2. _____

3. _____

4. _____

5. _____

6. _____

7. _____

8. _____

9. _____

10. _____

GOAL: Set priorities in a business setting

_____ NAME

_____ CLASS

Below is a list of activities that might occur during a typical day in an office. You will need to determine the order the activities should be completed. Read the activities, then write them on the *Things To Do Today* form on the next page in the order you believe they should be completed. *Read all ten activities before you complete the form.* Note that specific completion times are not given for some of the activities. Use your judgment as to when those activities would best be completed.

Write only the necessary information about each activity on the form. You do not need to copy each activity word for word as it is shown in the list. Write the activity to be completed first on Line 1 of the form. The activity to be completed last should be written on Line 10. Use the current date. Office hours are 8 a.m. to 5 p.m.

1. Place a call to Ms. Namesnik, CPA, at 11 a.m.

2. Make a bank deposit.

3. Call the repairperson for the office photocopier.

4. Attend 3:15 p.m. department meeting in conference room.

5. Submit travel expense report to finance department by 1 p.m.

6. Post department vacation schedule.

7. Leave reminder to night staff to prepare conference room for meeting tomorrow morning.

8. Finish filing miscellaneous reports.

9. Remind receptionist of important telephone call expected from France.

10. Just prior to 3:15 p.m. department meeting, hand out agenda to participants.

THINGS TO DO
TODAY

DATE: _____

1. _____

2. _____

3. _____

4. _____

5. _____

6. _____

7. _____

8. _____

9. _____

10. _____

GOAL: Understand ethics

Ethics is defined as the moral principles that govern personal and professional conduct. A person or group's behavior is guided by a sense of right and wrong. It is knowing the difference between right and wrong and then conducting oneself according to those principles that defines an ethical person. Individuals and companies make decisions based on a code of ethics.

Read the following quotations regarding ethical behavior. These quotations from distinguished people and organizations in history can provide good direction for us.

> "Is life so dear, or peace so sweet, as to be purchased at the price of chains and slavery? Forbid it, Almighty God! I know not what course others may take; but as for me, give me liberty, or give me death!" (Patrick Henry)
>
> "Associate with men of good quality if you esteem your own reputation, for it is better to be alone than in bad company." (President George Washington)
>
> "Leadership is a potent combination of strategy and character. But if you must be without one, be without the strategy." (General H. Norman Schwarzkopf)
>
> "A people that values its privileges above its principles soon loses both." (President Dwight D. Eisenhower)
>
> "An Aggie does not lie, cheat, or steal, or tolerate those who do." (Aggie Honor Code, Texas A&M University)

Ethical behavior is required of us daily. Someone once said that ethical behavior is doing the right thing, even when no one is watching. If you work in an office and take home pencils or pens that belong to the firm, are you acting ethically? If you work in a fast-food restaurant and provide food to your friends, is this ethical behavior? If you are a teacher's assistant at your school and provide test answers to fellow students, are you behaving ethically?

Think about situations you might have encountered that could be considered unethical. On the next page, write about an unethical situation that you have been part of or that you have heard about. Do not use real names. Describe the situation, what happened, how you reacted (if you were a part of this situation), and how the matter was resolved. Also include your feelings about the situation. If you were involved, did your peers pressure you in any way? Should you have acted in a different manner? Were you pleased with your actions? How did you feel about the resolution? Use additional sheets of paper, if necessary. There are no right or wrong answers for this exercise.

WRITING ON ETHICS

_____

_____

_____

_____

_____

_____

_____

_____

_____

_____

_____

_____

_____

_____

_____

_____

GOAL: Explore e-mail ethics

_____ NAME

_____ CLASS

Many people use e-mail regularly to communicate at work. It is quick, easy, convenient, and inexpensive. As an employee, it is important that you be aware of the ethical issues surrounding the use of e-mail at work.

- *Do not assume that e-mail is private.* Courts have supported the rights of employers to read employee e-mail. People have been fired for e-mailing sensitive or unethical information, such as company secrets or offensive jokes. Even deleted e-mails can often be retrieved from company backup systems. Do not put anything in an e-mail that you would not want everyone in the company to see.

- *Do not put anything in an e-mail that would embarrass you or your company.* When you write e-mail at work, you are writing on behalf of your company. The same ethical rules that apply to speaking or writing letters or memos at work apply to e-mail as well.

- *Do not use e-mail for unacceptable private purposes.* Check whether your employer has a policy on personal e-mail. Often, occasional personal use is acceptable, but regular, excessive, or improper use is not.

- *Do not read other people's e-mail.*

- *Do not forward or quote e-mail without permission.*

Read each e-mail scenario that follows. In the space provided below each scenario, write whether or not you think the employee's action is unethical and, if so, in what way.

If your instructor requests, be prepared to share your answers with other students. Discuss any answers that may differ. Share stories that you have heard or read about regarding e-mail ethics at work.

1. Mark includes a joke about women in an e-mail to a friend at work. By mistake, he sends it to an entire mailing list (13 employees).

   _____

   _____

2. Ellen is angry about a change in company policy, so she sends an e-mail to everyone in the company complaining about it.

   _____

   _____

3. Jim e-mails his wife, who often works at her computer, to let her know that there is a tornado watch for that afternoon.

_____

_____

4. Alicia sends an e-mail to a friend describing a product her company is testing that might interest her friend.

_____

_____

5. Kunio collects humorous stories and frequently sends them in e-mails to his friends.

_____

_____

6. Terri e-mails a dozen co-workers asking for contributions to her son's school debate team.

_____

_____

7. Roger is furious with the sales manager and sends her a blistering e-mail.

_____

_____

8. Guadalupe mistakenly receives a copy of an e-mail from her supervisor to the company president. She reads it.

_____

_____

GOAL: Write effective e-mail

E-mail is quick and easy to send and tends to be less formal than letters or memos. These features can be disadvantages, however. People are sometimes less careful in writing e-mail than in writing other correspondence. E-mail can contain mistakes and can be misinterpreted. In one survey, 51 percent of respondents said their e-mail is often misunderstood—as abrupt or angry, for example. How can you avoid such problems and write effective e-mail?

- *Do not send an e-mail when a meeting or phone call would be better.* If you have criticism or bad news to deliver, or if you think your message is likely to be misunderstood, call or meet with the person.

- *Use a short, specific subject line.* Some e-mail software abbreviates the subject line, so make it short. Be specific so the recipient understands the topic at a glance. Use a subject that accurately describes the content of your e-mail.

- *Be brief.* Keep messages to one screen, if possible. If you have several points to make, consider numbering them so it is easier for the recipient to read and respond to your e-mail.

- *Do a last check.* Spell check e-mail, if your software has that feature. Read through your e-mail one last time before sending it.

- *Use care with the Reply feature.* This feature can result in long e-mails when you are answering a lengthy message or when several replies go back and forth. Edit long original messages, leaving enough material so the most recent messages will not be misunderstood.

- *Do not assume privacy.* As mentioned previously, e-mail is not secure. Do not put anything in an e-mail that would not be suitable for everyone in the company to see.

EXERCISE 94a   Rewrite the following subject lines so they are short and specific. Invent details as necessary.

FOUND THIS ON THE INTERNET; THOUGHT YOU MIGHT LIKE IT

_____

IT'S DONE

_____

EXERCISE 94b   Would e-mail be the best way to communicate the following messages? Check the appropriate box.

1. A request from your supervisor for project information ☐ Yes ☐ No

2. News that a product has a safety hazard ☐ Yes ☐ No

3. A funny story about an employee at your workplace ☐ Yes ☐ No

4. A reply to a report that criticizes your work ☐ Yes ☐ No

5. A reminder about next week's project meeting ☐ Yes ☐ No

EXERCISE 94c   The following is an example of an ineffective e-mail. Critique the e-mail. On the lines provided below, list five or six things that are wrong with this e-mail.

To: Debbie Wilson debbiew@companynet.com

Subject: COPY ATTACHED

Attachment: ecreport.doc

You haven't been in your office, so I'll try an e-mail instead.

I have attached a copy of the employee compensation report for your review. There's some confidential information in the report, so don't share it around with just anyone. The Human Resources Departmetn did a terrible job on it, but I think I was able to save the situation.

I have proofread the report carfully, so you shouldn't find much wrong with it. Get it back to me by Tuesday, or I'll be after you!

---

1. _____

2. _____

3. _____

4. _____

5. _____

6. _____

GOAL: Use cell phones responsibly

_____ NAME

_____ CLASS

In cars, walking along the street, in restaurants, at schools, in libraries, even on hayrides—everywhere, people are talking on their wireless phones. The number of cell phone users is growing. By June 2011, there were 327.6 million wireless subscribers in the United States, an increase of 108 million in just five years.[1]

In certain places and situations, however, cell phones are not acceptable. Some restaurants, businesses, and schools have forbidden their use or have limited their use to certain areas within that space. Many countries have placed restrictions on the use of hand-held cellular phones in moving vehicles. The Federal Aviation Administration has banned in-flight use of wireless devices because they could interfere with the aircraft's communication and navigation systems.

EXERCISE 95a Put a checkmark in the appropriate box beside each statement. Be prepared to explain why you agree or disagree with the statements about cell phone use.

		Agree	Disagree
1.	Everyone should have a cell phone.	☐	☐
2.	People should be able to talk on cell phones in restaurants.	☐	☐
3.	People should be able to talk on cell phones at airports.	☐	☐
4.	People should be able to talk on cell phones while driving.	☐	☐
5.	People should be able to talk on cell phones at school.	☐	☐
6.	Cell phones can endanger lives.	☐	☐
7.	Talking on cell phones in cars is no more distracting than eating or tuning the radio.	☐	☐
8.	People should be able to talk on cell phones in theaters.	☐	☐
9.	People should be able to talk on cell phones on moving airplanes.	☐	☐
10.	Cell phones should be used in cars only for emergencies.	☐	☐
11.	Only emergency professionals need to carry cell phones with them at all times.	☐	☐
12.	Cell phones can save lives.	☐	☐

[1]CTIA The Wireless Association, http://www.ctia.org/advocacy/research/index.cfm/aid/10323, accessed 10/31/11.

EXERCISE 95b   Use a separate sheet of paper to prepare four lists as follows.

List 1: List reasons that cell phones are so popular.

List 2: List examples of situations in which cell phones are useful and can even protect lives.

List 3: List laws that you think should govern cell phone use.

List 4: List guidelines for common sense and responsible cell phone use.

If your instructor requests, be prepared to discuss the answers that you provided in Exercise 95a and the lists that you prepared in Exercise 95b.

GOAL: Search efficiently on the Internet

NAME _____

CLASS _____

You can find useful information on the World Wide Web on almost any topic. A **search engine** is a software program that searches and retrieves information from a database or network, such as the Internet. Search engines such as Google, LookSmart, Bing, Yahoo!, and many others search websites for key words you specify and display the results for you. In seconds, search engines make available to you huge amounts of material that would be difficult, if not impossible, to access in any other way. You can access a selection of search engines by clicking the Search button in your Web browser.

You can also key the URL of a search engine to go directly to its website. A **URL** (Uniform Resource Locator) is the unique address of a website that is accessible on the Internet. URL is usually pronounced by sounding out each letter of the acronym, but in some areas it is pronounced "Earl." A common way to get to a website is to enter the website's URL into your Web browser's address line. For example, the URL for the home page of Omaha's Henry Doorly Zoo is www.omahazoo.com.

Sometimes a search engine is not the best tool to find information on the Web. For example, if you want a general discussion of Impressionism, you may get better results in a resource such as an encyclopedia (http://www.britannica.com).

Here are some tips for searching efficiently on the Internet:

- *Be specific.* This is the most important tip for effective searching. The more specific your key words are, the better your search results are likely to be. Avoid using common words or punctuation.

- To search for an exact phrase, put the phrase in quotation marks. The search engine will retrieve only those words in that order.

- To return to a website that you recently visited but do not remember the address for, locate the website by looking in your Web browser history.

- If you spend a lot of time searching on the Web, or if your search does not yield the results you want, read the search engine's suggestions for advanced searches or use the Help feature.

- If your search does not yield the desired results, try another search engine.

Use a search engine to complete the following tasks.

1a. You need to write a report on the theory that dinosaurs evolved into birds. Key the word *dinosaurs*.

b. Your search yielded many results. You could read through them and find some helpful information. Instead, try to save time by being more specific. Search for *dinosaurs birds*. In the first two pages of search results, how many likely "hits" did you get?

2a. You need a timeline of events in the Civil War. Key *Civil War.*

b. Try narrowing your search by keying *Civil War timeline.* Explore your results. Write down a good URL.

_____

3. Search for information about the book *Shiloh* by Phyllis Reynolds Naylor. Write down the key words that gave you the best results.

_____

4. You want sports news. What would be a good Internet resource?

_____

5. Search for general information about hands-free computing. Print one useful article.

6. The Bengal tiger is one subspecies of tiger. List all the subspecies of tigers in the world. Which are endangered?

_____

7. Use the Internet to find apartments for rent in your area. Print a description of an apartment that interests you.

8. Use your searching skills to locate information on three topics that interest you. Write down a helpful URL for each topic.

Topic   URL

_____

_____

_____

GOAL: Use the Internet for homework

_____ NAME

_____ CLASS

The Internet is a wonderful tool to help you do your homework. At your fingertips are dictionaries, encyclopedias, tutors, museums, laboratories, magazines, newspapers, books, and many other resources that otherwise would not be easily available to you.

Note: Be cautious when using information obtained from the Internet. Use only reputable sources that can be verified as accurate and reliable.

Use the Internet to complete the following tasks. Visit the websites shown and supply the information requested.

1. http://www.m-w.com

   Find the definition of the word *piscine*.

   _____

2. http://www.howstuffworks.com

   Print an article on how batteries work.

3. http://www.webmath.com

   Use this website to solve the following algebra word problem:

   60 is 20 percent of what number? _____

4. http://www.britannica.com

   Print an article on the Great Barrier Reef.

5. http://www.cia.gov/library/publications/the-world-factbook

   What are the main imports and exports of Belarus? Print a map of that country.

   Imports: _____

   Exports: _____

6. http://www.votesmart.org

   Examine the voting record of one of your state senators. Print information showing how the senator voted on two bills that interest you.

7. http://memory.loc.gov

   Print an original historical document on any topic in American history. (For example, a rough draft of the Declaration of Independence or a Civil War image.)

8. http://www.cws.uiuc.edu/workshop/writers

   What is a restrictive clause? _____

   _____

9. http://www.ajr.org

   Print a news report from a newspaper in another state.

10. http://www.schoolwork.org

   Print one piece of information that can help you with your homework this week.

GOAL: Use the Internet at work

_____ NAME

_____ CLASS

Using the Internet can save you time in completing common workplace tasks and can save your company money. For example, you can now download federal tax forms and publications from the Internal Revenue Service website. Compare the few minutes it takes to do this to the amount of time it takes to drive to a government office and get the forms. Buying office products, purchasing stamps from the U.S. Postal Service, holding meetings online, doing research, and taking online courses are just a few examples of ways in which people use the Internet at work.

Use the Internet to complete the following tasks.

1. Write down the street address of a nearby location where you can get a passport, and write down the amount of time it will take to get a passport. Print information on the items you need to provide to get a first-time adult passport book.

   _____

   _____

2. You work for a city with a growing number of homeless people. Go to the U.S. Department of Housing and Urban Development website at http://www.hud.gov. Find a grant for which you can apply to help the homeless. Print the specifications.

3. Your company is going to do some remodeling and needs to contact a local electric company to obtain bids for electrical work. Go to www.yellowpages.com. Search for an electric company in your area and write down the company's name, address, and telephone number.

   _____

   _____

4. You need some good accounting software. Find it through an online vendor. List the vendor website address, the software, the price, and how long it will take to ship the software.

   _____

   _____

5. You are attending a conference at the Baltimore Convention Center. Get the convention center's street address, telephone and fax numbers, and e-mail address (for general information).

_____

_____

6. Print flight and rate information for a round-trip coach flight to arrive in Baltimore (Baltimore-Washington International Airport) on August 2nd and to leave on August 6th. If you live near Baltimore, pretend that you live in another city and state.

7. Find a hotel in Baltimore. Note the street address, telephone number, fax number (if available), e-mail address (if available), and single-room rate for August 2–5. Print information on the hotel's facilities.

_____

_____

8. Print directions and maps for driving from the Baltimore-Washington International Airport to your hotel and from your hotel to the Baltimore Convention Center (unless the convention center is within walking distance of your hotel).

9. Write down a rental car company in Baltimore, type of car, and rate (airport pick up and drop off).

_____

_____

10. Print information about two tourist attractions that you may want to visit while in Baltimore.

GOAL: Explore online shopping

NAME _____

CLASS _____

How does buying something online actually work? How does it compare with going to a store to shop? How do you pay for items? Is shopping online fun? These are some of the questions that you will find answers for in this exercise.

EXERCISE 99a   Follow the steps below and supply the information requested.

1. Go to the Amazon website at http://www.amazon.com.

2. List two types of products that you can buy at Amazon.

   a. _____   b. _____

3. List two types of customer service that you can access from this home page.

   a. _____   b. _____

4. Use the Help feature to find out how you can pay for your purchase. List two methods of payment, then return to the Amazon home page.

   a. _____   b. _____

5. A friend's birthday is next week and their favorite author is John McPhee. In the Search box, key *McPhee, John* and click *Go* or press ENTER.

6. McPhee has written many books. How many books in hardcover format does Amazon carry?

   _____

7. Click the link that will let you see all the book results of your John McPhee search.

8. Click the link to the paperback edition of *Basin and Range*.

9. List two pieces of information about this book that you can get on this page.

   a. _____   b. _____

10. Scroll up and click the link to add *Basin and Range* to your Cart.

11. You would also like to order a DVD. Search for the DVD of *A Man for All Seasons* starring Paul Scofield and Wendy Hiller. Add the DVD to your Cart.

12. What is the subtotal of your order? _____

13. Remove both items from your Cart and exit the Amazon website.

EXERCISE 99b   When you have completed Exercise 99a, answer the following questions.

1. What factors should you consider when deciding whether it is more cost effective to shop online or go to a store?

   _____

   _____

   _____

   _____

   _____

2. Did the Amazon site seem well organized and easy to navigate? Why or why not?

   _____

   _____

   _____

   _____

   _____

3. Did you enjoy shopping online, or would you prefer going to a store? Give your reasons.

   _____

   _____

   _____

   _____

   _____

GOAL: Go on an Internet scavenger hunt

_____ NAME

_____ CLASS

The Internet makes it possible for you to get more information faster and easier than ever before. With search engines and effective searching skills, you can find information on almost any topic for personal or professional use.

Use the Internet to complete the following tasks.

1. Print today's weather forecast for Phoenix, Arizona.

2. Find the definition of the word _crepitate_.

   _____

3. You want to send flowers to your grandmother for her birthday. She lives in another state. You can spend between $25 and $60. Write down the name of a florist, a description of the floral arrangement you chose, and the price.

   _____

   _____

4. You are writing an article on nutrition. Print information about the United States Department of Agriculture's Food Guide Pyramid.

5. You will be in New York City next month and plan to visit the Metropolitan Museum of Art. Write down the hours that the museum's main building is open, the student general admission price, and directions for getting to the museum by bus from Penn Station. Are you allowed to make charcoal sketches of the museum's works of art?

   _____

   _____

   _____

   _____

6. Use the following ticker symbols to find the current price per share for each stock:

   PEP _____   WEN _____   SNE _____   PSUN _____

7. What is the current population of the world? _____

8. You are giving an oral report on Rachel Carson. Print a biographical article about her.

9. Who is the Prime Minister of Canada? _____

10. Go to the *Los Angeles Times* website and print a front-page article.

11. Find a site that gives product reviews for digital cameras. Print a review.

12. Go to the website for a college that interests you. Write down the name of the college and the tuition for one year. Note whether you can apply for admission online. Print the admission requirements.

_____

_____

If time permits and your instructor requests, compare URLs from the Internet scavenger hunt with classmates. At what different sites did others find their answers?

Well done! You have completed the exercises for Unit 6. Before your instructor administers the Unit 6 Test, review the exercises in this unit. Follow your instructor's directions for completing the study of *Business Skills Exercises*.

Go Digital!

For additional activities visit www.cengage.com/school/bse

REFERENCE SOURCES

CONTENTS

The airport codes shown below are alphabetized by the code letters. They are not alphabetized by city names. Sometimes airport codes and city names do not start with the same letter. For example, the airport code for the New Orleans, LA, airport is MSY. You may have to read the list carefully to find the airport you are looking for.

AIRPORT CODES

Code	City, State	Code	City, State
ABE	Allentown, PA	LAS	Las Vegas, NV
ABQ	Albuquerque, NM	LAX	Los Angeles, CA
AMA	Amarillo, TX	LBB	Lubbock, TX
ANC	Anchorage, AK	LEX	Lexington, KY
ATL	Atlanta, GA	LNK	Lincoln, NE
AUS	Austin, TX	MCI	Kansas City, MO
BDL	Hartford, CT	MCO	Orlando, FL
BHM	Birmingham, AL	MEM	Memphis, TN
BNA	Nashville, TN	MGM	Montgomery, AL
BOS	Boston, MA	MIA	Miami, FL
BTR	Baton Rouge, LA	MOB	Mobile, AL
BUF	Buffalo, NY	MSY	New Orleans, LA
CAE	Columbia, SC	OMA	Omaha, NE
CVG	Cincinnati, OH	ONT	Ontario, CA
DCA	Washington, DC	ORD	Chicago, IL
DEN	Denver, CO	PDX	Portland, OR
DFW	Dallas/Fort Worth, TX	PHX	Phoenix, AZ
DSM	Des Moines, IA	RDU	Raleigh/Durham, NC
DTW	Detroit, MI	ROC	Rochester, NY
ELP	El Paso, TX	SAN	San Diego, CA
EWR	Newark, NJ	SAT	San Antonio, TX
FAI	Fairbanks, AK	SEA	Seattle/Tacoma, WA
FLL	Ft. Lauderdale, FL	SFO	San Francisco, CA
FOE	Topeka, KS	SHV	Shreveport, LA
HNL	Honolulu, HI	SLC	Salt Lake City, UT
IAH	Houston, TX	TPA	Tampa, FL
ICT	Wichita, KS	TUL	Tulsa, OK
IND	Indianapolis, IN	TUS	Tucson, AZ
JAN	Jackson, MS	TYS	Knoxville, TN
JFK	New York, NY	YKM	Yakima, WA

	FLIGHT INFORMATION						
Flight Number	Cities Served	Air Miles	Flying Time	Stops	Trip Time	Aircraft Used
4206	FLL-HNL	5,323	12:34	2	15:42	757
3100	ATL-ANC	4,133	10:11	1	11:18	A319
726	OMA-FAI	3,679	9:38	2	12:11	737
258	YKM-MIA	3,140	7:30	2	9:44	A320
132	BOS-SFO	3,082	7:13	1	8:13	717
281	SEA-DFW	2,527	6:14	1	8:44	737
185	JFK-LAX	2,459	5:53	0	5:53	A319
4624	LAS-ABE	2,170	5:55	2	10:20	757
778	MGM-TUS	1,699	5:24	2	8:35	737
505	PHX-DTW	1,678	3:37	0	3:37	A319
242	AUS-DEN	775	2:10	0	2:10	MD80
290	ORD-LAS	1,519	3:48	0	3:48	A320
1110	ABQ-SEA	1,357	4:09	1	6:17	757
304	EWR-FLL	1,338	4:22	2	6:07	737
355	DSM-IAH	1,327	4:46	2	7:23	MD80
190	MCO-BDL	1,257	3:42	1	4:27	A320
435	LBB-LEX	1,068	3:15	1	4:24	RJ
825	MCI-ELP	1,017	3:27	1	4:57	RJ
636	IND-YKM	2,161	6:24	2	8:44	EMB145
704	TYS-BNA	980	3:43	1	4:52	RJ
592	LNK-OMA	889	3:00	1	3:50	RJ
166	TPA-MSY	876	2:56	1	6:45	737
333	MEM-DCA	873	2:56	1	3:32	717
555	JAN-BTR	770	2:46	1	4:03	EMB145
901	RDU-CAE	631	2:32	1	3:16	RJ
625	SHV-MOB	630	2:27	1	3:16	EMB145
411	SLC-PDX	630	1:40	0	1:40	737
895	ICT-TUL	569	2:18	1	3:40	MD80
972	BUF-ROC	448	2:10	1	2:30	1900
642	SAN-ONT	167	1:19	1	2:00	EMB120

CODES FOR AIRCRAFT USED

A319	Airbus A319
A320	Airbus A320
1900	Beechcraft 1900
717	Boeing 717
737	Boeing 737
757	Boeing 757
RJ	Canadair Regional Jet
EMB120	Embraer EMB-120
EMB145	Embraer EMB-145
MD80	McDonnell Douglas MD80

FLYING TIME

12:34 = 12 hours, 34 minutes
Flying time is actual time in the air.

TRIP TIME

Trip time includes time spent in airport stopovers.

AIRPORT EXPRESS SHUTTLE SCHEDULE

Newport Outrigger	Baymont Hotel	Pacific Palms	Lemon Tree Inn	Arrive Airport
0450A	0500A	0505A	0510A	0555A
0520A	0530A	0535A	0540A	0625A
0550A	0600A	0605A	0610A	0655A
0620A	0630A	0635A	0640A	0725A
0650A	0700A	0705A	0710A	0755A
0720A	0730A	0735A	0740A	0825A
0750A	0800A	0805A	0810A	0855A
0820A	0830A	0835A	0840A	0925A
0850A	0900A	0905A	0910A	0955A
0920A	0930A	0935A	0940A	1025A
0950A	1000A	1005A	1010A	1055A
1020A	1030A	1035A	1040A	1125A
1050A	1100A	1105A	1110A	1155A
1120A	1130A	1135A	1140A	1225P
1150A	1200P	1205P	1210P	1255P
1220P	1230P	1235P	1240P	0125P
1250P	0100P	0105P	0110P	0155P
0120P	0130P	0135P	0140P	0225P

Newport Outrigger	Baymont Hotel	Pacific Palms	Lemon Tree Inn	Arrive Airport
0150P	0200P	0205P	0210P	0255P
0220P	0230P	0235P	0240P	0325P
0250P	0300P	0305P	0310P	0355P
0320P	0330P	0335P	0340P	0425P
0350P	0400P	0405P	0410P	0455P
0420P	0430P	0435P	0440P	0525P
0450P	0500P	0505P	0510P	0555P
0520P	0530P	0535P	0540P	0625P
0550P	0600P	0605P	0610P	0655P
0620P	0630P	0635P	0640P	0725P
0650P	0700P	0705P	0710P	0755P
0720P	0730P	0735P	0740P	0825P
0750P	0800P	0805P	0810P	0855P
0820P	0830P	0835P	0840P	0925P
0850P	0900P	0905P	0910P	0955P
0920P	0930P	0935P	0940P	1025P
0950P	1000P	1005P	1010P	1055P

All schedules are subject to change due to delays caused by traffic and/or weather conditions.

GRAMMAR, STYLE, AND PUNCTUATION

Baugh, L. Sue. *Essentials of English Grammar*. 3rd Ed. New York: McGraw-Hill Companies, 2005.

Good, C. Edward. *A Grammar Book for You and I... Oops, Me!* Virginia: Capital Books, Inc., 2002.

Elliott, Rebecca, Ph.D. *Painless Grammar*. 3rd Ed. New York: Barron's Educational Series, 2011.

Garner, Bryan A. *Garner's Modern American Usage*. 3rd Ed. New York: Oxford University Press, Inc., 2009.

Loberger Gordon, Ph.D., and Kate Shoup. *Webster's New World English Grammar Handbook*. 2nd Ed. New Jersey: Wiley Publishing, Inc., 2009.

Stilman, Anne. *Grammatically Correct*. 2nd Ed. Ohio: Writer's Digest Books, an imprint of F+W Media, Inc., 2010.

Truss, Lynne. *Eats, Shoots & Leaves: The Zero Tolerance Approach to Punctuation*. New York: Gotham Books, a division of Penguin Group, Inc., 2008.

JOB SEARCH

Beshara, Tony. *The Job Search Solution*. New York: AMACOM, a division of American Management Association, 2006.

Farr, Michael. *100 Fastest-Growing Careers*. Indiana: JIST Works, Inc., an imprint of JIST Publishing, 2010.

Nemko, Marty, Ph.D. *Cool Careers for Dummies*. 3rd Ed. New Jersey: Wiley Publishing, Inc., 2007.

Porot, Daniel, and Frances Bolles Haynes. *101 Toughest Interview Questions... and Answers that Win the Job!* New York: Ten Speed Press, an imprint of the Crown Publishing Group, 2009.

Powers, Dr. Paul. *Winning Job Interviews*. New Jersey: Career Press, Inc., 2010.

Taylor, Jeff, with Doug Hardy. *Monster Careers: How to Land the Job of Your Life*. New York: Penguin Books, 2004.

www.career.com

www.monster.com

PERSONAL AND PROFESSIONAL DEVELOPMENT

Brooks, Robert, Ph.D., and Sam Goldstein, Ph.D. *The Power of Resilience: Achieving Balance, Confidence, and Personal Strength in Your Life*. New York: McGraw-Hill Companies, 2004.

Canfield, Jack, with Janet Switzer. *The Success Principles*. New York: HarperCollins Publishers, 2005.

Chandler, Steve. *Reinventing Yourself*. New Jersey: Career Press, Inc., 2005.

Covey, Stephen R. *The 7 Habits of Highly Effective People: Powerful Lessons in Personal Change*. New York: Free Press, a division of Simon & Schuster, Inc., 2004.

Cushnir, Raphael. *The One Thing Holding You Back*. New York: HarperOne, a trademark of HarperCollins Publishers, 2008.

DuPont, Robert L., M.D., Elizabeth DuPont Spencer, M.S.W., and Caroline M. DuPont, M.D. *The Anxiety Cure*. New Jersey: John Wiley & Sons, Inc., 2003.

www.umano.com

	LONG-DISTANCE CALLS REGISTER			Month of ___April___,		20 --

Date	Time	O/I*	Caller	Person Called	City Called	Number
4-1	8:45	O	Gwynne Askew	Toshi Kato	Detroit, MI	313-555-0177
4-1	3:00	O	Eula Garber	Phyllis Frazer	Hyattsville, MD	240-555-0141
4-4	2:36	O	Danny Lavant	Annette Dano	Omaha, NE	402-555-0157
4-8	10:04	I	Colleen Scott	Tim Taylor	Duluth, MN	218-555-0181
4-8	10:40	O	Geneva Farrell	Gary Idens	Bend, OR	541-555-0186
4-10	9:06	O	Dennis Upshaw	Nolan Payne	Smyrna, GA	678-555-0174
4-11	10:30	O	Li-ming Chang	Harley Mason	Loveland, CO	970-555-0131
4-11	3:58	O	Lachanda Potts	Ester Salas	Dayton, OH	937-555-0125
4-15	2:45	O	Antonio Reese	Rosa Vasquez	Abilene, TX	325-555-0100
4-15	3:50	I	Willie Turkel	Clarke Ashley	White Plains, NY	914-555-0144
4-18	9:00	O	Nell Free	Rufus Vestal	Camden, AL	334-555-0110
4-18	11:16	O	Zoe Ann Elkins	Sherry Ruhlman	Mobile, AL	251-555-0119
4-18	1:45	O	Margo Barma	Eugene New	Dover, DE	302-555-0137
4-19	9:37	O	Juanita Ham	Goro Akama	Sumter, SC	803-555-0127
4-19	1:17	O	Lillie Sue Olden	Butch Medina	Monroe, LA	318-555-0189
4-22	10:14	O	Randall Hattaway	Calvin Ivey	Hilo, HI	808-555-0113
4-23	11:00	O	Leroy Norton	Eduardo Lamas	West Chester, PA	610-555-0199
4-23	11:37	O	Rebekah Caffon	Carlos Ruiz	Nashua, NH	603-555-0161
4-24	10:16	O	Lamar Russ	Doreen Keepers	Dunlap, IN	574-555-0148
4-25	9:04	O	Kevin Huang	Betty Dilbeck	Columbus, OH	614-555-0166
4-25	2:47	I	Howard Epps	Elise Mays	Anaheim, CA	714-555-0135
4-26	11:12	O	Max Logan	Saul Klein	St. Louis, MO	314-555-0104
4-30	9:23	O	Lu-yin Wu	Wylene Jenson	Camden, NJ	856-555-0193
4-30	12:10	O	Norma Briggs	Grace Speer	Joliet, IL	815-555-0128

*O = Outgoing; I = Incoming Collect

SINGLE Persons–MONTHLY Payroll Period

If the wages are–		And the number of withholding allowances claimed is–						
At least	But less than	0	1	2	3	4	5	6
		the amount of income tax to be withheld is–						
$0	$220	$0	$0	$0	$0	$0	$0	$0
220	230	5	0	0	0	0	0	0
680	720	53	22	0	0	0	0	0
720	760	57	26	0	0	0	0	0
760	800	61	30	0	0	0	0	0
800	840	65	34	3	0	0	0	0
840	880	69	38	7	0	0	0	0
880	920	73	42	11	0	0	0	0
920	960	79	46	15	0	0	0	0
960	1,000	85	50	19	0	0	0	0
1,000	1,040	91	54	23	0	0	0	0
1,040	1,080	97	58	27	0	0	0	0
1,080	1,120	103	62	31	0	0	0	0
1,120	1,160	109	66	35	4	0	0	0
1,160	1,200	115	70	39	8	0	0	0
1,200	1,240	121	75	43	12	0	0	0
1,240	1,280	127	81	47	16	0	0	0

MARRIED Persons–MONTHLY Payroll Period

If the wages are–		And the number of withholding allowances claimed is–						
At least	But less than	0	1	2	3	4	5	6
		the amount of income tax to be withheld is–						
$0	$680	$0	$0	$0	$0	$0	$0	$0
680	720	4	0	0	0	0	0	0
720	760	8	0	0	0	0	0	0
1,440	1,480	80	49	19	0	0	0	0
1,480	1,520	84	53	23	0	0	0	0
1,520	1,560	88	57	27	0	0	0	0
1,560	1,600	92	61	31	0	0	0	0
1,600	1,640	96	65	35	4	0	0	0
1,640	1,680	100	69	39	8	0	0	0
1,680	1,720	104	73	43	12	0	0	0
1,720	1,760	108	77	47	16	0	0	0
1,760	1,800	112	81	51	20	0	0	0
1,800	1,840	116	85	55	24	0	0	0
1,840	1,880	120	89	59	28	0	0	0
1,880	1,920	124	93	63	32	1	0	0
1,920	1,960	128	97	67	36	5	0	0
1,960	2,000	132	101	71	40	9	0	0
2,000	2,040	136	105	75	44	13	0	0
2,040	2,080	140	109	79	48	17	0	0
2,080	2,120	145	113	83	52	21	0	0
2,120	2,160	151	117	87	56	25	0	0
2,160	2,200	157	121	91	60	29	0	0
2,200	2,240	163	125	95	64	33	2	0

Source: Publication 15 (Circular E), Employer's Tax Guide for use in 2011; December 29, 2010

SINGLE Persons–WEEKLY Payroll Period

If the wages are–		And the number of withholding allowances claimed is–						
At least	But less than	0	1	2	3	4	5	6
		the amount of income tax to be withheld is–						
$0	$55	$0	$0	$0	$0	$0	$0	$0
55	60	2	0	0	0	0	0	0
60	65	2	0	0	0	0	0	0
65	70	3	0	0	0	0	0	0
175	180	14	7	0	0	0	0	0
180	185	14	7	0	0	0	0	0
185	190	15	8	0	0	0	0	0
190	195	15	8	1	0	0	0	0
195	200	16	9	1	0	0	0	0
200	210	17	9	2	0	0	0	0
210	220	18	10	3	0	0	0	0
220	230	20	11	4	0	0	0	0
230	240	21	12	5	0	0	0	0
240	250	23	13	6	0	0	0	0
250	260	24	14	7	0	0	0	0
260	270	26	15	8	1	0	0	0
270	280	27	16	9	2	0	0	0
280	290	29	18	10	3	0	0	0
290	300	30	19	11	4	0	0	0

MARRIED Persons–WEEKLY Payroll Period

If the wages are–		And the number of withholding allowances claimed is–						
At least	But less than	0	1	2	3	4	5	6
		the amount of income tax to be withheld is–						
$0	$155	$0	$0	$0	$0	$0	$0	$0
155	160	1	0	0	0	0	0	0
160	165	1	0	0	0	0	0	0
240	250	9	2	0	0	0	0	0
250	260	10	3	0	0	0	0	0
260	270	11	4	0	0	0	0	0
270	280	12	5	0	0	0	0	0
280	290	13	6	0	0	0	0	0
290	300	14	7	0	0	0	0	0
300	310	15	8	1	0	0	0	0
310	320	16	9	2	0	0	0	0
320	330	17	10	3	0	0	0	0
330	340	18	11	4	0	0	0	0
340	350	19	12	5	0	0	0	0
350	360	20	13	6	0	0	0	0
360	370	21	14	7	0	0	0	0
370	380	22	15	8	1	0	0	0
380	390	23	16	9	2	0	0	0
390	400	24	17	10	3	0	0	0
400	410	25	18	11	4	0	0	0
410	420	26	19	12	5	0	0	0
420	430	27	20	13	6	0	0	0
430	440	28	21	14	7	0	0	0

Source: Publication 15 (Circular E), Employer's Tax Guide for use in 2011; December 29, 2010

6.5% SALES TAX SCHEDULE 6.5%

Amount of Sale	Tax	Amount of Sale	Tax	Amount of Sale	Tax
.01— .10	.00	7.62— 7.76	.50	15.31—15.46	1.00
.11— .20	.01	7.77— 7.92	.51	15.47—15.61	1.01
.21— .35	.02	7.93— 8.07	.52	15.62—15.76	1.02
.36— .51	.03	8.08— 8.23	.53	15.77—15.92	1.03
.52— .67	.04	8.24— 8.38	.54	15.93—16.07	1.04
.68— .83	.05	8.39— 8.53	.55	16.08—16.23	1.05
.84— .99	.06	8.54— 8.69	.56	16.24—16.38	1.06
1.00— 1.15	.07	8.70— 8.84	.57	16.39—16.53	1.07
1.16— 1.30	.08	8.85— 8.99	.58	16.54—16.69	1.08
1.31— 1.46	.09	9.00— 9.15	.59	16.70—16.84	1.09
1.47— 1.61	.10	9.16— 9.30	.60	16.85—16.99	1.10
1.62— 1.76	.11	9.31— 9.46	.61	17.00—17.15	1.11
1.77— 1.92	.12	9.47— 9.61	.62	17.16—17.30	1.12
1.93— 2.07	.13	9.62— 9.76	.63	17.31—17.46	1.13
2.08— 2.23	.14	9.77— 9.92	.64	17.47—17.61	1.14
2.24— 2.38	.15	9.93—10.07	.65	17.62—17.76	1.15
2.39— 2.53	.16	10.08—10.23	.66	17.77—17.92	1.16
2.54— 2.69	.17	10.24—10.38	.67	17.93—18.07	1.17
2.70— 2.84	.18	10.39—10.53	.68	18.08—18.23	1.18
2.85— 2.99	.19	10.54—10.69	.69	18.24—18.38	1.19
3.00— 3.15	.20	10.70—10.84	.70	18.39—18.53	1.20
3.16— 3.30	.21	10.85—10.99	.71	18.54—18.69	1.21
3.31— 3.46	.22	11.00—11.15	.72	18.70—18.84	1.22
3.47— 3.61	.23	11.16—11.30	.73	18.85—18.99	1.23
3.62— 3.76	.24	11.31—11.46	.74	19.00—19.15	1.24
3.77— 3.92	.25	11.47—11.61	.75	19.16—19.30	1.25
3.93— 4.07	.26	11.62—11.76	.76	19.31—19.46	1.26
4.08— 4.23	.27	11.77—11.92	.77	19.47—19.61	1.27
4.24— 4.38	.28	11.93—12.07	.78	19.62—19.76	1.28
4.39— 4.53	.29	12.08—12.23	.79	19.77—19.92	1.29
4.54— 4.69	.30	12.24—12.38	.80	19.93—20.07	1.30
4.70— 4.84	.31	12.39—12.53	.81	20.08—20.23	1.31
4.85— 4.99	.32	12.54—12.69	.82	20.24—20.38	1.32
5.00— 5.15	.33	12.70—12.84	.83	20.39—20.53	1.33
5.16— 5.30	.34	12.85—12.99	.84	20.54—20.69	1.34
5.31— 5.46	.35	13.00—13.15	.85	20.70—20.84	1.35
5.47— 5.61	.36	13.16—13.30	.86	20.85—20.99	1.36
5.62— 5.76	.37	13.31—13.46	.87	21.00—21.15	1.37
5.77— 5.92	.38	13.47—13.61	.88	21.16—21.30	1.38
5.93— 6.07	.39	13.62—13.76	.89	21.31—21.46	1.39
6.08— 6.23	.40	13.77—13.92	.90	21.47—21.61	1.40
6.24— 6.38	.41	13.93—14.07	.91	21.62—21.76	1.41
6.39— 6.53	.42	14.08—14.23	.92	21.77—21.92	1.42
6.54— 6.69	.43	14.24—14.38	.93	21.93—22.07	1.43
6.70— 6.84	.44	14.39—14.53	.94	22.08—22.23	1.44
6.85— 6.99	.45	14.54—14.69	.95	22.24—22.38	1.45
7.00— 7.15	.46	14.70—14.84	.96	22.39—22.53	1.46
7.16— 7.30	.47	14.85—14.99	.97	22.54—22.69	1.47
7.31— 7.46	.48	15.00—15.15	.98	22.70—22.84	1.48
7.47— 7.61	.49	15.16—15.30	.99	22.85—22.99	1.49

7% SALES TAX SCHEDULE 7%

Amount of Sale	Tax	Amount of Sale	Tax	Amount of Sale	Tax
.01— .07	.00	9.22— 9.35	.65	18.50—18.64	1.30
.08— .21	.01	9.36— 9.49	.66	18.65—18.78	1.31
.22— .35	.02	9.50— 9.64	.67	18.79—18.92	1.32
.36— .49	.03	9.65— 9.78	.68	18.93—19.07	1.33
.50— .64	.04	9.79— 9.92	.69	19.08—19.21	1.34
.65— .78	.05	9.93—10.07	.70	19.22—19.35	1.35
.79— .92	.06	10.08—10.21	.71	19.36—19.49	1.36
.93—1.07	.07	10.22—10.35	.72	19.50—19.64	1.37
1.08—1.21	.08	10.36—10.49	.73	19.65—19.78	1.38
1.22—1.35	.09	10.50—10.64	.74	19.79—19.92	1.39
1.36—1.49	.10	10.65—10.78	.75	19.93—20.07	1.40
1.50—1.64	.11	10.79—10.92	.76	20.08—20.21	1.41
1.65—1.78	.12	10.93—11.07	.77	20.22—20.35	1.42
1.79—1.92	.13	11.08—11.21	.78	20.36—20.49	1.43
1.93—2.07	.14	11.22—11.35	.79	20.50—20.64	1.44
2.08—2.21	.15	11.36—11.49	.80	20.65—20.78	1.45
2.22—2.35	.16	11.50—11.64	.81	20.79—20.92	1.46
2.36—2.49	.17	11.65—11.78	.82	20.93—21.07	1.47
2.50—2.64	.18	11.79—11.92	.83	21.08—21.21	1.48
2.65—2.78	.19	11.93—12.07	.84	21.22—21.35	1.49
2.79—2.92	.20	12.08—12.21	.85	21.36—21.49	1.50
2.93—3.07	.21	12.22—12.35	.86	21.50—21.64	1.51
3.08—3.21	.22	12.36—12.49	.87	21.65—21.78	1.52
3.22—3.35	.23	12.50—12.64	.88	21.79—21.92	1.53
3.36—3.49	.24	12.65—12.78	.89	21.93—22.07	1.54
3.50—3.64	.25	12.79—12.92	.90	22.08—22.21	1.55
3.65—3.78	.26	12.93—13.07	.91	22.22—22.35	1.56
3.79—3.92	.27	13.08—13.21	.92	22.36—22.49	1.57
3.93—4.07	.28	13.22—13.35	.93	22.50—22.64	1.58
4.08—4.21	.29	13.36—13.49	.94	22.65—22.78	1.59
4.22—4.35	.30	13.50—13.64	.95	22.79—22.92	1.60
4.36—4.49	.31	13.65—13.78	.96	22.93—23.07	1.61
4.50—4.64	.32	13.79—13.92	.97	23.08—23.21	1.62
4.65—4.78	.33	13.93—14.07	.98	23.22—23.35	1.63
4.79—4.92	.34	14.08—14.21	.99	23.36—23.49	1.64
4.93—5.07	.35	14.22—14.35	1.00	23.50—23.64	1.65
5.08—5.21	.36	14.36—14.49	1.01	23.65—23.78	1.66
5.22—5.35	.37	14.50—14.64	1.02	23.79—23.92	1.67
5.36—5.49	.38	14.65—14.78	1.03	23.93—24.07	1.68
5.50—5.64	.39	14.79—14.92	1.04	24.08—24.21	1.69
5.65—5.78	.40	14.93—15.07	1.05	24.22—24.35	1.70
5.79—5.92	.41	15.08—15.21	1.06	24.36—24.49	1.71
5.93—6.07	.42	15.22—15.35	1.07	24.50—24.64	1.72
6.08—6.21	.43	15.36—15.49	1.08	24.65—24.78	1:73
6.22—6.35	.44	15.50—15.64	1.09	24.79—24.92	1.74
6.36—6.49	.45	15.65—15.78	1.10	24.93—25.07	1.75
6.50—6.64	.46	15.79—15.92	1.11	25.08—25.21	1.76
6.65—6.78	.47	15.93—16.07	1.12	25.22—25.35	1.77
6.79—6.92	.48	16.08—16.21	1.13	25.36—25.49	1.78
6.93—7.07	.49	16.22—16.35	1.14	25.50—25.64	1.79
7.08—7.21	.50	16.36—16.49	1.15	25.65—25.78	1.80
7.22—7.35	.51	16.50—16.64	1.16	25.79—25.92	1.81
7.36—7.49	.52	16.65—16.78	1.17	25.93—26.07	1.82
7.50—7.64	.53	16.79—16.92	1.18	26.08—26.21	1.83
7.65—7.78	.54	16.93—17.07	1.19	26.22—26.35	1.84
7.79—7.92	.55	17.08—17.21	1.20	26.36—26.49	1.85
7.93—8.07	.56	17.22—17.35	1.21	26.50—26.64	1.86
8.08—8.21	.57	17.36—17.49	1.22	26.65—26.78	1.87
8.22—8.35	.58	17.50—17.64	1.23	26.79—26.92	1.88
8.36—8.49	.59	17.65—17.78	1.24	26.93—27.07	1.89
8.50—8.64	.60	17.79—17.92	1.25	27.08—27.21	1.90
8.65—8.78	.61	17.93—18.07	1.26	27.22—27.35	1.91
8.79—8.92	.62	18.08—18.21	1.27	27.36—27.49	1.92
8.93—9.07	.63	18.22—18.35	1.28	27.50—27.64	1.93
9.08—9.21	.64	18.36—18.49	1.29	27.65—27.78	1.94

7¾% SALES TAX COLLECTION SCHEDULE 7¾%

TO	TAX	TO	TAX	TO	TAX	TO	TAX	TO	TAX
0.06	0.00	8.32	0.64	16.58	1.28	24.83	1.92	33.09	2.56
0.19	0.01	8.45	0.65	16.70	1.29	24.96	1.93	33.22	2.57
0.32	0.02	8.58	0.66	16.83	1.30	25.09	1.94	33.35	2.58
0.45	0.03	8.70	0.67	16.96	1.31	25.22	1.95	33.48	2.59
0.58	0.04	8.83	0.68	17.09	1.32	25.35	1.96	33.61	2.60
0.70	0.05	8.96	0.69	17.22	1.33	25.48	1.97	33.74	2.61
0.83	0.06	9.09	0.70	17.35	1.34	25.61	1.98	33.87	2.62
0.96	0.07	9.22	0.71	17.48	1.35	25.74	1.99	33.99	2.63
1.09	0.08	9.35	0.72	17.61	1.36	25.87	2.00	34.12	2.64
1.22	0.09	9.48	0.73	17.74	1.37	25.99	2.01	34.25	2.65
1.35	0.10	9.61	0.74	17.87	1.38	26.12	2.02	34.38	2.66
1.48	0.11	9.74	0.75	17.99	1.39	26.25	2.03	34.51	2.67
1.61	0.12	9.87	0.76	18.12	1.40	26.38	2.04	34.64	2.68
1.74	0.13	9.99	0.77	18.25	1.41	26.51	2.05	34.77	2.69
1.87	0.14	10.12	0.78	18.38	1.42	26.64	2.06	34.90	2.70
1.99	0.15	10.25	0.79	18.51	1.43	26.77	2.07	35.03	2.71
2.12	0.16	10.38	0.80	18.64	1.44	26.90	2.08	35.16	2.72
2.25	0.17	10.51	0.81	18.77	1.45	27.03	2.09	35.29	2.73
2.38	0.18	10.64	0.82	18.90	1.46	27.16	2.10	35.41	2.74
2.51	0.19	10.77	0.83	19.03	1.47	27.29	2.11	35.54	2.75
2.64	0.20	10.90	0.84	19.16	1.48	27.41	2.12	35.67	2.76
2.77	0.21	11.03	0.85	19.29	1.49	27.54	2.13	35.80	2.77
2.90	0.22	11.16	0.86	19.41	1.50	27.67	2.14	35.93	2.78
3.03	0.23	11.29	0.87	19.54	1.51	27.80	2.15	36.06	2.79
3.16	0.24	11.41	0.88	19.67	1.52	27.93	2.16	36.19	2.80
3.29	0.25	11.54	0.89	19.80	1.53	28.06	2.17	36.32	2.81
3.41	0.26	11.67	0.90	19.93	1.54	28.19	2.18	36.45	2.82
3.54	0.27	11.80	0.91	20.06	1.55	28.32	2.19	36.58	2.83
3.67	0.28	11.93	0.92	20.19	1.56	28.45	2.20	36.70	2.84
3.80	0.29	12.06	0.93	20.32	1.57	28.58	2.21	36.83	2.85
3.93	0.30	12.19	0.94	20.45	1.58	28.70	2.22	36.96	2.86
4.06	0.31	12.32	0.95	20.58	1.59	28.83	2.23	37.09	2.87
4.19	0.32	12.45	0.96	20.70	1.60	28.96	2.24	37.22	2.88
4.32	0.33	12.58	0.97	20.83	1.61	29.09	2.25	37.35	2.89
4.45	0.34	12.70	0.98	20.96	1.62	29.22	2.26	37.48	2.90
4.58	0.35	12.83	0.99	21.09	1.63	29.35	2.27	37.61	2.91
4.70	0.36	12.96	1.00	21.22	1.64	29.48	2.28	37.74	2.92
4.83	0.37	13.09	1.01	21.35	1.65	29.61	2.29	37.87	2.93
4.96	0.38	13.22	1.02	21.48	1.66	29.74	2.30	37.99	2.94
5.09	0.39	13.35	1.03	21.61	1.67	29.87	2.31	38.12	2.95
5.22	0.40	13.48	1.04	21.74	1.68	29.99	2.32	38.25	2.96
5.35	0.41	13.61	1.05	21.87	1.69	30.12	2.33	38.38	2.97
5.48	0.42	13.74	1.06	21.99	1.70	30.25	2.34	38.51	2.98
5.61	0.43	13.87	1.07	22.12	1.71	30.38	2.35	38.64	2.99
5.74	0.44	13.99	1.08	22.25	1.72	30.51	2.36	38.77	3.00
5.87	0.45	14.12	1.09	22.38	1.73	30.64	2.37	38.90	3.01
5.99	0.46	14.25	1.10	22.51	1.74	30.77	2.38	39.03	3.02
6.12	0.47	14.38	1.11	22.64	1.75	30.90	2.39	39.16	3.03
6.25	0.48	14.51	1.12	22.77	1.76	31.03	2.40	39.29	3.04
6.38	0.49	14.64	1.13	22.90	1.77	31.16	2.41	39.41	3.05
6.51	0.50	14.77	1.14	23.03	1.78	31.29	2.42	39.54	3.06
6.64	0.51	14.90	1.15	23.16	1.79	31.41	2.43	39.67	3.07
6.77	0.52	15.03	1.16	23.29	1.80	31.54	2.44	39.80	3.08
6.90	0.53	15.16	1.17	23.41	1.81	31.67	2.45	39.93	3.09
7.03	0.54	15.29	1.18	23.54	1.82	31.80	2.46	40.06	3.10
7.16	0.55	15.41	1.19	23.67	1.83	31.93	2.47	40.19	3.11
7.29	0.56	15.54	1.20	23.80	1.84	32.06	2.48	40.32	3.12
7.41	0.57	15.67	1.21	23.93	1.85	32.19	2.49	40.45	3.13
7.54	0.58	15.80	1.22	24.06	1.86	32.32	2.50	40.58	3.14
7.67	0.59	15.93	1.23	24.19	1.87	32.45	2.51	40.70	3.15
7.80	0.60	16.06	1.24	24.32	1.88	32.58	2.52	40.83	3.16
7.93	0.61	16.19	1.25	24.45	1.89	32.70	2.53	40.96	3.17
8.06	0.62	16.32	1.26	24.58	1.90	32.83	2.54	41.09	3.18
8.19	0.63	16.45	1.27	24.70	1.91	32.96	2.55	41.22	3.19

8.25% SALES TAX COLLECTION SCHEDULE 8.25%

TO	TAX	TO	TAX	TO	TAX	TO	TAX	TO	TAX
58.24	4.80	67.93	5.60	77.63	6.40	87.33	7.20	97.03	8.00
58.36	4.81	68.06	5.61	77.75	6.41	87.45	7.21	97.15	8.01
58.48	4.82	68.18	5.62	77.87	6.42	87.57	7.22	97.27	8.02
58.60	4.83	68.30	5.63	77.99	6.43	87.69	7.23	97.39	8.03
58.72	4.84	68.42	5.64	78.12	6.44	87.81	7.24	97.51	8.04
58.84	4.85	68.54	5.65	78.24	6.45	87.93	7.25	97.63	8.05
58.96	4.86	68.66	5.66	78.36	6.46	88.06	7.26	97.75	8.06
59.09	4.87	68.78	5.67	78.48	6.47	88.18	7.27	97.87	8.07
59.21	4.88	68.90	5.68	78.60	6.48	88.30	7.28	97.99	8.08
59.33	4.89	69.03	5.69	78.72	6.49	88.42	7.29	98.12	8.09
59.45	4.90	69.15	5.70	78.84	6.50	88.54	7.30	98.24	8.10
59.57	4.91	69.27	5.71	78.96	6.51	88.66	7.31	98.36	8.11
59.69	4.92	69.39	5.72	79.09	6.52	88.78	7.32	98.48	8.12
59.81	4.93	69.51	5.73	79.21	6.53	88.90	7.33	98.60	8.13
59.93	4.94	69.63	5.74	79.33	6.54	89.03	7.34	98.72	8.14
60.06	4.95	69.75	5.75	79.45	6.55	89.15	7.35	98.84	8.15
60.18	4.96	69.87	5.76	79.57	6.56	89.27	7.36	98.96	8.16
60.30	4.97	69.99	5.77	79.69	6.57	89.39	7.37	99.09	8.17
60.42	4.98	70.12	5.78	79.81	6.58	89.51	7.38	99.21	8.18
60.54	4.99	70.24	5.79	79.93	6.59	89.63	7.39	99.33	8.19
60.66	5.00	70.36	5.80	80.06	6.60	89.75	7.40	99.45	8.20
60.78	5.01	70.48	5.81	80.18	6.61	89.87	7.41	99.57	8.21
60.90	5.02	70.60	5.82	80.30	6.62	89.99	7.42	99.69	8.22
61.03	5.03	70.72	5.83	80.42	6.63	90.12	7.43	99.81	8.23
61.15	5.04	70.84	5.84	80.54	6.64	90.24	7.44	99.93	8.24
61.27	5.05	70.96	5.85	80.66	6.65	90.36	7.45	100.06	8.25
61.39	5.06	71.09	5.86	80.78	6.66	90.48	7.46	100.18	8.26
61.51	5.07	71.21	5.87	80.90	6.67	90.60	7.47	100.30	8.27
61.63	5.08	71.33	5.88	81.03	6.68	90.72	7.48	100.42	8.28
61.75	5.09	71.45	5.89	81.15	6.69	90.84	7.49	100.54	8.29
61.87	5.10	71.57	5.90	81.27	6.70	90.96	7.50	100.66	8.30
61.99	5.11	71.69	5.91	81.39	6.71	91.09	7.51	100.78	8.31
62.12	5.12	71.81	5.92	81.51	6.72	91.21	7.52	100.90	8.32
62.24	5.13	71.93	5.93	81.63	6.73	91.33	7.53	101.03	8.33
62.36	5.14	72.06	5.94	81.75	6.74	91.45	7.54	101.15	8.34
62.48	5.15	72.18	5.95	81.87	6.75	91.57	7.55	101.27	8.35
62.60	5.16	72.30	5.96	81.99	6.76	91.69	7.56	101.39	8.36
62.72	5.17	72.42	5.97	82.12	6.77	91.81	7.57	101.51	8.37
62.84	5.18	72.54	5.98	82.24	6.78	91.93	7.58	101.63	8.38
62.96	5.19	72.66	5.99	82.36	6.79	92.06	7.59	101.75	8.39
63.09	5.20	72.78	6.00	82.48	6.80	92.18	7.60	101.87	8.40
63.21	5.21	72.90	6.01	82.60	6.81	92.30	7.61	101.99	8.41
63.33	5.22	73.03	6.02	82.72	6.82	92.42	7.62	102.12	8.42
63.45	5.23	73.15	6.03	82.84	6.83	92.54	7.63	102.24	8.43
63.57	5.24	73.27	6.04	82.96	6.84	92.66	7.64	102.36	8.44
63.69	5.25	73.39	6.05	83.09	6.85	92.78	7.65	102.48	8.45
63.81	5.26	73.51	6.06	83.21	6.86	92.90	7.66	102.60	8.46
63.93	5.27	73.63	6.07	83.33	6.87	93.03	7.67	102.72	8.47
64.06	5.28	73.75	6.08	83.45	6.88	93.15	7.68	102.84	8.48
64.18	5.29	73.87	6.09	83.57	6.89	93.27	7.69	102.96	8.49
64.30	5.30	73.99	6.10	83.69	6.90	93.39	7.70	103.09	8.50
64.42	5.31	74.12	6.11	83.81	6.91	93.51	7.71	103.21	8.51
64.54	5.32	74.24	6.12	83.93	6.92	93.63	7.72	103.33	8.52
64.66	5.33	74.36	6.13	84.06	6.93	93.75	7.73	103.45	8.53
64.78	5.34	74.48	6.14	84.18	6.94	93.87	7.74	103.57	8.54
64.90	5.35	74.60	6.15	84.30	6.95	93.99	7.75	103.69	8.55
65.03	5.36	74.72	6.16	84.42	6.96	94.12	7.76	103.81	8.56
65.15	5.37	74.84	6.17	84.54	6.97	94.24	7.77	103.93	8.57
65.27	5.38	74.96	6.18	84.66	6.98	94.36	7.78	104.06	8.58
65.39	5.39	75.09	6.19	84.78	6.99	94.48	7.79	104.18	8.59
65.51	5.40	75.21	6.20	84.90	7.00	94.60	7.80	104.30	8.60
65.63	5.41	75.33	6.21	85.03	7.01	94.72	7.81	104.42	8.61
65.75	5.42	75.45	6.22	85.15	7.02	94.84	7.82	104.54	8.62
65.87	5.43	75.57	6.23	85.27	7.03	94.96	7.83	104.66	8.63
65.99	5.44	75.69	6.24	85.39	7.04	95.09	7.84	104.78	8.64
66.12	5.45	75.81	6.25	85.51	7.05	95.21	7.85	104.90	8.65
66.24	5.46	75.93	6.26	85.63	7.06	95.33	7.86	105.03	8.66
66.36	5.47	76.06	6.27	85.75	7.07	95.45	7.87	105.15	8.67
66.48	5.48	76.18	6.28	85.87	7.08	95.57	7.88	105.27	8.68
66.60	5.49	76.30	6.29	85.99	7.09	95.69	7.89	105.39	8.69
66.72	5.50	76.42	6.30	86.12	7.10	95.81	7.90	105.51	8.70
66.84	5.51	76.54	6.31	86.24	7.11	95.93	7.91	105.63	8.71
66.96	5.52	76.66	6.32	86.36	7.12	96.06	7.92	105.75	8.72
67.09	5.53	76.78	6.33	86.48	7.13	96.18	7.93	105.87	8.73
67.21	5.54	76.90	6.34	86.60	7.14	96.30	7.94	105.99	8.74
67.33	5.55	77.03	6.35	86.72	7.15	96.42	7.95	106.12	8.75
67.45	5.56	77.15	6.36	86.84	7.16	96.54	7.96	106.24	8.76
67.57	5.57	77.27	6.37	86.96	7.17	96.66	7.97	106.36	8.77
67.69	5.58	77.39	6.38	87.09	7.18	96.78	7.98	106.48	8.78
67.81	5.59	77.51	6.39	87.21	7.19	96.90	7.99	106.60	8.79

1314	BALANCE BROUGHT FORWARD	2,065	65
March 1 20—			
General Gas Co.			
Monthly service			
DEPOSIT			
BALANCE			
AMOUNT THIS CHECK		85	65

1318	BALANCE BROUGHT FORWARD	2,919	80
March 9 20—			
City of Kent			
License			
DEPOSIT			
BALANCE			
AMOUNT THIS CHECK		75	00

1322	BALANCE BROUGHT FORWARD	4,079	05
March 22 20—			
S & S Office			
Supplies			
Invoice 1386			
DEPOSIT			
BALANCE			
AMOUNT THIS CHECK		176	90

1315	BALANCE BROUGHT FORWARD	1,980	00
March 3 20—			
The Ching Co.			
Invoice 278			
March 2 DEPOSIT		1,350	00
BALANCE		3,330	00
AMOUNT THIS CHECK		527	75

1319	BALANCE BROUGHT FORWARD	2,844	80
March 10 20—			
Boxwood Gardens			
Florist bill			
DEPOSIT			
BALANCE			
AMOUNT THIS CHECK		85	75

1323	BALANCE BROUGHT FORWARD	3,902	15
March 25 20—			
Corner Service			
Auto Repairs			
DEPOSIT			
BALANCE			
AMOUNT THIS CHECK		526	10

1316	BALANCE BROUGHT FORWARD	2,802	25
March 6 20—			
United Parcel			
Service for Feb.			
DEPOSIT			
BALANCE			
AMOUNT THIS CHECK		622	45

1320	BALANCE BROUGHT FORWARD	2,759	05
March 18 20—			
Daily News			
Ads			
March 15 DEPOSIT		1,850	00
BALANCE		4,609	05
AMOUNT THIS CHECK		350	00

1324	BALANCE BROUGHT FORWARD	3,376	05
March 31 20—			
Salvation Army			
Contribution			
March 27 DEPOSIT		2,209	95
BALANCE		5,586	00
AMOUNT THIS CHECK		500	00

1317	BALANCE BROUGHT FORWARD	2,179	80
March 8 20—			
Postmaster			
Meter service			
March 8 DEPOSIT		1,240	00
BALANCE		3,419	80
AMOUNT THIS CHECK		500	00
BALANCE		2,919	80

1321	BALANCE BROUGHT FORWARD	4,259	05
March 19 20—			
Your Choice			
Answering Service			
April service			
DEPOSIT			
BALANCE			
AMOUNT THIS CHECK		180	00
BALANCE		4,079	05

1325	BALANCE BROUGHT FORWARD	5,086	00
March 31 20—			
Kent Power Co.			
Electric bill			
DEPOSIT			
BALANCE			
AMOUNT THIS CHECK		230	00
BALANCE		4,856	00

Checkbook Register

ACCOUNTING DEPARTMENT
INVENTORY

Month Ended   June, 20--

Product Number	Item	Unit Size	Closing Inventory	Unit Price	Inventory Value
AP738	Appointment Book, Desk	each	4	12.99	51.96
CD368	CD-R, 700MB, 10/pack	pack	18	6.99	125.82
CD394	CD-RW, 700MB, 10/pack	pack	8	8.49	67.92
DV592	DVD-R, 10/pack	pack	7	13.95	97.65
DV599	DVD-RW, 10/pack	pack	10	17.99	179.90
EN145	Envelopes, Interoffice, 100/box	box	7	18.99	132.93
EN211	Envelopes, Standard #10	box	9	16.15	145.35
EN215	Envelopes, Window #10	box	7	14.09	98.63
FI429	File Folders, Standard, 100/box	box	15	8.19	122.85
IC340	Index Cards, Ruled	pkg.	30	.64	19.20
LA330	Labels, File Folder, 450/pkg	pkg.	12	15.25	183.00
PA492	Paper, Calculator Roll, 12/pack	pack	6	9.25	55.50
PA500	Paper, Fax, 6/pack	pack	10	11.49	114.90
PA581	Paper, Printer, 5,000/case	case	25	28.45	711.25
PA598	Paper, Phone Message, 512/cube	cube	15	6.99	104.85
PC600	Paper Clips, Regular, 1,000/box	box	12	1.79	21.48
PC615	Paper Clips, Jumbo, 1,000/box	box	15	5.49	82.35
PE211	Pencils, #2	dozen	25	2.08	52.00
PE234	Pens, Ballpoint Med. Black	dozen	10	13.99	139.90
RU296	Rubber Bands, 2,500/box	box	10	3.79	37.90
RL308	Ruler, 12" Finger-grip	each	25	3.68	92.00
SP732	Stamp Pad, 2 3/4" x 4 1/4"	each	10	3.35	33.50
SP740	Stamp Pad Ink, Black	each	12	1.85	22.20
ST629	Stapler	each	20	13.99	279.80
ST722	Staples, 5,000/box	box	25	2.90	72.50
TA821	Tape, Invisible, 16/pack	pack	3	14.99	44.97
				Total	3,090.31

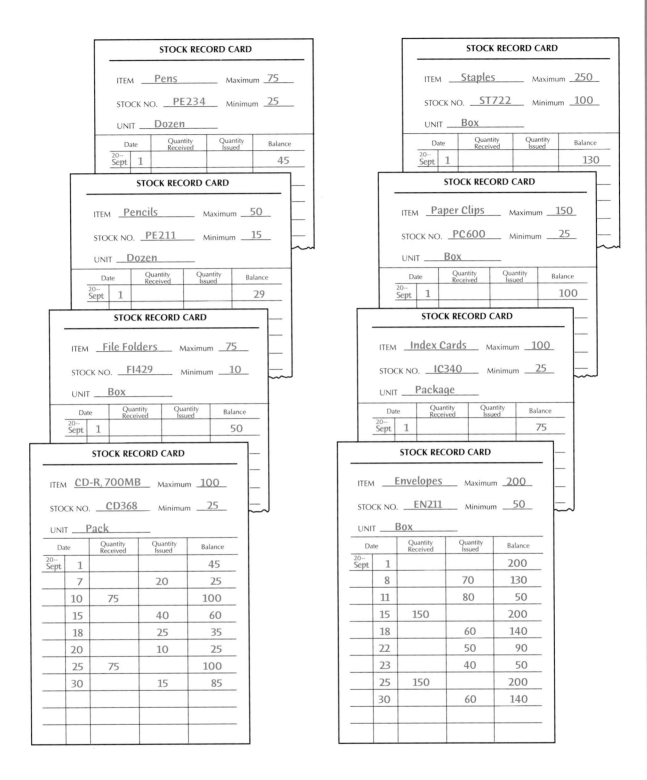

STOCK RECORD CARD

ITEM __Pens__ Maximum __75__
STOCK NO. __PE234__ Minimum __25__
UNIT __Dozen__

Date		Quantity Received	Quantity Issued	Balance
20-- Sept	1			45

STOCK RECORD CARD

ITEM __Pencils__ Maximum __50__
STOCK NO. __PE211__ Minimum __15__
UNIT __Dozen__

Date		Quantity Received	Quantity Issued	Balance
20-- Sept	1			29

STOCK RECORD CARD

ITEM __File Folders__ Maximum __75__
STOCK NO. __FI429__ Minimum __10__
UNIT __Box__

Date		Quantity Received	Quantity Issued	Balance
20-- Sept	1			50

STOCK RECORD CARD

ITEM __CD-R, 700MB__ Maximum __100__
STOCK NO. __CD368__ Minimum __25__
UNIT __Pack__

Date		Quantity Received	Quantity Issued	Balance
20-- Sept	1			45
	7		20	25
	10	75		100
	15		40	60
	18		25	35
	20		10	25
	25	75		100
	30		15	85

STOCK RECORD CARD

ITEM __Staples__ Maximum __250__
STOCK NO. __ST722__ Minimum __100__
UNIT __Box__

Date		Quantity Received	Quantity Issued	Balance
20-- Sept	1			130

STOCK RECORD CARD

ITEM __Paper Clips__ Maximum __150__
STOCK NO. __PC600__ Minimum __25__
UNIT __Box__

Date		Quantity Received	Quantity Issued	Balance
20-- Sept	1			100

STOCK RECORD CARD

ITEM __Index Cards__ Maximum __100__
STOCK NO. __IC340__ Minimum __25__
UNIT __Package__

Date		Quantity Received	Quantity Issued	Balance
20-- Sept	1			75

STOCK RECORD CARD

ITEM __Envelopes__ Maximum __200__
STOCK NO. __EN211__ Minimum __50__
UNIT __Box__

Date		Quantity Received	Quantity Issued	Balance
20-- Sept	1			200
	8		70	130
	11		80	50
	15	150		200
	18		60	140
	22		50	90
	23		40	50
	25	150		200
	30		60	140

Inventory—Stock Record Cards

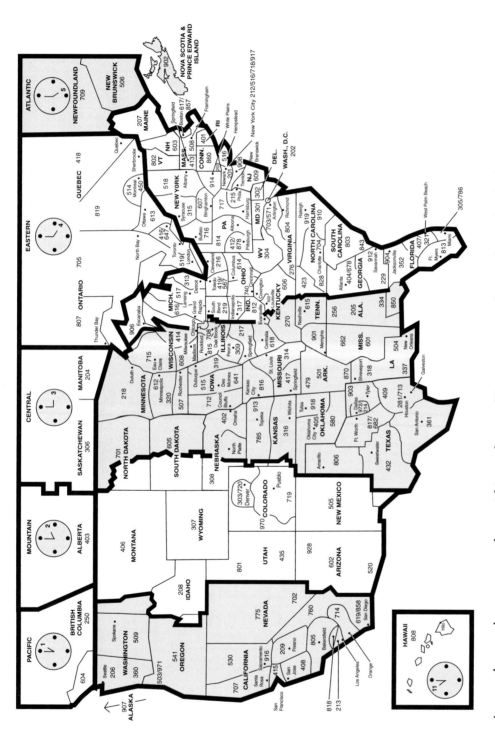

Area codes are shown as numbers within each state. Time zones are shown above the clocks at the top of the map. Read across the top of the map to see the names of the time zones and the times: Pacific, 1:00; Mountain, 2:00; Central, 3:00; Eastern, 4:00; and Atlantic, 5:00. All times shown are standard times (not daylight savings times). From these time zone clocks, you can learn that if it is 1 o'clock in the Pacific time zone, it is 4 o'clock in the Eastern time zone.

Map—Area Codes and Time Zones

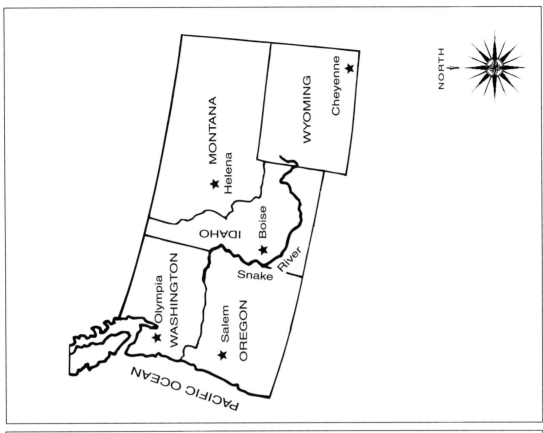

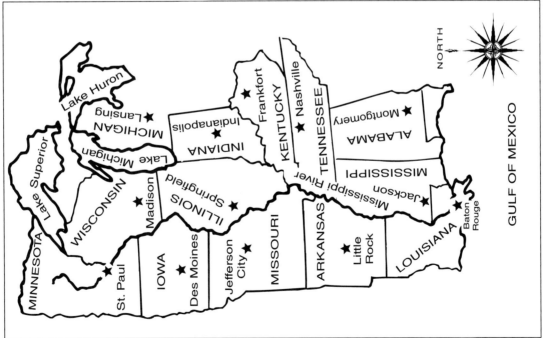

Map—Central States and Northwestern States

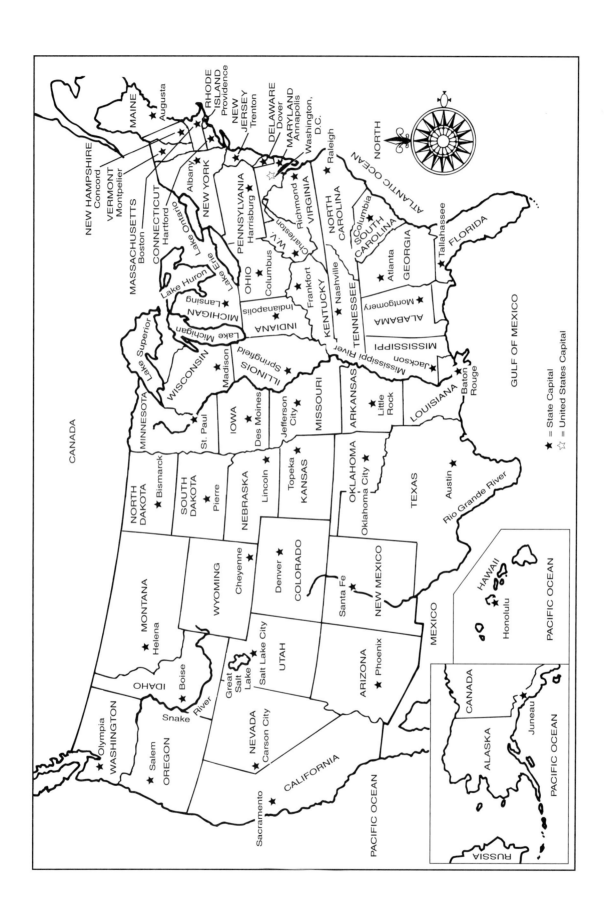

Map—United States with Capitals

FROM/TO	ALBUQUERQUE, NM	CHICAGO, IL	HOUSTON, TX	LOS ANGELES, CA	MILWAUKEE, WI	ORLANDO, FL
			NUMBER OF DRIVING MILES			
Atlanta, GA	1471	754	793	2256	844	437
Baltimore, MD	1889	703	1445	2675	793	899
Boston, MA	2239	986	1847	2985	1076	1303
Charlotte, NC	1647	781	1057	2435	875	524
Cleveland, OH	1606	346	1390	2345	436	1035
Denver, CO	448	1004	1119	1016	1045	1848
Kansas City, MO	891	527	789	1618	567	1243
Louisville, KY	1303	297	1031	2088	387	863
Minneapolis, MN	1331	408	1229	1926	336	1567
Myrtle Beach, SC	1810	949	1144	2594	1036	474
Nashville, TN	1225	507	846	2009	882	685
New Orleans, LA	1265	924	347	1898	1014	639
New York, NY	2024	791	1635	2790	880	1086
Oklahoma City, OK	543	800	444	1329	876	1338
Philadelphia, PA	1937	780	1546	2724	869	998
Portland, OR	1434	2121	2364	960	2065	3083
Salt Lake City, UT	606	1397	1648	688	1439	2359
Seattle, WA	1507	2063	2437	1142	1992	3136
Toronto, ON	1832	521	1664	2519	1485	970
Washington, DC	1886	701	1409	2673	790	849

SERVICES

CLASSIC AUTO PARTS
5963 Beverly Drive
Hollywood, CA 90028
(323)555-0145

Part No.	Price (each)	Part No.	Price (each)	Part No.	Price (each)
00053473	$151.65	00411611	$ 56.65	32363878	$ 67.70
00053474	86.70	00411612	66.65	32638370	44.50
00053475	15.50	00556328	123.00	36338637	55.40
00053476	23.35	00556329	132.00	38863783	45.00
00053477	36.90	00556330	135.50	43516653	8.75
00145570	5.55	00556331	155.30	43536655	7.85
00145571	4.35	00556332	135.50	43558658	8.85
00145572	7.00	00683382	87.50	48356685	7.85
00145573	3.35	00683383	88.80	51173714	66.00
00145574	5.20	00683384	78.80	51177341	65.50
00204833	117.75	00683385	77.75	57117437	57.50
00204834	106.60	00683386	87.50	57717337	77.50
00204835	115.00	11745905	45.50	57773374	220.00
00204836	139.75	11749505	55.75	64036893	115.75
00204837	108.80	11838233	45.50	64366389	88.70
00399455	65.00	11883283	75.75	64554369	11.75
00399456	43.40	11935575	57.75	64649693	9.90
00399457	95.50	11985357	175.00	77173947	135.65
00399458	37.50	25787385	175.50	77474197	15.90
00399459	25.75	25873758	170.75	77477947	37.75
00411608	55.55	25961608	177.75	77744749	88.30
00411609	65.35	25996808	178.85	91179771	103.50
00411610	60.65	32268357	87.75	91797974	44.40

BUSINESS FORMS
(packs of 100)

Code	Price	Code	Price	Code	Price
AA35	$12.24	JA25	$32.67	SE23	$5.88
AB53	22.43	JA52	36.35	SE32	5.08
AD35	11.45	JM53	38.00	SF38	5.58
AD53	21.50	JN55	38.25	SF88	8.58
BA85	8.87	KA16	4.55	TC95	13.35
BB38	7.70	KA66	5.45	TC98	13.85
BD81	6.95	KR02	3.88	TG17	18.35
BD88	9.65	KR20	8.33	TG77	18.55
CC40	32.88	LC19	6.39	US04	41.50
CD34	43.38	LC94	3.69	US40	44.50
CE80	23.46	LQ38	8.15	UZ23	41.05
CF08	23.58	LZ83	8.75	UZ28	44.00
DD16	18.48	MM34	14.45	VI53	17.75
DE76	11.25	MM48	15.55	VI58	17.70
DG92	17.52	MN44	14.45	VT63	17.77
DO29	17.85	MN48	15.45	VT68	17.57
EA38	5.55	MN18	8.53	WA17	2.95
EE83	7.75	NM81	8.35	WA77	2.59
EF88	9.09	NN18	3.38	WC59	2.90
EP88	5.39	NN81	5.83	WC99	2.99
FA02	8.06	OA35	8.05	WO99	2.09
FE20	8.86	OA55	8.80	XE25	23.05
FF22	6.88	OY85	8.08	XE28	22.35
FP32	8.88	OY88	8.80	XF38	23.30
GC44	27.50	PJ30	12.25	XF88	22.35
GC74	20.00	PJ38	12.55	XP38	23.35
GG77	25.35	PO80	12.35	YB11	23.85
GQ27	27.70	PO88	12.45	YB17	28.35
HB22	41.50	QV72	9.00	YP11	32.85
HB82	44.65	QV77	9.90	YP27	38.35
HD33	40.90	QW41	9.45	YR11	35.58
HD83	43.38	QW44	9.54	ZC47	6.88
IA91	7.30	RB09	22.74	ZC74	8.85
II32	7.53	RB90	27.47	ZO61	8.55
II91	7.33	RP89	24.75	ZO66	5.85
IT99	7.55	RP98	25.75	ZQ61	5.05

MURPHY'S OFFICE SUPPLIES
2673 Garden Plaza
Woodstown, NJ 08098

OFFICE EQUIPMENT

Printers and Accessories	Price
PB472 Inkjet Printer (up to 23 pages per minute)	$ 99.98
PB472A Black Ink	19.98
PC509 Color Inkjet Printer (up to 20 ppm)	120.98
PC509A Black Ink	24.39
PC509B Tricolor Ink	34.99
PL647 Laser Printer (up to 15 ppm)	179.98
PL647A Toner	77.49
PL647B Drum	140.19

Facsimile Machines and Accessories	
FI376 Inkjet Fax	$ 99.98
FI376A Cartridge	35.55
FP415 Plain-Paper Fax	115.78
FP415A Toner	75.23
FP415B Drum	89.25
FC692 Color Inkjet Fax	119.98
FC692A Black Ink	21.99
FC692B Cyan Ink	11.99
FC692C Magenta Ink	11.99
FC692D Yellow Ink	11.99

Copiers and Accessories	
SG478 Copier (up to 16 copies per minute)	$399.98
SG478A Toner	132.39
SG478B Drum	183.55
RJ605 Copier (up to 21 cpm)	449.98
RJ605A Toner	173.29
RJ605B Drum	183.55

Laser All-in-One Machines (Print/Fax/Copy)	
LS445 Sheet-Fed All-in-One	$199.98
LF621 Flatbed All-in-One	299.98
LSF Fax Cartridge	20.29

Symbol	Instruction	Example	Result
∧	insert copy	Te proof the	The proof of the
⌒	close up	The pr oof	The proof
#	add space	Theproof	The proof
∪	transpose	The porof the of	The proof of the
lc or /	lowercase	The Proof	The proof
ℓ	delete	The proof of of thee	The proof of the
/	replace	The proof in the	The proof of the
⊙	insert period	the proof However,	the proof. However,
___	underline or italicize	The proof	The proof
≡	capitalize	the best proof	The BEST proof
sp	spell out	sp 5 WP centers	five word processing centers
¶	n paragraph	proof. ¶ However, the	proof. However, the
No ¶	no paragraph (run together)	proof. No ¶ However, the	proof. However, the
.... or stet	leave as is; ignore the correction	The stet proof of the	The proof of the
∧	insert punctuation	the proof however	the proof; however,
‾∧‾	insert hyphen	The age old proof	The age-old proof
⌄	insert apostrophe	The proofs effect	The proof's effect
⌄ ⌄	insert quotation mark	The proof of the	The "proof" of the
⌐¬	move right	The proof	The proof
L	move left	The proof	The proof
⟲	move copy as indicated	The matter proof of the is	The proof of the matter is
SS	single space	600 Broad Street SS Mt. Pleasant, PA 15666	600 Broad Street Mt. Pleasant, PA 15666
DS	double space	DS Dear Mr. Sofranko	Dear Mr. Sofranko
QS	quadruple space	THE PROOF QS The proof of the	THE PROOF The proof of the

NATIONAL WIRE WORKS
11734 Telford Rd 555-0101
National Youth Foundation
3298 Congress Blvd. 555-0196
Nations Cheryl M atty
437 Candler Blvd 555-0183
Nation's Gardeners
958 Old Yale Rd. 555-0164
Nationwide Business Forms
117 Rainbow Dr. 555-0112
NATIONWIDE FLORAL SERVICE
11545 Circle 85 Pkwy 555-0147
Nationwide Haulers
1037 Gordon St 555-0123
Native Thos J CPA
945 Tara Cir. 555-0134
NATKIN PERSONNEL
775 Dogwood Hwy. 555-0154
Natural Health Foods, Inc.
2348 Phoenix Byway 555-0195
Natural You Hair Styles
654-E Exchange Pl 555-0171
Naturally Nutritious Co.
655 Business Park Dr. 555-0158

Navy Recruiting Station–
3529 Lake Plaza 555-0106
847 Cobb Pkwy 555-0151
Naylon G Philip DDS
633 Hembree Cir. 555-0129
Naylor Kim B DVM
3487 Armour Hwy 555-0166
NBS Car Rentals
937 Northcliff Ter 555-0102
NECCO SEWING CENTER
554 Ford Road Ext 555-0180
238 Lake Hearn Dr 555-0188
955 Light Cir. 555-0159
Needle George G rl est 555-0139
Needle Point Village 555-0121
Needlepoint Junction 555-0153
Neel Thelma J MC PC
11947 N Landing Run 555-0155
Neil M Thomas Rev 555-0191
NELSON-JOHNSON, INC. investments
Municipal Bldg 555-0168
News-Daily
3458 Old Dayton Hwy 555-0198
Classified Want Ads 555-0197

Government Section

United States

Continued from Last Page

Continued from Last Column

U.S. Government—
LABOR DEPT OF—
Bureau of Apprenticeship & Training
11543 Pierce Ave—
Area Office 555-0176
Regional Office 555-0194
State Office 555-0162
Bureau of Labor Statistics—
Administrative 555-0107
Regional Commissioner 555-0152
Statistical Information 555-0132
Employment & Training 555-0136
Federal Workers' Compensation 555-0146
Job Safety & Health 555-0105
Labor Statistics 555-0156
Minimum Wage/Overtime 555-0103
Pensions 555-0173
Public Affairs 555-0192
Women's Activities 555-0160

U.S. Government—
POSTAL SERVICE—
Airport Mail Facility 555-0184
Claims and Inquiry 555-0187
Customer Services 555-0172
Employee & Labor Relations 555-0163
Express Mail Service 555-0111
Finance 555-0175
Mail Processing 555-0165
Passport Information 555-0150
Personnel 555-0130
Philately/Stamp Collecting 555-0170
Postique/Stamp Collecting Ctr 555-0167
Postmaster 555-0104
Public Affairs 555-0138
Rates and Information 555-0190
Retail Sales and Service 555-0143
Special Delivery 555-0133
ZIP Code Information 555-0114

The U.S. Postal Service (USPS) recommends the abbreviations listed here. By using the state abbreviations, it is possible to enter the city, state, and nine-digit ZIP Code on the last line of an address within a maximum of 28 positions: 13 positions for the city, 1 space between the city and state abbreviation, 2 positions for the state abbreviation, 2 spaces between the state abbreviation and ZIP Code, and 10 positions for the ZIP+4 Code.

U.S. State, District, Possession, or Territory	Two-Letter Abbreviation	U.S. State, District, Possession, or Territory	Two-Letter Abbreviation
Alabama	AL	Ohio	OH
Alaska	AK	Oklahoma	OK
American Samoa	AS	Oregon	OR
Arizona	AZ	Palau	PW
Arkansas	AR	Pennsylvania	PA
California	CA	Puerto Rico	PR
Colorado	CO	Rhode Island	RI
Connecticut	CT	South Carolina	SC
Delaware	DE	South Dakota	SD
District of Columbia	DC	Tennessee	TN
Federated States of Micronesia	FM	Texas	TX
Florida	FL	Utah	UT
Georgia	GA	Vermont	VT
Guam	GU	Virgin Islands	VI
Hawaii	HI	Virginia	VA
Idaho	ID	Washington	WA
Illinois	IL	West Virginia	WV
Indiana	IN	Wisconsin	WI
Iowa	IA	Wyoming	WY
Kansas	KS		
Kentucky	KY	Armed Forces the Americas	AA
Louisiana	LA	Armed Forces Europe	AE
Maine	ME	Armed Forces Pacific	AP
Marshall Islands	MH		
Maryland	MD		

		Canadian Province, Possession, or Territory	Two-Letter Abbreviation
Massachusetts	MA		
Michigan	MI		
Minnesota	MN		
Mississippi	MS	Alberta	AB
Missouri	MO	British Columbia	BC
		Manitoba	MB
Montana	MT	New Brunswick	NB
Nebraska	NE	Newfoundland & Labrador	NL
Nevada	NV	Northwest Territories	NT
New Hampshire	NH	Nova Scotia	NS
New Jersey	NJ		
		Nunavut	NU
New Mexico	NM	Ontario	ON
New York	NY	Prince Edward Island	PE
North Carolina	NC	Quebec	PQ
North Dakota	ND	Saskatchewan	SK
Northern Mariana Islands	MP	Yukon Territory	YT

Source: U.S. Postal Service, 1998

ABBREVIATIONS FOR STREET DESIGNATORS

Word	Abbreviation	Word	Abbreviation	Word	Abbreviation	Word	Abbreviation
Alley	ALY	Estates	EST	Lakes	LKS	Ridge	RDG
Annex	ANX	Expressway	ESPY	Landing	LNDG	River	RIV
Arcade	ARC	Extension	EXT	Lane	LN	Road	RD
Avenue	AVE	Falls	FLS	Light	LGT	Row	ROW
Bayou	BYU	Ferry	FRY	Loaf	LF	Run	RUN
Beach	BCH	Field	FLD	Locks	LCKS	Shoal	SHL
Bend	BND	Fields	FLDS	Lodge	LDG	Shoals	SHLS
Bluff	BLF	Flats	FLT	Loop	LOOP	Shore	SHR
Bottom	BTM	Ford	FRD	Mall	MALL	Shores	SHRS
Boulevard	BLVD	Forest	FRST	Manor	MNR	Spring	SPG
Branch	BR	Forge	FRG	Meadows	MDWS	Springs	SPGS
Bridge	BRG	Fork	FRK	Mill	ML	Spur	SPUR
Brook	BRK	Forks	FRKS	Mills	MLS	Square	SQ
Burg	BG	Fort	FT	Mission	MSN	Station	STA
Bypass	BYP	Freeway	FWY	Mount	MT	Stravenue	STRA
Camp	CP	Gardens	GDNS	Mountain	MTN	Stream	STRM
Canyon	CYN	Gateway	GTWY	Neck	NCK	Street	ST
Cape	CPE	Glen	GLN	Orchard	ORCH	Summit	SMT
Causeway	CSWY	Green	GRN	Oval	OVAL	Terrace	TER
Center	CTR	Grove	GRV	Park	PARK	Trace	TRCE
Circle	CIR	Harbor	HBR	Parkway	PKWY	Track	TRAK
Cliffs	CLFS	Haven	HVN	Pass	PASS	Trafficway	TRFY
Club	CLB	Heights	HTS	Path	PATH	Trail	TRL
Corner	COR	Highway	HWY	Pike	PIKE	Tunnel	TUNL
Corners	CORS	Hill	HL	Pines	PNES	Turnpike	TPKE
Court	CT	Hills	HLS	Place	PL	Union	UN
Courts	CTS	Hollow	HOLW	Plains	PLNS	Valley	VLY
Cove	CV	Inlet	INLT	Plaza	PLZ	Viaduct	VIA
Creek	CRK	Island	IS	Point	PT	View	VW
Crescent	CRES	Islands	ISS	Port	PRT	Village	VLG
Crossing	XING	Isle	ISLE	Prairie	PR	Ville	VL
Dale	DL	Junction	JCT	Radial	RADL	Vista	VIS
Dam	DM	Key	KY	Ranch	RNCH	Walk	WALK
Divide	DV	Knolls	KNLS	Rapids	RPDS	Way	WAY
Drive	DR	Lake	LK	Rest	RST	Wells	WLS

ABBREVIATIONS FOR SECONDARY UNIT DESIGNATORS

Word	Abbreviation	Word	Abbreviation	Word	Abbreviation	Word	Abbreviation
Apartment	APT	Hangar	HNGR	Pier	PIER	Stop	STOP
Basement	BSMT	Lobby	LBBY	Rear	REAR	Suite	STE
Building	BLDG	Lot	LOT	Room	RM	Trailer	TRLR
Department	DEPT	Lower	LOWR	Side	SIDE	Unit	UNIT
Floor	FL	Office	OFC	Slip	SLIP	Upper	UPPR
Front	FRNT	Penthouse	PH	Space	SPC		

Source: U.S. Postal Service, 1998

UNITED STATES POSTAL SERVICE
DOMESTIC POSTAL RATES AND SERVICES
Effective July 5, 2011

FIRST CLASS

First-Class Mail includes postcards, letters, large envelopes (flat) and small packages. This service, along with Priority Mail and Express Mail, is ideal for sending personal correspondence, handwritten or typewritten letters, and bills or statements of account. It may also be used for advertisements and lightweight merchandise. First-Class Mail prices are based on both the shape and weight of the item being mailed.

1st ounce	$0.44
Each additional ounce up to 13 oz.	0.20

For pieces not exceeding (oz.)	The rate is	For pieces not exceeding (oz.)	The rate is
1	$0.44		
2	0.64	8	$1.88
3	0.84	9	2.04
4	1.04	10	2.24
5	1.24	11	2.44
6	1.44	12	2.64
7	1.64	13	2.84

Over 13 ounces—use Priority Mail

Postcards	$0.29	Large Postcards	0.44

PRIORITY MAIL

Fast and affordable delivery to every address in the United States. You can take the guesswork out of shipping with Priority Mail Flat Rates. Whatever fits in the box or envelope ships for one low rate—anywhere in the United States. There's virtually no weighing or calculating. And your packages reach their destinations in 2-3 days.

Flat Rate Envelope	$4.95	12-1/2" x 9-1/2"
Padded Flat Rate Envelope	4.95	12-1/2" x 9-1/2"
Legal Flat Rate Envelope	4.95	15" x 9-1/2"
Gift Card Flat Rate Envelope	4.95	10" x 7"
Small Flat Rate Envelope	4.95	10" x 6"
Window Flat Rate Envelope	4.95	10" x 5"
Small Flat Rate Box	5.20	8-5/8" x 5 3/8" x 1-5/8"
Medium Flat Rate Box (FRB1)	10.95	11" x 8-1/2" x 5-1/2"
Medium Flat Rate Box (FRB2)	10.95	13-5/8" x 11-7/8" x 3-3/8"
Large Flat Rate Box (domestic)	14.95	12" x 12" x 5-1/2"
Large Flat Rate Box APO/FPO/DPO Destinations	12.95	12" x 12" x 5-1/2"

EXPRESS MAIL

Express Mail is the fastest service for time-sensitive letters, documents, or merchandise. Overnight delivery is guaranteed to most locations 365 days a year—even Sundays and holidays—or your money back. Express Mail envelopes, labels, and boxes are available at no additional charge.

For pieces not exceeding	The rate is
8 ounces	$13.25
1 pound	15.25
2 pounds	16.55
3 pounds	17.60
4 pounds	18.90
5 pounds	19.60
6 pounds	22.95
7 pounds	26.35
8 pounds	27.65
9 pounds	29.15
10 pounds	30.10

Over 10 pounds—consult Postmaster or USPS web site

PARCEL POST

Used for mailing certain items: books, circulars, catalogs, and other printed matter, and merchandise weighing 1 pound or more, but not more than 70 pounds. Parcel post must measure 130 inches or less in combined length and girth. Pieces exceeding 108 inches but not more than 130 inches in combined length and girth are mailable at Parcel Post oversized rates.

Weight Not Over (lbs.)	The rate is	Weight Not Over (lbs.)	The rate is
1	$5.10	8	$8.70
2	5.15	9	8.95
3	5.65	10	9.18
4	6.10	11	9.49
5	7.23	12	9.80
6	7.92	13	10.11
7	8.37		

Over 13 lbs.—consult Postmaster or USPS web site

Source: United States Postal Service, Notice 123, July 5, 2011, and USPS web site: http://www.usps.com

SPECIAL SERVICES

CERTIFICATE OF MAILING

Provides evidence of mailing (but not evidence of receipt). Must be purchased at time of mailing.

Fee in addition to postage—$1.15

CERTIFIED MAIL

Provides the sender with a mailing receipt. A record is kept at the post office of delivery. A return receipt can also be purchased for an additional fee. Available only with First-Class and Priority Mail.

Fee in addition to postage—$2.85

DELIVERY CONFIRMATION

Provides information about the date and time of delivery or attempted delivery. Mailers may retrieve delivery status through the Internet or the toll-free number 1-800-222-1811. Available for Priority Mail, Parcel Post, Bound Printed Matter, Special Standard Mail, and Library Mail.

Fee in addition to postage .... Priority Mail—$0.70
.... First-Class Mail (parcels only)—0.80
.... Electronic—0.19

INSURED MAIL

Provides coverage against loss or damage.

Insurance Coverage Desired (merchandise)	Fee in addition to postage
$0.01 to $50	$1.80
$50.01 to $100	2.30
$100.01 to $200	2.85
$200.01 to $300	4.75
$300.01 to $400	5.80
$400.01 to $500	6.85
$500.01 to $600	7.90

For coverage over $600—consult Postmaster or USPS web site

MONEY ORDERS

Provides safe transmission of money. Available in amounts up to $700.

Postal military money order	$0.30
Domestic money order	1.10
Inquiry fee	5.40

RETURN RECEIPT

Provides the sender with a mailing receipt. A delivery record is kept at the post office of address, but no record is kept at the post office of mailing.

Fee in addition to postage:

Showing to whom delivered, signature, date, and addressee's address (if different)
Requested at time of mailing $2.30
   (received by mail)
Requested at time of mailing $1.15
   (received electronically)
Requested after mailing $4.70
   (received by fax, mail, or e-mail)

REGISTERED MAIL

Provides maximum protection and security for valuables. Available only for items posted in Priority Mail and First-Class Mail rates. Postal insurance is provided for articles with a declared value up to a maximum of $25,000.

Declared Value (without postal insurance)	Fee (in addition to postage)
$0.00	$10.75

(with postal insurance)

$0.01 to $100	11.50
$100.01 to $500	13.25
$500.01 to $1,000	14.65
$1,000.01 to $2,000	16.05
$2,000.01 to $3,000	17.45

For higher values—consult Postmaster or USPS web site

SPECIAL HANDLING

Weight	Fee
Not more than 10 pounds	$7.55
More than 10 pounds	10.60

SIZE STANDARDS FOR DOMESTIC MAIL

Shape	Length	Height	
Postcards	minimum	5 inches	3 ½ inches
	maximum	6 inches	4 ½ inches
	maximum thickness	0.016 inches	
Letters	minimum	5 inches	3 ½ inches
	maximum	11 ½ inches	6 1/8 inches
	maximum thickness	¼ inch	
Large Envelopes	minimum	11 ½ inches	6 1/8 inches
	maximum	15 inches	12 inches
	maximum thickness	¾ inch	
Packages	maximum length plus girth 108 inches (130 inches for Parcel Post)		

MEDIA MAIL

Media Mail is a cost efficient way to mail books, sound recordings, recorded video tapes, printed music, and recorded computer-readable media (such as CDs, DVDs, and diskettes). Media Mail cannot contain advertising except for incidental announcements of books. The maximum weight for Media Mail is 70 lbs.

Weight Not Over (lbs.)	The rate is	Weight Not Over (lbs.)	The rate is
1	$2.41	6	$4.46
2	2.82	7	4.87
3	3.23	8	5.26
4	3.64	9	5.65
5	4.05	10	6.04

Over 10 lbs.—consult Postmaster or USPS web site

Source: United States Postal Service, Notice 123, July 5, 2011, and USPS web site: http://www.usps.com

USPS—Rates and Services

VERMONT

(Abbreviation: VT)

Post office and county	ZIP Code
Adamant, Washington	05640
Albany, Orleans	05820
Alburg, Grand Isle	05440
Arlington, Bennington	05250
Ascutney, Windsor N	05030
Averill, Essex N	05901
Bakersfield, Franklin	05441
Barnard, Windsor N	05031
Barnet, Caledonia	05821
Barre, Washington G C	05641
Barton, Orleans	
West Glover CPO	05822
Beebe Plain, Orleans N	05823
Beecher Falls, Essex	05902
Bellows Falls, Windham G C	05101
Belmont, Rutland	05730
Belvidere Center, Lamoille	05442
Bennington, Bennington C	05201
Benson, Rutland C N	05731
Benson, CPO Fair Haven	05743
Bethel, Windsor	05032
Bolton Valley, CPO Richmond	05477
Bomoseen, Rutland	05732
Bondville, Bennington	05340
Bradford, Orange	05033
Braintree, P Randolph	05060
Brandon, Rutland C	05733
BRATTLEBORO, Windham GC	
(SEE PAGE 3-3216)	
Bread Loaf, CPO Middlebury	05753
Bridgewater, Windsor	05034
Bridgewater Corners, Windsor	05035
Bridport, Addison	05734
Bristol, Addison C	05443
Brookfield, Orange	05036
Brownsville, Windsor	05037
BURLINGTON, Chittenden G C	
(SEE PAGE 3-3216)	
Cabot, Washington	05647
Calais, Washington	05648
Cambridge, Chittenden	05444
Cambridgeport, Windham	05141
Canaan, Essex	05903
Castleton, Rutland	05735
Cavendish, Windsor	05142
Center Rutland, Rutland	05736
Charlotte, Chittenden	05445
Chelsea, Orange	05038
Chester, Windsor	05143
Chester Depot, Windsor N	05144
Chittenden, Rutland	05737
COLCHESTER, Chittenden (SEE PAGE 3-3216)	
Concord, Essex	05824
Corinth, Orange	05039
Coventry, Orleans	05825
Craftsbury, Orleans	05826
Craftsbury Common, Orleans	05827
Cuttingsville, Rutland Shrewsbury	05738
Danby, Rutland	05739
Danville, Caledonia	05828
Derby, Orleans	05829
Derby Line, Orleans G	05830
Dorset, Bennington	05251
East Arlington, Bennington	05252
East Barre, Washington	05649
East Berkshire, Franklin	05447
East Burke, Caledonia	05832
East Calais, Washington	05650
East Charleston, Orleans	05833
EAST CORINTH, Orange (SEE PAGE 3-3216)	
East Dorset, Bennington	05253
East Dover, Windham	05341
East Fairfield, Franklin	05448
East Hardwick, Caledonia	05836
East Haven, Essex	05837
East Middlebury, Addision N	05740
East Montpelier, Washington	05651
East Poultney, Rutland C N	05741
East Randolph, Orange	05041
East Ryegate, Caledonia Rygate B	05042
East San Johnsbury, Caledonia N	05838
East Thetford, Orange	05043
East Wallingford, Rutland	05742
Eden, Lamoille	05652
Eden Mills, Lamoille	05653
Ely, P Fairlee	05045
Enosburg Falls, Franklin	05450
Essex, Chittenden C N	05451
ESSEX JUNCTION, Chittenden G C (SEE PAGE 3-3216)	
Fairfax, Chittenden	05454
Fairfield, Franklin	05455
Fair Haven, Rutland C Benson CPO	05743
Fairlee, Orange Ely P	05045

BRATTLEBORO, VT

POSTMASTER AND GENERAL DELIVERY

General Delivery	05301
Postmaster, 204 Main St.	05301

POST OFFICE BOXES MAIN OFFICE, STATIONS, AND BRANCHES

Box Nos.

1-1998	Brattleboro	05302
2001-2740	Brattleboro	05303
6001-7451	Brattleboro	05302
8001-8480	Brattleboro	05304
9476-9576	Brattleboro	05302

RURAL ROUTES

01, 02, 03, 04, 05, 06, 07.	05301

HIGHWAY CONTRACTS

32	05301

NAMED STREETS

All Street Addresses.	05301

BURLINGTON, VT

POSTMASTER AND GENERAL DELIVERY

General Delivery	05401
Postmaster, 320 Pine St.	05401

POST OFFICE BOXES MAIN OFFICE, STATIONS, AND BRANCHES

Box Nos.

1-1916 Burlington (Elmwood)	05402
3001-3360 North Burlington	05401
4001-4638 Champlain Station	05406
5001-10000 Burlington (Elmwood)	05402
64641-65425 Champlain Station	05406

APARTMENTS, HOTELS, MOTELS

Radisson Hotel, 60 Battery St	05401
Town Country Motel, 490 Shelburne Rd	05401

BUILDINGS

Chase Mill, 1 Mill St.	05401

GOVERNMENT OFFICES

Champlain Station, 30 Shelburne Rd	05401
City Hall, 149 Church St	05401
City of Burlington, 149 Church St	05401
FBI, 11 Elmwood Ave	05401
Federal Bldg, 11 Elmwood Ave	05401
State Office Bldg, 1193 North Ave	05401

UNIVERSITIES AND COLLEGES

Burlington College, 95 North Ave	05401

NAMED STREETS

All Street Addresses.	05401

COLCHESTER, VT

POSTMASTER AND GENERAL DELIVERY

General Delivery	05446
Postmaster, 218 Mallets Bay Ave	05446

POST OFFICE BOXES MAIN OFFICE, STATIONS, AND BRANCHES

Box Nos.

1-1068 Colchester	05446
2002-2212 Colchester	05449

UNIVERSITIES AND COLLEGES

St. Michaels College, 109 Place St. Michael	05446

NAMED STREETS

All Street Addresses.	05446

EAST CORINTH, VT

POSTMASTER AND GENERAL DELIVERY

General Delivery	05040
Postmaster, 749 Village Rd	05040

POST OFFICE BOXES MAIN OFFICE, STATIONS, AND BRANCHES

Box Nos.

A-D	East Corinth	05040
11-167	East Corinth	05076
151-1137 East Corinth		05040

RURAL ROUTES

01	05040
02	05040

NAMED STREETS

Ben Dexter Rd	05076
Benjamin Rd	05040
Bowen Rd	05040
Brainard Ln	05040
Bruleigh Rd	05040
Carter Pl	05040
Cheney 4 Corner Rd	05040
Chicken Farm Rd	05040
Clark Rd.	05076
Colby Rd	05076
E Corinth Rd	05040
Corinth Topsham Rd	05076
Crosby Rd	05076
Currier Rd	05076
Currier Hill Rd	05040
Dickey Rd	05040
Downing Rd	05076
Eames Pl	05040
Emerson Rd.	05076
Emma Jane Rd.	05076
Erwin Rd	05040
Fairground Rd.	05040
Fiske Rd.	05076
Flanders Brook Rd	05040
Frost Rd	05076
Fulton Rd.	05076
Gahn Rd	05040
Galusha Hill Rd.	05076
Harold White Rd	05040
Harris Priv Dr	05076
Harts Rd.	05076
Harts Cross Rd	05076
Hutchison Rd	05040
Israel Ln.	05040
James Downing Rd	05040
Jewell Ln	05040
John White Rd	05076
Karl Nye Rd.	05076
Kasson Rd	05040
Keenan Pond Rd.	05076
Lime Kiln Rd	05076
Macdonald Rd	05076
Mctaggert Rd	05076
Ordway Rd	05040
Page Hill Rd.	05040
Powder Spring Rd	05076
Powers Rd	05076
Rachina Rd	05076
Sanborn Rd	05040
School House Rd	05076
Short St	05040
Stryker Rd	05076
Swamp Rd	05076
Taplin Hill Rd	05040
Thompson Pl & Rd.	05040
Topsham Corinth Rd 1-99 (ODD)	05040
1-399	05040
Town Highway 32	05040
Tucker Mt Rd	05040
Unindona Rd	05040
Vermont Route 25	05040
Village Rd	05040
Vt Route 25	05076
Waits River Vly School Rd	05040
Wayne Hill Rd.	05040
Welchs Rd	05040
Wiley Hill Rd.	05076
Woodward Lane	05040

Worthley Rd	05076
Worthley Way	05040
Wrights Mtn Rd	05040

ESSEX JUNCTION, VT

POSTMASTER AND GENERAL DELIVERY

General Delivery	05701
Postmaster, 151 West St.	05701

POST OFFICE BOXES MAIN OFFICE, STATIONS, AND BRANCHES

Box Nos.

All PO Boxes	05453

HIGHWAY CONTRACTS

64	05452

NAMED STREETS

All Street Addresses.	05452
Except Pearl St 78-80	05453

MONTPELIER, VT

POSTMASTER AND GENERAL DELIVERY

General Delivery	05602
Postmaster, 87 State St.	05602

POST OFFICE BOXES MAIN OFFICE, STATIONS, AND BRANCHES

Box Nos.

All PO Boxes	05601

RURAL ROUTES

03, 04, 05, 06	05602

HIGHWAY CONTRACTS

32	05305

UNIVERSITIES AND COLLEGES

Norwich Univ at Vt, 36 College St	05602
Vermont College, 36 College St	05602

NAMED STREETS

All Street Addresses.	05602

RUTLAND, VT

POSTMASTER AND GENERAL DELIVERY

General Delivery	05701
Postmaster, 151 West St.	05701

POST OFFICE BOXES MAIN OFFICE, STATIONS, AND BRANCHES

Box Nos.

1-999	Rutland	05702
1001-1858 Rutland		05701
6001-6999 Rutland		05702

RURAL ROUTES

01, 02, 03, 04	05701

HIGHWAY CONTRACTS

34	05701

NAMED STREETS

All Street Addresses.	05701

SOUTH BURLINGTON, VT

POST OFFICE BOXES MAIN OFFICE, STATIONS, AND BRANCHES

Box Nos.

All PO Boxes	05407

RURAL ROUTES

01, 02	05403

APARTMENTS, HOTELS, MOTELS

Anchorage Motor Inn 108 Dorset St	05403

County Parks Apts 635 Hinesburg Rd	05403
Dorset Commons, 435 Dorset St	05403
Econo Lodge, 1076 Williston Rd	05403
Ho Hum Motel 1200 Shelburne Rd	05403
Holiday Inn, 1068 Williston Rd	05403
Horizon Heights 102 Quarry Hill Rd	05403
Meadow Brook, 69 Joy Dr	05403
Sheraton Motor Inn 870 Williston Rd	05403
Uno Pizza, 1330 Shelburne Rd	05403
Wellesley Grove, 630 Hinesburg Rd	05403
Windridge, 175 Kennedy Dr	05403

BUILDINGS

Burlington Intl Airport 1200 Airport Dr	05403
Dorset Square Mall 150 Dorset St.	05403
Town Square, 425 Dorset St.	05403

GOVERNMENT OFFICES

Comm Correctional Center 7 Farrell St.	05403
So Burl City Offices, 575 Dorset St.	05403

NAMED STREETS

All Street Addresses.	05403

Source: U.S. Postal Service, 2003

THE NATION

City	Wednesday Hi	Lo	W	Thursday Hi	Lo	W	Friday Hi	Lo	W
Albany................	41	34	r	47	34	r	46	34	pc
Albuquerque..........	62	39	s	64	38	s	63	38	s
Amarillo	56	36	s	65	40	s	63	38	s
Anchorage	24	12	pc	22	10	pc	22	12	pc
Asheville	62	21	s	65	31	pc	63	35	c
Atlanta................	66	46	sh	62	40	s	65	44	s
Atlantic City.........	54	47	r	59	35	pc	56	40	s
Austin..................	74	42	s	68	38	s	70	40	s
Baltimore.............	50	42	r	58	36	pc	58	37	pc
Billings	48	38	pc	65	42	s	60	42	s
Birmingham	65	43	c	63	36	s	63	38	s
Bismarck	36	25	s	54	27	pc	55	32	r
Boise	54	34	s	54	34	s	56	35	pc
Boston	52	42	pc	52	37	r	53	39	pc
Brownsville...........	78	56	c	81	66	pc	79	64	s
Buffalo	45	38	r	45	36	sh	45	38	pc
Charleston, SC......	54	40	s	66	37	s	50	38	s
Charlotte, NC	66	44	r	64	36	pc	65	40	t
Cheyenne	42	29	sf	61	35	sf	62	35	s
Chicago	50	34	r	50	36	pc	50	38	s
Cincinnati	59	39	r	50	33	pc	55	37	s
Cleveland	55	40	r	44	38	c	50	42	pc
Dallas	66	46	s	68	47	s	66	47	pc
Dayton	65	20	pc	52	35	c	60	32	pc
Denver	45	29	sh	65	36	s	58	36	s
Des Moines	53	28	pc	56	41	s	54	38	s
Detroit	48	36	r	48	34	pc	47	36	pc
Fairbanks..............	9	-4	sf	4	-10	sn	8	-10	i
Fargo	40	26	c	50	34	s	45	30	s
Flagstaff................	37	25	s	52	22	pc	50	23	pc
Grand Rapids	48	35	r	47	37	pc	48	37	s
Hartford	44	39	r	49	34	sh	47	35	pc
Helena.................	46	26	s	61	32	s	50	28	s
Honolulu..............	87	71	s	87	71	pc	87	70	s
Houston	70	46	s	68	46	s	70	48	s
Indianapolis..........	52	36	r	51	34	pc	52	36	s
Jacksonville...........	65	32	s	73	36	s	72	38	s
Juneau	41	34	sf	41	32	pc	42	33	pc
Kansas City	53	32	s	60	43	s	58	42	s
Knoxville..............	63	40	sh	57	35	pc	60	38	s

Weather (**W**): **s**-sunny, **pc**-partly cloudy, **c**-cloudy, **sh**-showers, **t**-thunderstorms, **r**-rain, **sf**-snow flurries, **sn**-snow, **i**-ice

Weather Forecasts

THE NATION

City	Wednesday Hi	Lo	W	Thursday Hi	Lo	W	Friday Hi	Lo	W
Las Vegas	69	51	s	74	53	pc	74	55	s
Little Rock	60	41	pc	62	38	s	62	40	s
Los Angeles	69	46	s	70	49	s	72	50	s
Louisville	69	34	pc	62	42	c	65	41	c
Lubbock	52	39	r	54	36	pc	54	40	s
Memphis	57	42	pc	58	41	s	58	42	s
Miami	86	72	pc	83	65	t	83	70	pc
Milwaukee.............	48	34	r	50	38	pc	50	36	r
Minneapolis...........	47	28	r	50	36	s	48	30	s
Nashville................	60	41	sh	58	34	s	60	37	s
New Orleans	68	54	pc	68	51	s	69	53	s
New York	52	44	r	52	40	sh	50	42	sh
Norfolk..................	62	49	r	63	43	s	62	50	s
Oklahoma City.......	60	40	s	62	44	s	64	46	s
Omaha	54	27	pc	63	35	s	60	30	s
Orlando.................	88	66	pc	76	56	sh	80	60	t
Philadelphia............	50	44	r	54	38	pc	52	40	pc
Phoenix	82	58	s	85	58	s	83	56	s
Pittsburgh..............	57	38	pc	48	37	s	52	30	s
Portland, ME..........	48	38	pc	45	34	r	45	36	sf
Portland, OR..........	56	36	s	58	42	s	59	43	s
Raleigh-Durham.....	57	21	s	65	31	c	56	42	c
Rapid City..............	52	27	pc	66	38	s	63	40	pc
Reno......................	50	29	pc	56	29	pc	54	32	c
Sacramento............	64	44	s	65	44	s	68	42	pc
Salt Lake City........	54	34	pc	54	33	s	55	36	s
San Antonio	74	44	s	68	46	s	70	48	s
San Diego..............	66	54	s	66	52	s	65	55	s
San Francisco..........	65	50	pc	60	48	pc	62	50	r
Seattle...................	52	38	s	54	40	pc	52	40	r
Shreveport	75	40	t	68	50	c	62	45	c
Sioux Falls	47	26	pc	55	35	pc	50	35	r
Spokane.................	46	26	s	48	32	c	47	30	pc
St. Louis	71	48	sh	58	38	sh	55	39	r
St. Pete/Tampa	75	37	s	75	46	pc	78	51	pc
Topeka...................	55	33	s	65	39	s	60	37	s
Tucson...................	81	52	s	82	55	s	80	53	s
Tulsa......................	57	38	s	64	46	s	60	40	pc
Washington, D.C. ..	59	43	r	58	38	pc	58	45	r
Wichita..................	59	33	s	62	41	s	62	37	s

Weather (**W**): **s**-sunny, **pc**-partly cloudy, **c**-cloudy, **sh**-showers, **t**-thunderstorms, **r**-rain, **sf**-snow flurries, **sn**-snow, **i**-ice

Weather Forecasts

GLOSSARY

A

ABA American Bankers Association

accession log a list of the code numbers assigned to records in a numeric filing system

acronym a word formed from the first letters of several words

action verb a verb that describes an action

alphabetic index an alphabetic list of names or subjects and their assigned code numbers; used with an accession log

alphabetic order to put names in the same order as the letters of the alphabet, or in ABC order

ATM Automated Teller Machine

C

CD-ROM compact disc read-only memory

check register a log of all transactions in a checking account

chronological order in order of time, using dates to determine placement

common noun names general people, places, and things and is not capitalized unless it starts a sentence or is part of a title

complete subject tells who is speaking, who is spoken to, or who or what is spoken about in a sentence

consecutive order numbers that follow one after another from lowest to highest; for example, 1, 2, 3 and so on

count-back method counting change to customers one coin or bill at a time, beginning with the smallest coins and working up to the larger bills

cross-reference system a system used for indexing unusual names that might be easily confused or for records that might be filed in more than one place

cross-referencing putting a card or sheet in a file folder in every place a person might look for a record

D

deposit putting money into an account

deposit ticket a form that must be completed each time a deposit is made in an account; also called a deposit slip

DVD-ROM digital versatile (or video) disc read-only memory

E

endorse to sign the back of a check to be deposited into an account

ethics the moral principles that govern personal and professional conduct

H

helping verbs verbs used in combination with a main verb to make a verb phrase; also called auxiliary verbs

I

indexing putting the name of a person or business in a certain order according to the rules of filing

infinitive a verb form following the word to; for example, to sleep

invoice a document issued by a seller that lists the details of a transaction between a seller and a buyer

L

linking verb a verb that links, or connects, the subject of a sentence to information about that subject

M

main idea the single most important idea in a group of words; also called the topic sentence

N

nominative pronoun the subject of the verb and carries out the action; also called a subjective pronoun

noun the word used to name a person, place, or thing

O

objective pronoun the object of the verb and receives the action

P

petty cash cash kept on hand for payment of minor items

petty cash book a record of all petty cash paid from a petty cash fund

petty cash fund a specified amount of bills and coins for ready use when a petty cash payment is needed, typically kept in one place such as a metal box

petty cash receipt a form showing the details of a petty cash payment and placed with the petty cash fund

POS point of sale

possessive pronoun shows possession or ownership

predicate includes the verb and tells you something about the subject

prepositional object the noun or pronoun that ends a prepositional phrase

prepositional phrase a group of words beginning with a preposition and ending with a noun or pronoun

prepositions connecting words that show relationships between nouns or pronouns and other words in a sentence

primary number first in rank or importance; also called terminal digit; the group of numbers farthest right in terminal-digit filing

prioritizing the process of determining the order in which tasks should be completed

pronoun a word used to replace a noun, a group of nouns, or another pronoun

proofreading the skill of detecting errors in written documents; errors may be in keying, spelling, grammar, punctuation, format, or content

proper noun names a specific person, place, or thing and is capitalized no matter where it appears in a sentence

S

sales receipt a document issued by a business showing the details of a customer's purchase

search engine a software program that searches and retrieves information from a database or network, such as the Internet

secondary number second in rank or importance; the middle group of numbers in terminal-digit filing

sentence a group of words that expresses a complete thought

signature card a document a customer signs when opening an account at a financial institution; it identifies the depositor

simple subject the main word within the complete subject

T

terminal digit the end digits of a number; also called primary number

terminal-digit filing a method of numeric filing in which numbers are filed in consecutive order (lowest number to highest number); however, the numbers are divided into groups and are read from right to left

tertiary number third in rank or importance; the group of numbers farthest left in terminal-digit filing

time management the process of controlling the amount of time spent on specific tasks in order to increase efficiency

U

URL Uniform Resource Locator; the unique address of a website that is accessible on the Internet

V

verb the core of the predicate; describes a subject's action, condition, or state of being

verb phrase the combination of one or more helping verbs followed by the main verb

W

work order an order received by an organization from a customer or from a department within an organization for work to be completed